eLmL 2018

The Tenth International Conference on Mobile, Hybrid, and On-line Learning

March 25 – 29, 2018

Rome, Italy

eLmL 2018 Editors

Joseph C. Kush, Duquesne University, Pittsburgh, USA
Cynthia Lester, Georgia State University, USA

Printed from e-media with permission by:

Curran Associates, Inc.
57 Morehouse Lane
Red Hook, NY 12571

Some format issues inherent in the e-media version may also appear in this print version.

Printed by Curran Associates, Inc. (2018)

International Academy, Research, and Industry Association (IARIA)
412 Derby Way
Wilmington, DE 19810

Phone: (408) 893-6407
Fax: (408) 527-6351

petre@iaria.org

Additional copies of this publication are available from:

Curran Associates, Inc.
57 Morehouse Lane
Red Hook, NY 12571 USA
Phone: 845-758-0400
Fax: 845-758-2633
Email: curran@proceedings.com
Web: www.proceedings.com

eLmL 2018

Forward

The tenth edition of the International Conference on Mobile, Hybrid, and On-line Learning (eLmL 2018), held in Rome, Italy, March 25 - 29, 2018, focused on the latest trends in e-learning and also on the latest IT technology alternatives that are poised to become mainstream strategies in the near future and will influence the e-learning environment.

eLearning refers to on-line learning delivered over the World Wide Web via the public Internet or the private, corporate intranet. The goal of the eLmL 2018 conference was to provide an overview of technologies, approaches, and trends that are happening right now. The constraints of e-learning are diminishing and options are increasing as the Web becomes increasingly easy to use and the technology becomes better and less expensive.

eLmL 2018 provided a forum where researchers were able to present recent research results and new research problems and directions related to them. The topics covered aspects related to tools and platforms, on-line learning, mobile learning, and hybrid learning.

We take this opportunity to thank all the members of the eLmL 2018 Technical Program Committee as well as the numerous reviewers. The creation of such a broad and high-quality conference program would not have been possible without their involvement. We also kindly thank all the authors who dedicated much of their time and efforts to contribute to the eLmL 2018. We truly believe that, thanks to all these efforts, the final conference program consists of top quality contributions.

This event could also not have been a reality without the support of many individuals, organizations, and sponsors. We are grateful to the members of the eLmL 2018 organizing committee for their help in handling the logistics and for their work to make this professional meeting a success.

We hope that eLmL 2018 was a successful international forum for the exchange of ideas and results between academia and industry and for the promotion of progress in eLearning research.

We also hope that Rome provided a pleasant environment during the conference and everyone saved some time for exploring this beautiful city.

eLmL 2018 Chairs

eLmL Steering Committee

Herwig Mannaert, University of Antwerp, Belgium
Stephen White, The University of Huddersfield - Queensgate, UK
Maiga Chang, Athabasca University, Canada
Hironori Washizaki, Waseda University, Japan
Krzysztof Szklanny, Polish-Japanese Academy of Information Technology, Poland
Christian M. Stracke, Open University of the Netherlands, The Netherlands
Ivan Ganchev, University of Limerick, Ireland / Plovdiv University "Paisii Hilendarski", Bulgaria
Tomayess Issa, Curtin University, Australia
Yifat Ben-David Kolikant, Hebrew University of Jerusalem, Israel
Mudasser Wyne, National University - San Diego, USA

eLmL Industry/Research Advisory Committee

Michael Verhaart, Eastern Institute of Technology Hawke's Bay, New Zealand
Guglielmo Trentin, Institute of Educational Technology of the Italian National Research Council (ITD-CNR), Italy
Nick Louloudakis, Institute of Computer Science, Foundation of Research and Technology Hellas (ICS-FORTH), Greece

eLmL 2018

COMMITTEE

eLmL Steering Committee
Herwig Mannaert, University of Antwerp, Belgium
Stephen White, The University of Huddersfield - Queensgate, UK
Maiga Chang, Athabasca University, Canada
Hironori Washizaki, Waseda University, Japan
Krzysztof Szklanny, Polish-Japanese Academy of Information Technology, Poland
Christian M. Stracke, Open University of the Netherlands, The Netherlands
Ivan Ganchev, University of Limerick, Ireland / Plovdiv University "Paisii Hilendarski", Bulgaria
Tomayess Issa, Curtin University, Australia
Yifat Ben-David Kolikant, Hebrew University of Jerusalem, Israel
Mudasser Wyne, National University - San Diego, USA

eLmL Industry/Research Advisory Committee
Michael Verhaart, Eastern Institute of Technology Hawke's Bay, New Zealand
Guglielmo Trentin, Institute of Educational Technology of the Italian National Research Council (ITD-CNR), Italy
Nick Louloudakis, Institute of Computer Science, Foundation of Research and Technology Hellas (ICS-FORTH), Greece

eLmL 2018 Technical Program Committee

Ali Ahmad Alawneh, Philadelphia University, Jordan
Yayoi Anzai, Kyushu University, Japan
Cristina Azevedo Gomes, Polytechnic Institute of Viseu, Portugal
Juarez Bento da Silva, Universidade Federal de Santa Catarina, Brazil
Werner Beuschel, Technical University Brandenburg, Germany
Mohsin Bilal, Umm Al Qura University, Saudi Arabia
Julien Broisin, University of Toulouse, France
Eglė Butkevičienė, Kaunas University of Technology, Lithuania
José Carlos Metrolho, IPCB, Portugal
Maiga Chang, Athabasca University, Canada
Steven Chen, United Daily News, Taiwan
Lorraine Cleeton, Northcentral University / Walden University, USA
David Comiskey, Ulster University, Northern Ireland
Andre Constantino da Silva, Federal Institute of São Paulo – IFSP, Brazil
Ana de las Heras, Udima Universidad a Distancia de Madrid, Spain
Giuliana Dettori, Istituto per le Tecnologie Didattiche, Genova, Italy
Ramon Fabregat Gesa, University of Girona, Spain
Joseph Finkelstein, Center for Bioinformatics and Health Analytics - Columbia University, USA
Sue Folley, University of Huddersfield, UK
Ivan Ganchev, University of Limerick, Ireland / Plovdiv University "Paisii Hilendarski", Bulgaria
Leonardo Garrido, Tecnológico de Monterrey, Mexico
Henrique Gil, Escola Superior de Educação do Instituto Politécnico de Castelo Branco, Portugal

Giuliana Guazzaroni, Università Politecnica delle Marche, Italy
David Guralnick, Kaleidoscope Learning & Columbia University, New York, USA
Felix Hamza-Lup, Georgia Southern University, USA
Feifei Han, University of Sydney, Australia
Oriel Herrera, Universidad Católica de Temuco, Chile
Helen Hong, National Institute of Education, Singapore
Taketoshi Inaba, Tokyo University of Technology, Japan
Tsunenori Ishioka, The National Center for University Entrance Examinations, Japan
Tomayess Issa, Curtin University, Australia
Adel Jebali, Concordia University, Canada
Srećko Joksimović, Moray House School of Education | University of Edinburgh, UK
Mike Joy, University of Warwick, UK
Alex Jung, Aalto University, Finland
Katerina Kabassi, TEI of Ionian Islands, Greece
Konstantinos Kalemis, Kapodistrian University of Athens, Greece
Keiichi Kaneko, Tokyo University of Agriculture and Technology, Japan
Charalampos Karagiannidis, University of Thessaly, Greece
Ilias Karasavvidis, University of Thessaly, Greece
Yifat Ben-David Kolikant, Hebrew University of Jerusalem, Israel
Vitomir Kovanovic, University of South Australia, Adelaide, Australia
Bernd Krämer, FernUniversität in Hagen, Germany
Miroslav Kulich, Czech Technical University in Prague | Czech Institute of Informatics, Robotics, and Cybernetics, Czech Republic
Joseph C. Kush, Duquesne University, USA
Cynthia Y. Lester, Georgia State University, USA
Ken W. Li, Hong Kong Institute of Vocational Education (Tsing Yi), Hong Kong
Andreas Lingnau, Humboldt-Universität zu Berlin, Germany
Giorgos Liodakis, TEI of Crete, Greece
Martin Llamas Nistal, Universidade de Vigo, Spain
Nick Louloudakis, Institute of Computer Science, Foundation of Research and Technology Hellas (ICS-FORTH), Greece
Hwangji Sherrie Lu, Ashford University, USA
Luca Andrea Ludovico, Università degli Studi di Milano, Italy
Stefania Manca, Institute of Educational Technology - National Research Council of Italy, Italy
Giuseppina Rita Mangione, INDIRE (National Institute for Documentation, Innovation and Educational Research), Italy
Herwig Mannaert, University of Antwerp, Belgium
José Manuel Machado, University of Minho, Portugal
Alke Martens, University of Rostock, Germany
Paulo Martins, INESC TEC / University of Trás-os-Montes e Alto Douro, Portugal
Bruce R. Maxim, University of Michigan-Dearborn, USA
Natarajan Meghanathan, Jackson State University, USA
Santiago Mengual Andrés, University of Valencia, Spain
Begoña Montero-Fleta, Universitat Politecnica de Valencia, Spain
Rafael Morales Gamboa, Universidad de Guadalajara, Mexico
Umberto Nanni, Universita' di Roma "La Sapienza", Italy
Jari Palomaki, Tampere University of Technology - Pori, Finland
Andreas Papasalouros, University of the Aegean, Greece

Hugo Paredes, INESC TEC / University of Trás-os-Montes e Alto Douro, Portugal
Arna Peretz, Ben-Gurion University of the Negev, Israel
Maria Potes Barbas, Escola Superior de Educação de Santarém, Portugal
Tamara Powell, Kennesaw State University, USA
Francesca Pozzi, Istituto Tecnologie Didattiche - CNR, Genoa, Italy
Athanasios Priftis, HES, Geneva, Switzerland
Natālija Prokofjeva, Riga Technical University, Latvia
Yannis Psaromiligkos, Piraeus University of Applied Science, Greece
Maja Pušnik, University of Maribor, Slovenia
Sonja D. Radenkovic, University of Belgrade, Serbia
Juliana Elisa Raffaghelli, University of Florence, Italy
Thurasamy Ramayah, Universiti Sains Malaysia, Malaysia
Fabrizio Ravicchio, ITD-CNR, Italy
Laura Rayón, Universidad de Alcalá, Spain
Fernando Reinaldo Ribeiro, Polytechnic Institute of Castelo Branco, Portugal
Jan Renz, Hasso Plattner Institute | University of Potsdam, Germany
Anja Richert, RWTH Aachen University, Germany
Marina Rui, University of Genova, Italy
Demetrios Sampson, Curtin University, Australia
Juan Manuel Santos Gago, University of Vigo, Spain
Carol Savill-Smith, Independent Researcher, UK
Filippo Sciarrone, University of Roma Tre, Italy
Karim Sehaba, Université Lumière Lyon 2, France
Jirarat Sitthiworachart, Walailak University, Thailand
Eliza Stefanova, Sofia University St. Kl. Ohridski, Bulgaria
Monika Steinberg, Hochschule Hannover, Germany
Christian M. Stracke, Open University of the Netherlands, The Netherlands
Boštjan Šumak, University of Maribor, Slovenia
Jakub Swacha, University of Szczecin, Poland
Krzysztof Szklanny, Polish-Japanese Academy of Information Technology, Poland
John T. Thompson, Buffalo State College, USA
Lisette Toetenel, Oxford Brookes University, UK
Jean-Philippe Trabichet, Haute Ecole de Gestion de Genève, Switzerland
Guglielmo Trentin, Institute of Educational Technology of the Italian National Research Council (ITD-CNR), Italy
Thrasyvoulos Tsiatsos, Aristotle University of Thessaloniki, Greece
Carlos Vaz de Carvalho, Instituto Superior de Engenharia do Porto, Portugal
Esteban Vázquez-Cano, Spanish National University of Distance Education (UNED), Spain
Ioanna Vekiri, independent writer and researcher, Greece
Michael Verhaart, Eastern Institute of Technology Hawke's Bay, New Zealand
Minjuan Wang, San Diego State University, USA / Shanghai International Studies University, China
Hironori Washizaki, Waseda University, Japan
Stephen White, The University of Huddersfield - Queensgate, UK
Mudasser Wyne, National University - San Diego, USA
Rihito Yaegashi, Kagawa University, Japan
Ahmed Mohamed Fahmy Yousef, Fayoum University, Egypt
Katarina Zakova, Slovak University of Technology, Slovakia

Diego Zapata-Rivera, Educational Testing Service, USA
Qinglong Zhan, Tianjin University of Technology and Education, China

Copyright Information

For your reference, this is the text governing the copyright release for material published by IARIA.

The copyright release is a transfer of publication rights, which allows IARIA and its partners to drive the dissemination of the published material. This allows IARIA to give articles increased visibility via distribution, inclusion in libraries, and arrangements for submission to indexes.

I, the undersigned, declare that the article is original, and that I represent the authors of this article in the copyright release matters. If this work has been done as work-for-hire, I have obtained all necessary clearances to execute a copyright release. I hereby irrevocably transfer exclusive copyright for this material to IARIA. I give IARIA permission or reproduce the work in any media format such as, but not limited to, print, digital, or electronic. I give IARIA permission to distribute the materials without restriction to any institutions or individuals. I give IARIA permission to submit the work for inclusion in article repositories as IARIA sees fit.

I, the undersigned, declare that to the best of my knowledge, the article is does not contain libelous or otherwise unlawful contents or invading the right of privacy or infringing on a proprietary right.

Following the copyright release, any circulated version of the article must bear the copyright notice and any header and footer information that IARIA applies to the published article.

IARIA grants royalty-free permission to the authors to disseminate the work, under the above provisions, for any academic, commercial, or industrial use. IARIA grants royalty-free permission to any individuals or institutions to make the article available electronically, online, or in print.

IARIA acknowledges that rights to any algorithm, process, procedure, apparatus, or articles of manufacture remain with the authors and their employers.

I, the undersigned, understand that IARIA will not be liable, in contract, tort (including, without limitation, negligence), pre-contract or other representations (other than fraudulent misrepresentations) or otherwise in connection with the publication of my work.

Exception to the above is made for work-for-hire performed while employed by the government. In that case, copyright to the material remains with the said government. The rightful owners (authors and government entity) grant unlimited and unrestricted permission to IARIA, IARIA's contractors, and IARIA's partners to further distribute the work.

Table of Contents

Effects of Multiple Viewing of Captions and Subtitles on English Proficiency 1
Yayoi Anzai and Kanji Akahori

Mobile Learning Model for Zimbabwe Higher Education 4
Lydia Maketo

Frequency of Sticker Use for Expressing Emotions in Text Messaging: Effects of Gender and Text-Messaging Dependency 10
Yasuyuki Ozawa, Yuuki Kato, and Shogo Kato

The Potential of Support-Rich Environment for Teaching Meaningful Mathematics to Low-Achieving Students 13
Yifat Ben-David Kolikant and Orit Broza

A Introduction Of Scratch And Programming Education 19
Ruimeng Racic

An Introduction to Code.org 21
Bria Koch

Determining Pedagogically Sound Methods of Teaching and Learning Computational Skills 23
Cheryl Tkacs

Hybrid Learning: A Summary of Current Models and Research 30
Stefanie Graban

A Review of the Importance of Computational Thinking in K-12 32
Katharine McClelland and Lori Grata

Teaching ESL and Instruction Design with Computational Thinking and Robot-Assisted Language Learning 35
Jianan Zhou

Conversation: Loose Parts - A Pathway from Play to Technology 38
Julia Williams, David Carbonara, and Rose Mary Mautino

Proposal for a Lesson Support System using Computer Virtualization Technology 41
Yuto Terao, Kenta Morita, and Naoki Morita

Using Deep Learning Methods to Automate Collaborative Learning Process Coding Based on Multi-Dimensional Coding Scheme 45
Takahiro Kanayama, Kimihiko Ando, Chihiro Shibata, and Taketoshi Inaba

SmarTTeaching Pharmacology 54
Pieter van Wyk

Tracking Verb Phrases for Formative Feedback in Foreign Language Writing 58
Shuai Shao, Kazuhiro Ohtsuki, Hidenari Kiyomitsu, and Min Kang

An Approach toward Automatic Error Detection in Learners' English Writing Based on the Source Language 62
Koichi Kawamura, Harumi Kashiwagi, and Min Kang

Best Practices in a Redesigned Online Computer Ethics Course 66
Cynthia Lester

Educator-Oriented Tools for Managing the Attention-Aware Intelligent Classroom 72
Evropi Stefanidi, Maria Korozi, Asterios Leonidis, Maria Doulgeraki, and Margherita Antona

Integrating Office 365 Into Your Curriculum: A Backward Design Professional Learning Course 78
Katharine McClelland

Applying Mixed Reality Techniques for the Visualization of Programs and Algorithms in a Programming Learning Environment 84
Santiago Sanchez Sobrino, Maria Angeles Garcia Marin, Maria del Carmen Lacave Rodero, Ana Isabel Molina Diaz, Carlos Gonzalez Morcillo, David Vallejo Fernandez, and Miguel Angel Redondo Duque

Developing, Understanding and Evaluating Augmented Reality Framework for Universities in Saudi Arabia 90
Muteeb Alahmari

A User-centric Design and Pedagogical-based Approach for Mobile Learning 100
Mohammed Bahja and Rawad Hammad

Effects of Multiple Viewing of Captions and Subtitles on English Proficiency

Yayoi Anzai
Kyushu University,
Innovation Center for Educational Resource
Fukuoka, Japan
email: anzai.yayoi.450@m.kyushu-u.ac.jp

Kanji Akahori
Japan Association for Promotion of Educational Technology
Tokyo, Japan
email: akahori@japet.or.jp

***Abstract*— English as a Foreign Language (EFL) teachers and researchers in Japan have been seeking an effective way to determine how mobile learning can be best integrated in language learning. There are also some others who have been searching the best way to use captions and subtitles of the English videos to enhance effective language learning. They often investigate the effects of using computers. They generally agree that the use of captions or subtitles is helpful to acquire the target language, and English captions are found to be more effective than Japanese subtitles to enhance English proficiency. However, there is a gap between the state of the art and actual classroom situations. Students spend more time with smartphones than computers. They watch the same video a few times combining English captions and Japanese subtitles, not only English captions. Thus, the purpose of this study was to find out the immediate effects of both captions and subtitles on EFL proficiency after viewing the same English video multiple times, using a smartphone. The results showed that the group who used both Japanese subtitles and English captions performed better on the vocabulary section and had a higher total score compared to the group who only used English captions.**

Keywords-subtitles; captions; EFL; ESL; mobile learning.

I. INTRODUCTION

Online videos have been flourishing and getting much attention from language teachers using Computer Assisted Language Learning (CALL) because of their excellent educational contents [1]. Massive Open Online Courses, MOOCs and Technology Entertainment Design (TED) Talks are good examples. MOOCs consist of video lectures, an online community, and exams, while TED Talks are speeches promoted as "ideas worth spreading." What they have in common is that they use English as a global language, and captions and subtitles are of significant benefit to English as a Foreign Language (EFL), and English as a Second Language (ESL) learners [1]-[3].

The rest of the paper is structured as follows. In Section 2, we introduce the literature review. In Section 3, we describe the methods used in this study. In Section 4, we provide the results of our study. In Section 5, we provide discussion, and finally, in Section 6, we present our conclusions.

II. LITERATURE REVIEW

Ample research supports that captions and subtitles have positive effects on language acquisition [4]-[11]. In Table 1, we show studies related to subtitles and captions in English learning.

In the laboratory experimental settings, many studies have investigated the effects on the target language after viewing the edited video once. However, there have not been many studies on the effects of captions and subtitles after viewing the same video multiple times, though this is what is often happening in actual EFL/ESL classrooms, since the students cannot understand everything in the video after viewing it once. In addition, smartphones were not often used in the previous studies, though this is the device that the students carry all the time. Thus, what is missing are the effects of multiple viewings of both captions and subtitles together on EFL learners, when they use smartphones.

TABLE 1. STUDIES RELATED TO SUBTITLES AND CAPTIONS IN ENGLISH LEARNING

Author(s)	Year	Environment	Findings
T. Kikuchi [4]	1996	classroom	The study examined the potential of using English-captioned movies in the areas of rapid reading and listening comprehension. The results showed that the group who used English sound and captions made statistically much more progress than other groups who used captions, pictures and English sound, or English sound only.
S. Yoshino, E. Nojima, & K. Akahori [5]	1997	laboratory	English captions are more effective than Japanese subtitles to enhance English listening.
S. Yoshino [6]	2003	laboratory	The study examined the timing of the captions, and found that more information was recalled when L2, second language, captions were presented before the corresponding L2 audio.
K. Tomita [7]	2008	laboratory	Immediately after the experiment, the group who watched the news video with superimposed caption performed significantly higher than the group who studied without the caption. However, there was no

			significant difference after three months.
Y. Anzai [3]	2016	online class	Subtitles and captions support Japanese and international participants to MOOCs to learn the subject matter.
E.Peters, E. E. Heynes, & E. Puimege [8]	2016	classroom	Incidental vocabulary acquisition while watching a short video is possible and captions have more potential than subtitles for this purpose. Moreover, learners' vocabulary size and an item's frequency of occurrence in the video clip have positive correlation with vocabulary acquisition.
K. Hosogoshi [9]	2016	classroom	The Japanese subtitles group performed better in the use of imaginary and summarizing strategies throughout the listening.
M. P. H. Rodgers and S. Webb [10]	2017	classroom	The results revealed that captions on television programs are likely to aid comprehension when episodes are most difficult.
H. S. Mahdi [11]	2017	classroom	Studying the effect of keywords videos captioning on vocabulary acquisition using mobile devices. The study found that keyword captioning is a useful mode to improve learners' pronunciation.

Considering what was missing in the literature and its importance, this study was conducted in a laboratory setting. This approach was chosen not to be conducted in a classroom to eliminate confounding variables as much as possible while investigating the effects of captions and subtitles. In addition, the theory of instructional design was taken into consideration to decide the order in which captions and subtitles were presented to participants when watching the English video. Reigeluth states that "instructional design is concerned with understanding, improving, and applying methods of instruction" (p.7) [12]. The theory recommends designing instructions to allow learners to understand the framework before looking at the details of what they want to understand. Thus, since all the participants were Japanese, this study of the treatment group was first shown a video with Japanese subtitles to set them the framework of the video, and then they looked at the English subtitles to learn more details about English expressions.

Under the current educational context, the purpose of this study was to find out the immediate effects of captions and subtitles on EFL proficiency after viewing the same English video multiple times, using a smartphone. Captioning refers to "L2, second language, subtitled video," whereas subtitles refer to "L1, first language, subtitled video" of L2 aural input. The statistical design used was a series of two-way analysis of variance (ANOVA). The independent variable was Group (a control group vs the treatment group), and English proficiency (high vs low) was measured using the Oxford Placement Test. The dependent variables were the scores taken from the English tests about the video.

The hypothesis of this research was:
Using smartphones, the treatment group with Japanese captions and English subtitles would perform better in English tests than the control group who only had English subtitles.

III. Methods

The study was conducted in a university laboratory setting in September 2016 in Tokyo, Japan. The number of Japanese students was 60. The length of the video was 1 minute 30 seconds, in English, with English captions and Japanese subtitles added. Both groups viewed the same video three times (Figure 1). The control group used English captions three times, while the treatment group used Japanese subtitles twice and then, English captions once (Figure 2).

Figure 1.
Investigating the effects of the video with Japanese/English subtitles

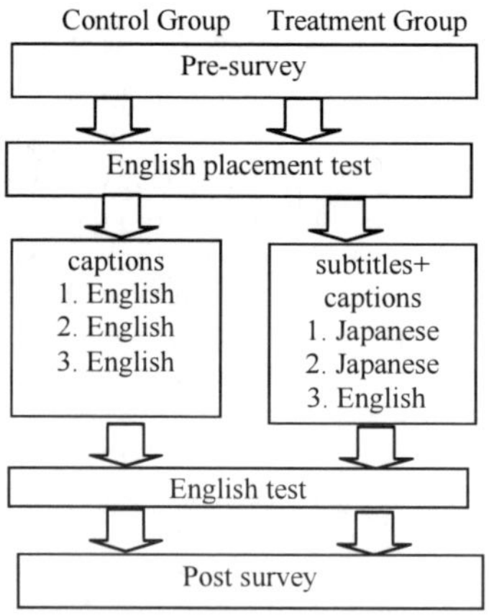

Figure 2. The process of the study

The effects were measured with a test that consisted of 1) vocabulary, 2) content comprehension, 3) summary, and 4) listening proficiency. In the first section, vocabulary, the students were asked to translate English words or phrases into Japanese. Examples of the tested vocabulary include "Confucius" and "evolution." In the second section, content and comprehension, they were asked to choose True or False questions based on the video. An example of the questions is "We are living in an age of Web2.0." In the third section, they were asked to summarize the English video in Japanese. In the fourth section, listening proficiency, they were asked to fill in the blanks while listening to the video. An example includes "Spring time in education for all of us, with the various new (3) of learning."

IV. RESULTS

We compared the control group who watched English captions three times with the treatment group who had Japanese subtitles twice followed by English captions once. The results showed that there was no significant interaction between the two groups. Regarding Group, the treatment group (M = 13.39, SD = 5.22) tended to perform better than the control group (M = 11.50, SD = 4.67). As for the other independent variable, English proficiency (high vs low), there was no significant difference between the two groups.

When we examined each section of the English test, we found no interaction, but there was a significant difference between the wo groups (F(1, 56) = 22.02, p < .001. The treatment group (M = 3.40, SD = 1.35) performed better than the control group (M = 2.00, SD = .98) on the vocabulary section, where they were able to translate English words into Japanese better. In other words, the students were able to process the two languages at the same time, and picked up the corresponding words in the other language quickly using the subtitles, and memorized them. There were no significant statistical differences between the two groups in the other parts of the English test.

V. DISCUSSION

This study revealed that the use of L1 subtitles does not necessarily hinder acquiring L2. That is, overall, a combination of L1 subtitles and L2 caption is more advantageous than using only L2 captions. Using L1 subtitles to grasp the whole picture before looking at the details in L2 is one approach to enhance learning.

In addition, as a result of this study, it is found that the group who used subtitles and captions tended to perform better than the group with only captions on the total score of the English test. According to Yoshino, Nojima, and Akahori [5], English captions are more effective than Japanese subtitles to enhance English listening. Thus, it may lead to the assumption that the effectiveness of the use of captions and subtitles may go in the order of Japanese subtitles with English captions, secondly English captions, and thirdly Japanese subtitles.

The results of this study would be useful to design English language learning using online videos, such as MOOCs or TED Talks, equipped with captions and subtitles. Learners should be flexible to choose when they use L1 and L2 in their language learning.

VI. CONCLUSION

In summary, this study aimed to find out the immediate effects of both captions and subtitles on EFL proficiency after viewing the same English video multiple times. Smartphones were used as a learning device for this experiment. The results showed that the group who watched both Japanese subtitles and English captions tended to perform better in the total score, and particularly on the vocabulary section, than the group who used only English captions.

ACKNOWLEDGMENT

This study was supported by a Grant-in-Aid for Scientific Research (C), JSPS KAKENHI Number 15K01034 from April 2015 - March 2019 with representative researcher: Dr. Kanji Akahori; research collaborator: Dr. Yayoi Anzai.

REFERENCES

[1] Y. Anzai, "English Education at Universities in Japan and Open Education." In Yoshida, H., & Nozawa, K. (Eds.), My foreign language class using ICT, Maruzen Pranet: Tokyo, pp. 63–76, 2014.

[2] R. Tabuchi, and E. Yufune, "Analysis on the display time of TED subtitles and tis educational use, Language education & technology Vol. 54, pp. 167-192, 2017.

[3] Y. Anzai, (2016, 12). Results from JMOOC, Science and technology of taste and odor, ICER Newsletter. Available from: http://www.icer.kyushu-u.ac.jp/sites/default/files/newsletter201612.pdf/ 2018.03.02

[4] T. Kikuchi, "The effects of an English-captioned movie on word recognition and rapid reading." Proceedings of Annual Convention of Japan Association of College English Teachers, Vol. 35, pp. 205-208, 1996.

[5] S. Yoshino, E. Nojima, and K. Akahori, "The effects of caption on English listening comprehension, Japan Society for Educational Technology, Vol. 21, Suppl, pp. 29 – 32, 1997..

[6] S. Yoshino, "The effective use of timing to increase caption effectiveness : An experiment." Japan Society for Educational Technolog, Vol. 27, 3, pp. 237–246, 2003

[7] K. Tomita, "Effects of a superimposed caption on learners' listening skills." Proceedings of Annual Convention of Japan Association of College English Teachers, Vol. 47, pp. 42-43, 2008

[8] E. Peters, E. Heynes, and E. Puimege (2016). "Learning vocabulary through audiovisual input: The differential effect of L1 subtitles and captions," Vol. 63, pp134-148, System.

[9] K. Hosokoshi, "Effects of captions and subtitles on the listening process: Insights from EFL learners' listening strategies," JALT CALL, Vol. 12, 3, pp. 153-178, 2016

[10] M. P. H. Rodgers and S. Webb, "The effects of captions on EFL learners' comprehensiion of English-language televisiion programs," CALICO Journal, Vol. 34, 1, pp. 20-38, 2017.

[11] H. S. Mahdi, "The effect of key-words video captions on vocabulary leaerning through mobile-assisted langage learning," Australian Educational Computig, Vol. 332, 1, 2017.

[12] C. Reigeluth, Instructional-design theories and models: an overview of their current status. Volume I. Hillsdale, NJ: Lawrence Erlbaum, 1983

Mobile Learning Model for Zimbabwe Higher Education

Lydia Maketo
School of information Systems
Curtin University
Perth, Australia
email:lydia.maketo@student.curtin.edu.au

***Abstract*—The benefits of mobile-learning (m-learning) have been widely publicised. Research on m-learning is predominantly from developed nations, with a paucity of empirical studies on the adoption and implementation of m-learning in the tertiary institutions of developing nations. Although there are numerous m-learning projects in developing countries, few research projects have investigated the feasibility of implementing m-learning in tertiary institutions in these developing countries including Zimbabwe. This study attempts to determine the feasibility of implementing m-learning in Zimbabwe by investigating factors that influence m-learning implementation and adoption, discovering students' and lecturers' attitudes towards m-learning, and discussing the potentials and challenges of m-learning. This study will develop a new model for m-learning, especially for Zimbabwean universities and other tertiary institutions in similar developing countries, thereby providing a conceptual foundation for future related research.**

Keywords-Mobile-learning; m-learning; developing countries; universities.

I. INTRODUCTION

The proliferation of mobile devices, particularly mobile phones, in developing nations, such as Namibia, Kuwait, India and Zimbabwe [1]-[4] has given hope to the integration of mobile technology into education practices. Studies from developing countries [5]-[9] have shown positive results for m-learning projects in supporting education in remote locations. In order for m-learning to succeed in higher education in the developing countries, it is necessary to understand the factors that influence m-learning implementation and adoption in such countries. To this end, this study addresses three research questions:

(1) What are the factors that influence the implementation of mobile learning in Zimbabwe?

(2) What are students' perceptions toward the mobile learning model?

(3) What are the academic staff perceptions toward the mobile learning model?

This paper is organized as follows: Section 2 introduces related studies followed by discussions on the importance of m-learning in Zimbabwe, m-learning potentials and challenges and the research gap. Section 3 discusses the research methodology. Section 4 presents the research outcomes. In Section 5, the proposed m-learning model is presented. Section 6 concludes the study.

II. BACKGROUND

A. *M-learning definition*

There is not yet a consensus on the definition of m-learning from an academic or professional standpoint which could be attributed to the rapidly evolving nature of the field. Literature shows varied definitions of m-learning revolving around the ambiguity of "mobile" in mobile learning [10]-[13]. Most studies focus on the mobility of the technology or the mobility of the learner, with one study highlighting the mobility of the content [14]. Earlier definitions of m-learning took a techno-centric perspective, defining m-learning as learning using mobile devices with an emphasis on the mobility of technologies [15]-[18]. The focus has shifted from the mobility of the devices to the mobility of the users [19]-[21]. There is a general consensus that m-learning involves the use of ubiquitous mobile devices for learning and teaching. This study focuses on learner-centred mobility, since learners use various technologies such as mobile devices, their own or other people's computers, as they move between settings.

B. *Why M-learning in Zimbabwe*

Education is widely accepted as a major factor in economic development [22]-[24]. Although educational indicators suggest that there have been improvements in Zimbabwe, such as increased enrolment across the different levels of education, the quality of education still faces noteworthy challenges.

Lack of access to quality education continues to be a major impediment to economic growth in developing countries. In Zimbabwe, universities are responsible for producing highly skilled manpower and are therefore central to the development of the country. There is a need to improve access to quality, cost-effective education in Zimbabwe. M-learning presents an opportunity to improve the quality of education in Zimbabwe given the availability of cheaper mobile devices, and that Zimbabwe can by-pass the fixed telephony network and increase mobile phone networks. Hence, m-learning has the potential to reach a wider segment of the population, facilitating the expansion of educational projects.

Zimbabwe has sixteen universities and eight polytechnic colleges, these institutions are yet to fully embrace m-learning. The information and communication technologies (ICT) infrastructure in some of these institutions is underutilised. In teaching and learning, ICT is largely used for placement of course outlines, notes, assignments and website links [25][26]. The integration of ICT with education is not uniform in Zimbabwe tertiary institutions.

C. M-learning potentials

M-learning provides a relatively cheaper means of integrating education with technology. Mobile devices are less expensive than personal computers (PCs) or laptops. The mobile phone density in Zimbabwe is above 100% [2]. Hence, m-learning has the potential to provide more access to information. Three important benefits of integrating education with technology are access, support and communication [27][28].

The mobile learning research community has proved that m-learning can enhance, extend and enrich the concept and activity of learning itself, beyond earlier conceptions of learning [29]. Some of the possibilities of m-learning include situated learning, context-aware learning, and personalised learning. M-learning enables learners to have access to a variety of resources and communities that share the same interests even in different locations, which produces a dynamic educational experience [30].

M-learning enables interaction between learners and lecturers and amongst learners themselves. M-learning fosters collaboration opportunities for learners [7] [30] [31]. There is evidence that collaboration produces better understanding [32]. Learners can now benefit from a range of user-generated content that can be accessed through various mobiles such as podcasts, which is native to mobiles; Wikipedia, that can be accessed on low-end mobiles and YouTube, which is accessed on high-end mobiles.

Most learners own and love mobile technologies and use them regularly in their personal lives [33][34]. It seems likely that these same learners would want to use their mobile devices to personalize their education and make it more engaging.

There are a number of m-learning pilot projects that have been carried out in developing countries, such as m-learning curriculum framework in South Africa [19], smartphone-based m-learning with physician trainees in Botswana [35], using mobile phone cameras for science learning and teaching in Sri-Lanka [36]. The pilot projects in developing countries have yielded positive results, which is encouraging so far. All countries need to educate the next generation's workforce. For developing countries, there is a need to provide education of an acceptable standard in order to produce a workforce that is effective and can support economic growth.

D. M-learning challenges

M-learning initiatives are infeasible in some developing nations because of a myriad of obstacles. A major impediment to m-learning adoption is inadequate infrastructure in the form of unreliable electricity supplies [37][38] and poor Internet connectivity [29][39][40].

Another major barrier to m-learning adoption is the high initial investment costs. There are high costs associated with equipment, connectivity, technical support, training and maintenance [31][41].

Some developing countries have educational policies restricting the use of mobile devices for learning, and some have government officials who are unaware of the potential of mobile phones to enhance education [27][38].

Academics have raised curriculum issues associated with m-learning from both pedagogical and practical perspectives [30]. Lecturers also expressed concerns regarding privacy and security [42]. There are fears that confidential information could be potentially exposed to students and that quality of content could be compromised when transferred to mobile learning activities [42]. Educators' concerns about security and privacy can prevent the effective penetration of mobile technology in the educational realm [43]. It is important to acknowledge the concerns raised by the lecturers as downplaying these concerns may prevent these key stakeholders from capitalizing on the benefits of mobile technologies in education.

Technological constraints such as size of device, multiple standards, numerous operating systems, and low battery life should also be considered when implementing m-learning [20][39][44][45]. It is difficult to address all barriers to m-learning as the obstacles are wide-ranging because of the diversity of developing nations.

E. Research Gap

There is a lack of m-learning models and frameworks grounded in empirical research in the context of developing countries. Literature [16][41] attributes this gap in research to lack of resources, in sharp contrast to developed countries where m-learning was facilitated by adequate resources and infrastructure. Previous researchers have examined the various combinations of aspects which influence m-learning implementation [45]-[50]. There are suggestions that models from developed countries can be applied to developing nations [41]. However, [38] argues that in developing countries various factors need to be considered. These include different levels of infrastructure, the needs and challenges due to unique cultures, as well as the various views of what constitutes learning if learners are to benefit from m-learning.

A review of the available m-learning frameworks from both developing and developed countries shows that the existing m-learning frameworks cannot be adopted as there are gaps in these conceptual models, making them inadequate for implementation in the Zimbabwean context with respect to (1) factors influencing m-learning adoption (2) challenges to m-learning (3) m-learning characteristics and (4) pedagogy. There is a need to conduct research which includes the various aspects as in the proposed conceptual model to examine how they *collectively* influence m-learning implementation.

III. RESEARCH METHODS

The mixed-methods approach will be employed for this study. Participants for this study will be drawn from m-learning stakeholders in tertiary institutions comprising students, lecturers, administrators, librarians and information technology (IT) personnel and the relevant government ministries in Zimbabwe.

The study will adopt an exploratory design because of the scant previous research on m-learning in tertiary education in Zimbabwe, starting with the in-depth interviews followed by focus groups.

In-depth interviews will be used to collect data from the lecturers, library staff, administrative staff, university IT staff, mobile service providers, the Ministry of Higher Education, and the Ministry of ICT. Based on the proposed conceptual model, the themes to be discussed will include connectivity, educational policies, themes based on characteristics of m-learning and expectations of lecturers. It is anticipated that other themes will surface during the interviews.

Focus groups will be used to elicit learners' attitudes, experiences, beliefs and reactions which cannot easily be obtained by other methods. Purposeful sampling will be used to select focus groups. The pre-defined themes based on the proposed model will include usability, Human-Computer Interaction (HCI), cheaper mobile phones, culture and learners' expectations. It is anticipated that other themes will emerge from the focus group discussions.

IV. RESEARCH OUTCOMES

It is anticipated that this study will contribute to theoretical knowledge about various aspects underlying the successful implementation of m-learning in universities, both generally, and more specifically in relation to the mainstream higher education context of Zimbabwe. The latter poses a set of challenges that require careful investigation prior to the introduction of widespread m-learning in university pedagogy. This study will make a theoretical contribution in that it will show how each aspect of the proposed conceptual model is interacting (moderation/mediating) with others, and how all aspects will synergistically influence m-learning implementation. Furthermore, the study seeks to contribute to theoretical knowledge by offering recommendations regarding m-learning in developing countries. Students, researchers and academics will be able to use this model as a reference in future related studies.

From a practical perspective, the research aims to introduce an m-learning model for tertiary institutions in Zimbabwe, to facilitate the integration of technology in their teaching and learning approaches. It is anticipated that the m-learning model will encourage m-learning adoption and implementation in Zimbabwe and will be adopted by this country's other educational institutions. The m-learning model will provide guidelines for instructional designers and lecturers when designing m-learning activities, blending these with existing teaching and learning practices. Also, the universities, the education department of the Zimbabwean government and other stakeholders will benefit from this model. This model will enable students to experience dynamic learning anywhere anytime.

V. PROPOSED MODEL

The initial proposed m-learning model for Zimbabwe higher education will be drawn from existing frameworks in developing countries similar to Zimbabwe [5]-[9] and other m-learning studies [41][49][51].When reviewing m-learning studies, some studies emphasis on technical design and development of technologies. Some studies do not include challenges to m-learning implementation and do not explain the importance of learning theories in supporting m-learning. Although there are varied characteristics of m-learning and different factors that influence m-learning adoption, it is essential to examine the factors that influence m-learning adoption and the characteristics of m-learning. The factors and characteristics impact m-learning implementation and adoption especially where m-learning is in its infancy. The proposed model depicted in Figure 1 comprises the challenges of m-learning, factors that influence m-learning adoption, the key characteristics of m-learning, and pedagogy.

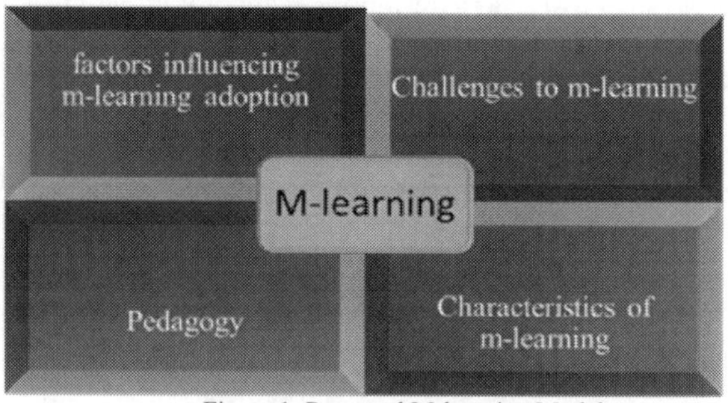

Figure 1. Proposed M-learning Model

A. *Factors influencing m-learning adoption*

There are a number of factors that influence m-learning implementation and adoption. Previous research has shown that m-learning has become attractive because of cheaper costs of mobile devices coupled with the increased capabilities of these devices [51]. There is a suggestion that the key factor in adopting m-learning in developing countries hinges on socio-cultural factors [52]. The study will investigate the various factors that affect m-learning adoption and implementation in developing countries, and seek to find how these factors interact with each other in influencing m-learning implementation and adoption.

B. Challenges to m-learning

In the proposed research model, the researcher has taken into account the challenges associated with m-learning. The researcher understands that these challenges can impede the effective design and implementation of m-learning in Zimbabwe. Literature shows that infrastructure is a major obstacle when implementing m-learning. This study will seek to identify and address challenges that can hinder m-learning implementation in Zimbabwe.

C. Characteristics of m-learning

The characteristics of m-learning will be identified in terms of tertiary institutions in Zimbabwe in order to produce an m-learning model for this country. Some key characteristics for m-learning from extant literature are: ubiquity, mobility, training and support, collaboration, blending, context, and communication [5]-[9] [48] [53].

D. Pedagogy

A study by P. Ramsden [54] indicates that there is a relationship between students' perceptions of their learning environment and their approach to learning. M-learning implementation should therefore take into consideration the learners' perceptions of their learning environments as they can potentially influence m-learning adoption. Early m-learning research was not explicitly grounded in learning theories [55]. It is likely that effective integration of mobile technologies with education will depend on whether m-learning has been based on sound learning theories.

VI. CONCLUSION

Although the benefits of m-learning have been widely publicised, there is a scarcity of empirical research on m-learning for tertiary institutions from developing countries, particularly in Africa. M-learning adoption and implementation by universities is technically complex given that the learning involves students, instructors, content and institutions. In developing countries like Zimbabwe, the implementation of m-learning is a complex process, made increasingly so by considerations of infrastructure and culture. It is anticipated that the proposed model will capture the various aspects of m-learning in the context of a developing country and that this model will serve as a conceptual foundation for future research in m-learning in Zimbabwe universities and tertiary institutions in other developing countries.

REFERENCES

[1] A. Al-Hunaiyyan, R. A. Alhajri, and S. Al-Sharhan, "Perceptions and challenges of mobile learning in Kuwait," *Journal of King Saud University - Computer and Information Sciences*, 2016.

[2] G. P. Kabanda, "Technology Affordances and Diffusion for Mobile Connectivity and Applications in Zimbabwe," International Journal of Emerging Technology and Advanced Engineering, 6 (6), p. 13-23, 2014

[3] R. Misra and S. Srivastava, "M-education in India: an effort to improve educational outcomes with a special emphasis on Ananya Bihar," *On the Horizon,* vol. 24, no. 2, pp. 153-165, 2016.

[4] J. Osakwe, N. Dlodlo, and N. Jere, "Where learners' and teachers' perceptions on mobile learning meet: A case of Namibian secondary schools in the Khomas region," *Technology in Society*, 2016.

[5] O. Adesope, S. Olubunmi, and J. McCracken, "Implementing mobile learning in developing countries: Prospects and challenges." *EdMedia: World Conference on Educational Media and Technology*, pp. 1249-1254. Association for the Advancement of Computing in Education (AACE), 2007.

[6] A. Barker, G. Krull, and B. Mallinson, "A proposed theoretical model for m-learning adoption in developing countries." *Proceedings of mLearn*, vol. 2005, p. 4th. 2005.

[7] T. H. Brown, "Towards a model for m-learning in Africa," *International journal on ELearning,* vol. 4, no. 3, pp. 299, 2005.

[8] M. Ford and A. Botha, "A pragmatic framework for integrating ICT into education in South Africa." *IST-Africa, 2010*, pp. 1-10. IEEE, 2010.

[9] K. Masters, "Low-key m-learning: a realistic introduction of m-learning to developing countries." *Sixth Conference on Communications in the 21st Century: Seeing, Understanding, Learning in the Mobile Age, Budapest*. 2005.

[10] M. O. M. El-Hussein and J. C. Cronje, "Defining Mobile Learning in the Higher Education Landscape," *Educational Technology & Society,* vol. 13, no. 3, pp. 12-21, 2010.

[11] Y.M. Huang, W.-Y. Hwang, and K.-E. Chang, "Guest Editorial-Innovations in Designing Mobile Learning Applications," *Educational Technology & Society,* vol. 13, no. 3, pp. 1-2, 2010.

[12] Y. Laouris and N. Eteokleous, "We need an educationally relevant definition of mobile learning. In mLearn 2005:4th World conference on mLearning" *Proceedings of mLearn.* (Vol. 2005).

[13] H. Peng, Y. J. Su, C. Chou, and C. C. Tsai, "Ubiquitous knowledge construction: Mobile learning re-defined and a conceptual framework," *Innovations in Education and Teaching International,* vol. 46, no. 2, pp. 171-183, 2009.

[14] D. E. Öngen, Ç. Hürsen, M. Halat, H. Boz, M. Hashemi, M. Azizinezhad, V. Najafi, and A. J. Nesari, "2nd World Conference on Psychology, Counselling and Guidance - 2011What is Mobile Learning? Challenges and Capabilities," *Procedia - Social and Behavioral Sciences,* vol. 30, pp. 2477-2481, 2011/01/01, 2011.

[15] K. Alsaadat, "Mobile learning and university teaching." *International Conference on Education and New Learning Technologies (EDULEARN09)*. Vol. 6, 2009.

[16] G. J. Hwang and C. C. Tsai, "Research trends in mobile and ubiquitous learning: A review of publications in selected

journals from 2001 to 2010," *British Journal of Educational Technology,* vol. 42, no. 4, pp. E65-E70, 2011.
[17] A. Kukulska-Hulme, *Mobile learning: A handbook for educators and trainers*: Psychology Press, 2005.
[18] J. Traxler, "Defining mobile learning." *IADIS International Conference Mobile Learning*, pp. 261-266. 2005.
[19] A. Botha, J. Batchelor, J. Traxler, I. de Waard, and M. Herselman, "Towards a mobile learning curriculum framework," *Proceedings of IIMC International Information Management Corporation. IST-Africa*, 2012.
[20] N. Pachler, B. Bachmair, and J. Cook, *Mobile devices as resources for learning: Adoption trends, characteristics, constraints and challenges*: Springer, 2010.
[21] M. Sharples, I. Arnedillo Sánchez, M. Milrad, and G. Vavoula, "Mobile Learning: Small devices, Big Issues. Book chapter to appear in Technology Enhanced Learning: Principles and Products, Kaleidoscope Legacy Book," Springer-Verlag, Berlin, 2008.
[22] D. E. Bloom, D. Canning, and K. Chan, *Higher education and economic development in Africa*: World Bank Washington, DC, 2006.
[23] T. Gylfason, "Natural resources, education, and economic development," *European economic review,* vol. 45, no. 4, pp. 847-859, 2001.
[24] P. P. Saviotti, A. Pyka, and B. Jun, "Education, structural change and economic development," *Structural Change and Economic Dynamics,* vol. 38, pp. 55-68, 9//, 2016.
[25] P. Mupfiga and M. Chirimumimba, "Application of mobile computing in tertiary institutions: case study of Midlands State University," 2015.
[26] S. Mavellas and M. Samuel, "Investigating The Use Of Mobile Computing In Zimbabwe Polytechnics: Case Of A Polytechnic In Zimbabwe," *International Journal of Scientific & Technology Research,* vol. 4, no. 7, pp. 121-125, 2015.
[27] Y. Mehdipour and H. Zerehkafi, "Mobile learning for education: Benefits and challenges," *International Journal of Computational Engineering Research,* vol. 3, no. 6, pp. 93-101, 2013.
[28] J. H. Valk, A. T. Rashid, and L. Elder, "Using mobile phones to improve educational outcomes: An analysis of evidence from Asia," *The International Review of Research in Open and Distributed Learning,* vol. 11, no. 1, pp. 117-140, 2010.
[29] J. Traxler, "Mobile learning: Shaping the frontiers of learning technologies in global context," *Reshaping Learning*, pp. 237-251: Springer, 2013.
[30] B. Handal, J. MacNish, and P. Petocz, "Adopting mobile learning in tertiary environments: Instructional, curricular and organizational matters," *Education Sciences,* vol. 3, no. 4, pp. 359-374, 2013.
[31] J. B. Ferreira, A. Z. Klein, A. Freitas, and E. Schlemmer, "Mobile Learning: Definition, Uses and Challenges," *Increasing Student Engagement and Retention Using Mobile Applications: Smartphones, Skype and Texting Technologies*, pp. 47-82, 2013.
[32] D. Parsons, H. Ryu, and M. Cranshaw, "A Study of Design Requirements for Mobile Learning Environments." *Advanced Learning Technologies, 2006. Sixth International Conference on.* IEEE, pp. 96-100, 2006.
[33] B. Jin and J. F. Pena, "Mobile communication in romantic relationships: Mobile phone use, relational uncertainty, love, commitment, and attachment styles," *Communication Reports,* vol. 23, no. 1, pp. 39-51, 2010.
[34] H. Thinyane, "Are digital natives a world-wide phenomenon? An investigation into South African first year students' use and experience with technology," *Computers & Education,* vol. 55, no. 1, pp. 406-414, 2010.
[35] A. Y. Chang, R. Littman-Quinn, D. Ketshogileng, A. Chandra, T. Rijken, S. Ghose, A. Kyer, A. K. Seymour, and C. L. Kovarik, "Smartphone-based mobile learning with physician trainees in Botswana," *International Journal of Mobile and Blended Learning (IJMBL),* vol. 4, no. 2, pp. 1-14, 2012.
[36] S. Ekanayake and J. Wishart, "Identifying the potential of mobile phone cameras in science teaching and learning: A case study undertaken in Sri Lanka," *Innovations in Mobile Educational Technologies and Applications*, pp. 162-177: IGI Global, 2013.
[37] L. E. Armey and L. Hosman, "The centrality of electricity to ICT use in low-income countries," *Telecommunications Policy,* vol. 40, no. 7, pp. 617-627, 7//, 2016.
[38] J. Traxler, "Mobile learning in international development," *Global mobile learning implementations and trends*, pp. 45, 2013.
[39] L. Adam, N. Butcher, F. Tusubira, C. Sibthorpe, and D. Souter, "Transformation-Ready: The strategic application of information and communication technologies in Africa," *Education sector study. Washington, DC: The World Bank Retrieved from worldbank.org/EXTINFORMATIONANDCOMMUNICATIONAND TECHNOLOGIES/Resources/282822-1346223280837/RegionalTradeandIntegration_Fullreport. pdf,* 2011.
[40] N. Y. Asabere, "Benefits and challenges of mobile learning implementation: Story of developing nations," *International Journal of Computer Applications,* vol. 73, no. 1, 2013.
[41] Y. C. Hsu and Y.-H. Ching, "A review of models and frameworks for designing mobile learning experiences and environments," *Canadian Journal of Learning and Technology,* 2015.
[42] S. A. Shonola and M. Joy, "Mobile learning security issues from lecturers' perspectives (Nigerian universities case study)," *EDULEARN14 Proceedings*, pp. 7081-7088, 2014.
[43] G. Kambourakis, "Security and Privacy in m-Learning and Beyond: Challenges and State-of-the-art," *International Journal of u-and e-Service, Science and Technology,* vol. 6, no. 3, pp. 67-84, 2013.
[44] G. Orr, "A review of literature in mobile learning: Affordances and constraints." *Wireless, Mobile and Ubiquitous Technologies in Education (WMUTE), 2010 6th IEEE International Conference on*, pp. 107-111. IEEE, 2010.
[45] F. B. Osang, J. Ngole, and C. Tsuma, "Prospects and challenges of mobile learning implementation in Nigeria: Case study National Open University of Nigeria (NOUN)." *International Conference on ICT for Africa*, pp. 20-23. 2013.
[46] T. D. Cochrane, "Critical success factors for transforming pedagogy with mobile Web 2.0," *British Journal of Educational Technology,* vol. 45, no. 1, pp. 65-82, 2014.
[47] A. Herrington and J. Herrington, "Authentic mobile learning in higher education," 2007.
[48] U. Imtinan, V. Chang, and T. Issa, "Common Mobile Learning Characteristics--An Analysis of Mobile Learning Models and Frameworks," *International Association for Development of the Information Society*, 2013.

[49] Y. Liu, H. Li, and C. Carlsson, "Factors driving the adoption of m-learning: An empirical study," *Computers & Education,* vol. 55, no. 3, pp. 1211-1219, 2010.

[50] M. Sharples, P. Lonsdale, J. Meek, P. Rudman, and G. N. Vavoula, "An evaluation of MyArtSpace: A mobile learning service for school museum trips," 2007.

[51] S. Iqbal and I. A. Qureshi, "M-learning adoption: A perspective from a developing country," *The International Review of Research in Open and Distributed Learning,* vol. 13, no. 3, pp. 147-164, 2012.

[52] J. Keengwe and M. Bhargava, "Mobile learning and integration of mobile technologies in education," *Education and Information Technologies,* vol. 19, no. 4, pp. 737-746, 2014.

[53] F. Ozdamli and N. Cavus, "Basic elements and characteristics of mobile learning," *Procedia-Social and Behavioral Sciences,* vol. 28, pp. 937-942, 2011.

[54] P. Ramsden, *Learning to teach in higher education*: Routledge, 2003.

[55] J. Traxler and A. Kukulska-Hulme, "Evaluating mobile learning: Reflections on current practice," 2005.

Frequency of Sticker Use for Expressing Emotions in Text Messaging

Effects of Gender and Text-Messaging Dependency

Yasuyuki Ozawa
Faculty of Education
Meisei University
Tokyo, Japan
e-mail: ozawa.yasuyuki@gmail.com

Yuuki Kato
Faculty of Arts and Sciences
Sagami Women's University
Kanagawa, Japan
e-mail: y-katou@star.sagami-wu.ac.jp

Shogo Kato
School of Arts and Sciences
Tokyo Woman's Christian University
Tokyo, Japan
e-mail: shogo@lab.twcu.ac.jp

***Abstract*—In online learning, emotional support for the learner is important for increasing learning effectiveness. Graphical symbols, such as emoticons, work as emotional expressions in text-based online interactions. This study focuses on "stickers", a new form of graphical expression. Using questionnaires, we asked participants how frequently they used stickers to express seven types of emotions. This study examined the effects of gender and text-messaging dependency on frequency of sticker use for expressing emotions in text messaging. As a result, the effects of gender and dependency were confirmed.**

Keywords—sticker; emotional expression; gender difference; text-messaging dependency; text messenger.

I. INTRODUCTION

In online learning, emotional support for the learner reduces dropout and is important for increasing learning effectiveness. Social presence theory frequently refers to such support as a theoretical framework [1]. This theory was proposed in early media research and holds that media offering few non-verbal cues have a low social presence in comparison with face-to-face communication [2]. Subsequent online learning research has shown that social presence can be increased by various means, even in Computer-Mediated Communication (CMC) [3][4]. Increased social presence is receiving more attention as an important factor for helping online learning students [5]. In personal CMC, emoticons and emoji, mutual greetings, shared empathy, and self-disclosure are important necessary means of increasing social presence [4]. Emoticons and emoji in particular are closely related to emotional expressions [6]. However, in recent years, a new type of graphical symbol known as "stickers" (illustrations, often containing characters or text, sent in lieu of messages on many messaging platforms) have emerged. These can be used in text messenger apps while using mobile devices. Originally, a sticker was an illustration that could be attached to a text message in LINE from 2011, an instant messenger application mainly used on smartphones in Japan [7]. By 2013, Facebook messenger was also equipped with similar features, followed by Facebook timeline in 2014. In 2016, iMessage for iPhone added sticker functionality.

As many previous studies have pointed out, given the impact of symbols such as emoticons on text-based CMC [6], stickers are considered to have potential capabilities [8]. However, few studies have investigated stickers in text messaging. In this study, we conducted a basic survey on stickers in text messaging with smartphones.

Specifically, we examined the effects of gender and text-messaging dependency on sticker use in text messaging. Many studies have shown gender differences in socioemotional interactions in online communication [9], and some studies have found that women use more emoticons [10]. Therefore, we aimed to clarify gender differences in sticker use for expressing emotions in text messaging. Further, studies on text-messaging dependency have shown that high-dependency users tend to exhibit excessive use of text messaging to build socioemotional relationships [11]. High-dependency users who place importance on text-based interactions to maintain human relationships are thought to make greater use of graphical symbols available for communications. Accordingly, we also investigated the effects of text-messaging dependency on sticker use for expressing emotions in text messaging.

The rest of the paper is structured as follows. In Section 2, we present the method of this study. In Section 3, we present the results of this study. Finally, we conclude in Section 4.

II. METHOD

The survey participants were 300 Japanese students (152 women, 148 men; mean age = 20.12; standard deviation (SD) = 1.26) at universities in the Tokyo area. They were not students in an online course. Participation in this survey was voluntary. Participants were asked to answer a paper-based questionnaire. We asked participants to report their frequency of sticker use in text message exchanges to express each of seven kinds of emotion (joy, surprise, sadness, anxiety, anger, guilt, and love) using a 6-point Likert-like scale from 1 (not at all) to 6 (almost every time). In addition, we asked participants about the frequency of their daily use of stickers in text-messaging. We measured messaging dependency using the 15-item short version of the Text-Message Dependency Scale [11] modified by the authors. This scale comprises emotional reaction, perception of excessive use, and relationship maintenance subscales, each with five questions scored on a 5-point Likert-like scale from 1 (strongly disagree) to 5 (strongly agree).

III. RESULTS

Participants were grouped according to degree of text-messaging dependency by calculating each participant's score on each subscale. Next, we used IBM SPSS Statistics 24, which is a statistical package for the social sciences, to perform a two-step cluster analysis using the three subscale scores as variables to comprehensively reflect their scores in this classification. This resulted in participants' division into two clusters: Cluster 1 (N = 154) contained the high text-messaging dependency group and Cluster 2 (N = 146) the low dependency group.

To investigate the influence of gender and degree of text-messaging dependency on usual frequency of sticker use, we assigned gender and dependency groups (high and low) as between-subjects factors and then performed a two-way analysis of variance. The results of the analysis of variance were as follows: the main effect of gender, $F(1, 295) = 46.92$, $p < 0.001$; and the main effect of dependency, $F(1, 295) = 0.93$, ns. There was no significant interaction. This result indicates that, compared with men, women used more stickers in text messaging on a daily basis.

Next, to investigate the influence of gender and degree of text-messaging dependency on frequency of sticker use for expressing each of seven emotions, we assigned gender and dependency groups as between-subjects factors, and then performed a two-way analysis of variance in each emotion. A significant main effect of gender was seen in the following five emotions: joy: $F(1, 296) = 73.79$, $p < 0.001$; surprise: $F(1, 296) = 6.03$, $p < 0.05$; sadness: $F(1, 295) = 40.71$, $p < 0.001$; guilt: $F(1, 296) = 22.66$, $p < 0.001$; love: $F(1, 295) = 45.72$, $p < 0.001$. A marginally significant main effect of dependency was seen in the following three emotions: joy: $F(1, 296) = 3.55$, $p = 0.061$; sadness: $F(1, 295) = 3.15$, $p = 0.077$; anxiety: $F(1, 295) = 3.19$, $p = 0.075$. There was no significant interaction for all seven emotions. These results are as follows. Joy and sadness were affected by both gender and dependency. Surprise, guilt and love were affected only by gender. Anxiety was affected only by dependency. Anger was not affected by either gender or dependency. These results are shown in Figure 1.

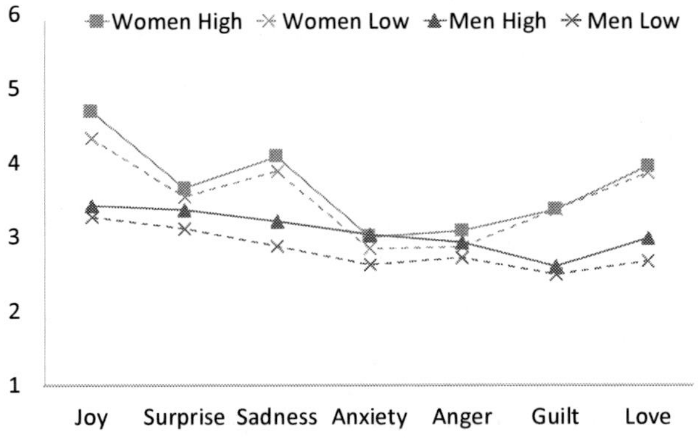

Figure 1. Comparison of frequencies of using stickers to express seven kinds of emotions by gender and dependency.

IV. CONCLUSION AND FUTURE WORK

This study investigated emotional expression using stickers as preliminary research into new emotional support in online learning via smartphones. To date, there have been almost no reports of research on stickers internationally. Our findings showed that, compared with men, women used stickers more frequently on a daily basis, and more frequently used them to express joy, surprise, sadness, guilt, and love. These gender differences are consistent with the results of previous studies on symbols such as emoticons used in text-based CMC [10]. In addition, our findings showed that individuals with high dependency use stickers more frequently than those with low dependency to express joy, sadness, and anxiety. Within the context of dependency, the most characteristic result was considered to be expression of anxiety, where no gender difference was noticed. This result may be attributable to individuals with high dependency tending to often feel uneasy about maintaining human relationships in online communication [11]. There was no difference between individuals with high dependency and individuals with low dependency regarding the usual use of stickers. Stickers are not only used to express emotions – they can also be used to convey various communicative intents such as expressing opinions and attitudes [8]. Individuals with low dependency may use stickers more for purposes other than emotional communication. Verification of this is work for future research. The findings of this study and subsequent works will provide valuable information for mentors who communicate (chat) with learners to increase social presence and prevent dropouts in online learning.

The primary limitation of this study was that all the participants were undergraduate students at Japanese universities. Thus, it is unclear whether the current findings can be generalized to users of various ages from other countries and cultural backgrounds. Finally, future work is needed to examine in detail the role of various graphical symbols (including stickers) collected in real online learning environments, to propose ways of increasing learners' social presence and fostering their learning activities.

ACKNOWLEDGMENT

This work was supported by JSPS KAKENHI Grant Numbers 15K01089, 15K01095.

REFERENCES

[1] C. N. Gunawardena and F. J. Zittle, "Social presence as a predictor of satisfaction within a computer-mediated conferencing environment," American Journal of Distance Education, vol. 11, no. 3, pp. 8-26, 1997, doi:10.1080/08923649709526970.

[2] J. A. Short, E. Williams, and B. Christie, The social psychology of telecommunications. London: Wiley, 1976.

[3] J. C. Richardson and K. Swan, "Examining social presence in online courses in relation to students' perceived learning and satisfaction," Journal of Asynchronous Learning Networks, vol. 7, pp. 68-88, 2003, Available from: http://hdl.handle.net/2142/18713.

[4] K. Swan, "Building communities in online courses: The importance of interaction. Education. Communication and

Information," vol. 2, pp. 23-49, 2002, doi:10.1080/146363 1022000005016.

[5] D. R. Garrison and T. Anderson, E-learning in the 21st century: A framework for research and practice. London: Routledge Falmer, 2003.

[6] A. Garrison, D. Remley, P. Thomas, and E. Wierszewski, "Conventional faces: Emoticons in instant messaging discourse," Computers and Composition, vol. 28, pp. 112-125, 2011, doi:10.1016/j.compcom.2011.04.001.

[7] Ministry of Internal Affairs and Communications, "White paper 2016: Information and communications in Japan," 2016, Available from http://www.soumu.go.jp/johotsusintokei/ whitepaper/eng/WP2016/2016-index.html.

[8] S. S. Wang, "More than words? The effect of Line character sticker use on intimacy in the mobile communication environment," Social Science Computer Review, vol. 34, pp. 456-478, 2016, doi:org/10.1177/0894439315590209.

[9] M. Timmers, A. H. Fischer, and A. S. R. Manstead, "Gender differences in motives for regulating emotions," Personality and Social Psychology Bulletin, vol. 24, pp. 974-985, 1998, doi:10.1177/0146167298249005.

[10] D. Derks, A. H. Fischer, and A. E. Bos, "The role of emoticon in computer-mediated communication: A review," Computers in Human Behavior, vol. 24, pp. 766-785, 2008, doi:10.1016/j. chb.2007.04.004.

[11] T. Igarashi, T. Motoyoshi, J. Takai, and T. Yoshida, "No mobile, no life: Self-perception and text-message dependency among Japanese high school students," Computers in Human Behavior, vol. 24, pp. 2311-2324, 2008, doi:10.1016/j.chb. 2007.12.001.

The Potential of Support-Rich Environment for Teaching Meaningful Mathematics to Low-Achieving Students

Yifat Ben-David Kolikant
School of Education
Hebrew University of Jerusalem
Jerusalem, Israel
Email: Yifat.kolikant@mail.huji.ac.il

Orit Broza
Levinsky College
Tel-Aviv, Israel
Email: Orit.broza1@gmail.com

***Abstract*— We have designed a collaborative, computer-supported, rich environment to promote meaningful mathematics among low-achieving students (LAS). Fifth-grade students interchangeably solved decimal subtraction tasks with peers in the context of a computer game and simulations, and in discussion sessions, led by their teachers, in foursomes. We describe the results of the first round of our design-based research, where we traced three such groups, using observations and interviews. We found that the computer context was both constructive and destructive, in terms of students' learning. The group discussions did not yield the rich discussions we had hoped for. Yet, overall, the environment was successful because students gained meaningful mathematical knowledge and practiced active, thoughtful, and collaborative socio-mathematical behavior, which is dramatically different from what they were used to.**

Keywords-low-achieving students; support-rich environment; computer games; scaffoldings; computer-supported collaborative learning.

I. Introduction

The question of how students' construction of meaningful knowledge can be supported presents an important challenge to researchers and teachers alike. Teaching the complex topic of mathematics to low-achieving students (LAS) poses a special challenge, owing to LAS's unique cognitive and behavioral characteristics [12]. The teaching and learning processes of LAS have been studied by examining different teaching methods, strategies, and tactics (e.g., [2]). However, we found sparse work on the effectiveness of rich environments, let alone environments of computer-supported collaborative-learning (CSCL), on the learning processes and outcomes of LAS.

In fact, LAS characteristics, which we describe next, might bring one to suspect the feasibility of teaching LAS basic mathematics, let alone in (Computer Supported) Collaborative Learning (CS)CL settings. Nonetheless, we hypothesized that a rich CSCL environment, involving a computer game, real context mathematics, peer discussions, and teacher mediation may be the key for addressing the LAS's unique and diversified needs. Here, we describe the results of the first round of a design-based research we have conducted to examine these hypotheses. We first describe the characteristics of LAS. Then, we review the literature and how it influenced our hypotheses and design. Next, we describe a study, the first round of a design-based research in which we examined our hypotheses. We traced the participation of 3 groups of four students each in the activities we had designed, using various data sources, such as the videotapes and audiotapes of the classes, interviews, and ad-hoc conversations with the students and the teachers, along with observations. We discuss our findings and the practical implications on our design framework and the broader community. Our main conclusion is that CSCL, when carefully designed, can promote LAS learning of meaningful mathematics as well as the development of socio-mathematical skills.

The rest of the paper is structured as follows. In Section II, we review the literature on LAS as well as on successful interventions in terms of meaningful learning. Then, we describe our pedagogical design (Section IV), and the literature that inspired us in the design, such as the decision to involve a computer-game session in which students work in pairs, and small-group discussions led by the teacher (Section III). We then describe the study (Section V). We examined how the rich environment either hinders or supports students' construction of mathematical meaning. Our focus was on the mutual interplay between the two contexts in which students worked (on the computer and in group discussions). We present the findings (Section VI) and discuss them (Section VII).

II. LAS and Meaningful Mathematics

There is no single, definitive profile for LAS [7][16]. In fact, most of studies have not focused on the methodological criteria used to identify those students with learning disabilities [16]. LAS are commonly identified based on two factors: teacher reports and their performance on standardized or informal tests (students' score below the 50th percentile on standardized tests; however, they are not diagnosed as having learning disabilities) [2]. In attempting to explain LAS's poor performance, the literature focuses on cognitive deficiencies and on behavioral manifestations of their failures. LAS find it difficult to retrieve basic mathematics knowledge from their memory [10]. Craik [5] terms this difficulty as 'fragile memory', a product of superficial data processing. They also lack meta-cognitive skills [9], and are sensitive to the learning contexts. They thus find it much harder than others to solve simple and complex addition and subtraction problems. These difficulties may lead them to use less sophisticated strategies and to make more errors.

Recently, Karagiannakis et al. [14] developed a model that can be used to sketch students' mathematical profiles for four domains (numbers, memory, number line, and reasoning); they empirically examined it to determine whether and how it can differentiate students with and without difficulties in learning mathematics. According to their analysis, students, both the normal/high achievers and the underachievers, do not all share the same sets of strong or weak mathematical skills. In addition, under achievement in mathematics is not related to weaknesses in a single domain (e.g., numbers, memory, number line, and reasoning). They also suggest that for LAS students, just like for the other students, cognitive strengths or weaknesses may rely on any of the four domains (mentioned above) of their model. Their findings empirically strengthen the heterogeneity of this population group.

Experiencing repeated failures and difficulties in keeping up with the class might in turn, decrease their motivation and sense of internal responsibility and make them more passive learners. It might also lead them to act impulsively, rely on the judgment and feedback of an external authority [12], and avoid collaborative work with peers [1]. Their schooling-purposed interaction in class is, for the most part, with the teacher.

These characteristics probably underlie many teachers' beliefs that LAS are unable to deal with tasks involving high-order thinking skills and that the most effective way of promoting mathematical performance in LAS is to 'drill and kill', that is, to focus more on the mathematical algorithms than on the mathematical meaning [15]. However, despite their difficulties, there is empirical evidence that in certain environments LAS are capable of enhancing their mathematical understanding. There is empirical evidence that LAS can exhibit mathematical reasoning orally when placed in intimate and supportive learning environments, such as in small groups where they are tutored [3][15]. Peltenburg et al. [20] show that, in a familiar context with the help of technological tools, LAS can succeed in solving subtraction problems by using an indirect addition strategy spontaneously, rather than the conventional direct subtraction strategy. Karagiannakis and Cooreman [13] suggest that these interventions should be designed for repeated success by building on a student's strengths, while avoiding use of repetitive tasks that cause repetitive failure experiences, thereby maximizing the learning opportunities of all students.

This led us to assume that a rich environment that includes technological tools, small groups, and teacher's support building on LAS' strengths might be the key for their success.

III. The Literature Inspiring the Design and Hypotheses

Our design was inspired by the socio-cultural theoretical perspective on learning, especially the notion of distributed scaffolding. Scaffolding is "titrated support that helps learners learn through activity. It helps learners perform tasks that are outside their independent reach and consequently develop the skills necessary for completing such tasks independently" [24, p.306] . Because LAS vary in their behavior, in our design we sought to design distributed scaffoldings [22], i.e., to integrate and sequence multiple forms of support via various means. Different scaffolds interact with each other; sometimes they produce a robust form of support, a synergy [24], and other times they might sabotage the learning processes and the outcome.

We were inspired by the Learning in Context approach, namely, the idea of presenting mathematical concepts and procedures in a context relevant to the child's day-to-day life [11], and in particular, the Realistic Mathematics Education (RME) theoretical framework. According to the RME framework, students should advance from contextual problems using significant models that are situation related, to mathematical activity at a higher level (e.g., engaging in more formal mathematical reasoning). As students progress from informal to more formal mathematics, their "*model of*" the situation is transformed into a "*model for*" reasoning. We hypothesized that RME could be the key to promote meaningful learning for LAS, because the subtraction tasks, the mathematics to be mastered, will be associated with real-life experiences, which might mitigate their fragile memory and tendency for superficial processing of new knowledge.

We aimed at transforming students' social and socio-mathematical norms, from passive to active, from isolated to social collaboration, from impulsive to thoughtful. We were motivated by the premise that digital games, by the nature of their design, have the potential to motivate students in becoming active rather than passive, by enabling experimentation and exploration without fear of failing in front of the entire class [8][23]. The use of games for teaching may be particularly beneficial for LAS because of their tendency to remain passive and to comply with authoritative voices. We were aware of the possibility that a hands-on, minds-off strategy might emerge, especially because of the tendency for impulsivity. This is one of the reasons students were asked to work with peers in front of the computer. We assumed that collaborative settings would trigger twofold interactions: with the system and with the co-learner. Peers would explain their calculations to each other, and question other actions, which would bring about reflection and thoughtfulness [6].

Every session was designed to include interchangeable students' work in front of the computer with their peers, along with group discussions, led by the teacher. Teachers' interactions with students can create zones of opportunities that can be directed to scaffold students' social and emotional development [19]. The teacher can mediate the use of tools (e.g., computer games, online units), orchestrate the students' activities, and reframe them conceptually [17].

The students, hence, experienced two different collaborative settings. When students worked (in pairs) in front of the computer (game or online units), the teachers were asked to observe them and to offer help when necessary (for instance, if students maintain trial and error strategies or are stuck in their calculation process). In the group discussions, the teachers were asked to focus the discussion on various strategies that can be used to solve subtraction tasks, encourage students to verbalize their thoughts, and encourage them to rely on each other's past experience, thereby facilitating students in learning the meaning of how to participate in the community, i.e., support the transformation of their sociomathematical norms [4]. In these discussions, the teachers also introduced students to new tasks and encouraged them to employ the strategies previously used in a supposedly new context. As we will explain in the next section, in our design we presented tasks sometimes as stories and sometimes as formal subtraction exercises, and gradually increased the difficulty of calculating the numbers whose decimals are half, to numbers, whose decimals include individual units. We assumed that students' sense of security when expressing themselves publicly would increase, since they are in a group of equals, and will experience active (and successful) work with their peers in front of the computer.

IV. THE INSTRUCTIONAL DESIGN

We developed an extracurricular program for fifth grade LAS. It consisted of ten weekly sessions that focus on subtraction with decimal numbers, a topic that students had not yet learned in their regular classes. Students were categorized into groups of four, according to their regular class, and each group worked with a teacher trained by the second author.

We utilized a *real life context* simulated by an ice-cream shop computer game. Specifically, during the sessions, students played a computer game in which they received orders from random customers, prepared the orders, calculated the price to be paid, and gave change as needed (Figure 1). Because of the heterogeneity of the LAS and their individual needs, we sought to provide a variety of support types. Therefore, students also worked on supplementary online study units concerned with the transition between money and formal representations, as well as change calculations. Students also enacted game-like situations with play money in Israeli bills and coins: New Israeli Shekels (NIS) and agorot (1NIS = 100 agorot, and the smallest coin is 10 agorot). In order to support the transition from the concrete to the abstract, real-paper worksheets were designed, which included exercises in concrete, graphic, and abstract forms.

In order to facilitate a delicate transition from the realistic environment (shop simulation) to formal mathematics, subtraction was first presented through monetary simulations and calculations only, and formal representations were interwoven at a later stage. The program progresses in a *spiral-like manner*. With the help of the teacher, students are expected to progress from one level to the next. The tasks at each level maintain an overall forward trend of increasing complexity, and students are able to revisit earlier levels and solve simpler exercises on the computer on their own. The teachers had the flexibility to attune the program, in response to students' emerging needs.

Figure 1. A screenshot of an online learning unit, where the task at hand is 50-38.6.

In each session, students spent almost half of their time in front of the computer, working in pairs. They were first introduced through online activity to two avatars, a girl and a boy, each of whom described a strategy for calculating the required change. Then they played or worked in pairs on the computer. The other half was devoted to class discussions, as described above. Specifically, in order to address LAS's tendency to passively rely on external authority and to encourage them to take personal responsibility, the teachers were not supposed to correct students' strategies directly, but rather, to ask questions to encourage them to talk aloud about their thinking processes, thus, making diagnosis easier and potentially leading them to correct their own mistakes, re-voicing when needed, and referring them to suitable tools in the environment when necessary. The teacher generally followed these instructions well.

V. THE STUDY

Our goal was to examine our design's hypotheses, i.e., to examine how the rich environment either hinders or supports students' construction of mathematical meaning, especially the mutual interplay between the two contexts in which students worked (on the computer and in group discussions).

A. Participants

We traced 12 LAS (4 male, 8 female) from 3 fifth grade classes in suburban schools within the same city, who participated in the program. All participants were chosen based on the recommendation of their mathematics teachers. They all performed under the 50th percentile on standardized tests, yet were not diagnosed as having learning disabilities.

B. Data Sources

In two groups all sessions were videotaped. In one group they were audiotaped. We observed students in their regular class two times before they began participating in our activities. We also observed all the sessions, and documented how the teacher presented the tasks, focusing on the sequence of activities—of both the teacher (e.g., presenting the tasks, intervening during the computer sessions, suggesting a tool, getting students' attention, answering questions) and the students (e.g., how they interact with the computer, with each other, with the teacher, and so forth). We conducted interviews with the CSCL teachers, after the activity as well as ad hoc conversations after every session. We also talked with the parents' class mathematics teachers and to each student after the CSCL activity.

C. Methods of Analysis

Our report mainly draws on the analysis of the videotapes. We were inspired by the analysis model of Powell et al. [21] for developing mathematical ideas and reasoning. We fully transcribed one group through videotapes. The transcripts were coded twice by two researchers. We segmented the text into episodes, each beginning with the presentation of a new task and ending with its being accomplished (or the work on it was terminated). For each episode we examined: (1) who participated in it; (2) the knowledge pieces that emerged; (3) the difficulties that arose, including whether they were solved, and if so, how and by whom, especially (d) the support provided by the teacher; and (5) whether the task was successfully accomplished independently or with help from others. We also coded affective utterances, both positive and negative. We compared the results with the video, audio, and notes taken during the observations in the other groups. Interviews were analyzed thematically.

VI. FINDINGS

As we hypothesized, the computerized environment, especially the computer game, encouraged the students to be active as well as engaged in their task. For the most part, they were observed to be very focused on the task in hand. In fact, in 5 sessions, students continued working (or playing) after the class had ended. The students reported in the interviews and ad hoc conversations that they had enjoyed the activity. The following quotes are but two examples of typical phrases heard throughout the entire program: "it was fun…not a regular class", "playing with the computer gives a sense of fun, [vs.] a blackboard, where you just sit and solve exercises".

On the computer the students usually decided to work in turns. In each turn the one on the keyboard gave ice-cream, calculated the price, the change, and returned change. For a few couples, we noticed a different division of labor: the one on the keyboard interacted with the avatar clients and in the meantime, the other did the calculations. In a few cases when one student took over the keyboard the teacher interfered.

During the play, each student solved many subtraction exercises, manifested by the need to give change to customers in the shop.

Failures in this context did not discourage them. On the contrary, this is when we observed collaboration, mathematical discussions with their peers and with the teacher. Usually, when they received a response from a "customer" indicating that the change they gave was incorrect, they were observed pausing to think and sometimes they turned to their peers and verbalized their "solution process". Sometimes this verbalization was performed after their peers asked them how they had worked. The discussion helped them many times to correct themselves. This behavior was dramatically different from the observed passivity (or impulsivity) in the regular classes. Moreover, in this context, the students generally welcomed the teachers' intervention and cooperated with them. Hence, the computer and the peers often generated a synergetic effect on the students.

However, we also observed an appreciable number of situations in which students merely employed trial and error, using the immediate feedback of the computer ("too much" and "too little") to guess the correct answer. Usually the partner became silent in these situations. From the conversations in these situations, we learned that the pressure of time and the wish to gain as many points as possible in the game in a designated time encouraged this behavior. In one extreme example, one student stopped working because the clients became angry, because it took her time to calculate. We also noticed that in the initial lessons the teacher had to compete with students' attention to their computer in these situations. We observed the teacher, in such situations, touching the students' hand or shoulder to get their attention.

We observed many expressions of frustration among the students during group discussions. The teacher borrowed the idea of students taking turns when at the computer and asked them to solve exercises in turns in the group discussions. However, this idea turned out to be less productive. For the most part, the interaction took the form of one student explaining his or her solution process, followed by the teacher's verbalization. The teacher sometimes told the peers to be quiet, in an attempt to assist the individual to think and (re-)calculate. We thus observed almost no rich peer discussions about strategies. In her interview she explained that students' poor discursive habits made her prioritize the individual's learning over building a community and discursive habits.

We expected that during the participation the students' ability and wiliness to provide explanations would increase. During the discussion with the teacher (with or without a computer) the students were constantly asked to describe and explain their strategies. The alienation of this request was prominent in their responses. They became silent, gave vague or non-informative answers (e.g., "I just did so"), and sometimes even said, "I don't remember".

In some of the students there was evidence of a change in their discursive manners. In these cases we found that students relied on the money model (especially the fact that 1 nis = 100 agorot) to explain their subtraction strategies even when the subtraction task was phrased in an abstract manner and not in money terms. Real context mathematics, hence, supported students' leaning.

We also expected that the students would develop many strategies for subtraction. Indeed, the teacher posed questions like "in what way would you like to solve this problem?" at least three times in each of the first three sessions. However, we did not observe the emergence of a new strategy. One possible explanation is rooted in our sequencing of students' activities. In the initial lessons, students were introduced by an online unit to two strategies, presented to them by two avatars, who dealt with the task of calculating change. Possibly, this early exposure, together with students' tendencies to rely on external authoritative voices, brought about a fixation in their thoughts. Moreover, sometimes we were not sure that students understood the meaning underlying these strategies.

Nonetheless, in conversations with the teachers in the regular classes after the program ended, the teachers reported that the behavior of most of the participants in their class improved; specifically, that despite their difficulties they were more motivated and less passive.

VII. Discussion and Conclusions

The findings support the premise that RME is valuable in facilitating LAS meaningful learning [11]. Students adapted the real-life money model to resolve the subtraction tasks, even when given in an abstract form.

The computer-peer setting was found to be both supportive and destructive in terms of students' learning. The computer played a major role in making students active and engaged in mathematical discussions about the subtraction task in hand with their peers and the teacher, despite the students' fragile knowledge. We saw moments of synergy [24] when the presence of peers brought about a reflection about a wrong calculation, and a discussion about the strategy applied. The teacher's intervention in this context was welcomed and fruitful. However, we also observed situations in which the computer *game* encouraged trial and error because of the time factor and the competitive nature of games.

The group discussions did not yield the rich discussions we had hoped for. Although we had observed that the ability of most students to provide explanations had developed during their participation, these students did not develop new strategies, but rather, used the strategies they had been introduced to at the beginning. This behavior aligns with the LAS's tendency to focus on a given algorithm, given by an external authority. In addition, in this context, students' discursive acts were mostly in response to the teacher and merely addressed her.

Finally, in our design we had expected a metaphorical diffusion between the two contexts in which students performed and collaborated—that students' activeness, ability, and wiliness to discuss with their peers when failing to solve a task on the computer would diffuse to the group discussion context and that the teacher-led discussions would enrich the mathematical discursive practices, which would then diffuse to the computer context.

Apparently, this diffusion is not straightforward and a fine-tuned design is required to support its occurrence. Therefore, in in the next round we re-designed the group discussions in consultation with the literature on Accountable Talk [18], aiming at better facilitation of establishing the norms of mathematical peer discussions. We minimized the time spent in front of the computer game and instead, added time to the online unit, in which students still simulated the ice-cream shop, but without the pressure of time and gaining points. Finally, we aimed at setting the students' mindset right from the beginning by explaining to them that this class is about ***their*** strategies. We omitted the introduction to the two strategies, and instead, simulated in class an affair where students brought personal items and had to give money and get change and then conducted a discussion on their calculation strategies.

More work is required to fine tune the design. A larger sample of participants is necessary in order to generalize and further explore LAS learning processes and outcomes in this environment and gain insights as to how to support their learning. Nonetheless, this study shows that overall the rich CSCL environment was successful not only because students gained mathematical knowledge—they also adapted strategies to solve subtraction tasks. These students also practiced socio-mathematical behavior different from what they were used to: from passive reliance on authority, impulsive, and individualistic interactions in class, to active, thoughtful collaboration about mathematical meaning. According to the regular class teachers, to some extent, this behavior has diffused to their regular classes. We thus can conclude that meaningful learning of LAS is feasible and furthermore, that LAS can benefit from CSCL settings, which stands in contrast to their characteristics in the literature as passive or even detached individualists [2]. In this aspect our work makes a modest step towards achieving equity in mathematics education by extending the teaching of mathematical meaning to academically diversified students.

References

[1] R. Alexander, "Culture, dialogue and learning: Notes on an emerging pedagogy". In N. Mercer and S. Hodgkinson (Eds.), Exploring talk in school, London: SAGE, 2008, pp.91-114.

[2] S. Baker, R. Gersten, and D. S. Lee, "A synthesis of empirical research on teaching Mathematics to Low Achieving Students," The Elementary School Journal, vol. 103, 2002, pp. 51–73.

[3] D. Chazan, "Beyond formulas in mathematics and teaching: Dynamics of the high school lgebra classroom", New York: Teachers College Press, 2000.

[4] P. Cobb, "Supporting the improvement of learning and teaching in social and institutional context", Cognition and instruction:Twenty-five years of progress, 78, 2001, pp 19-37.

[5] F.I.M Craik, "Memory: Levels of processing. International encyclopedia of the social & behavioral sciences", University of Toronto, Canada, 2002.

[6] P. Dillenbourg and F. Fischer, "Computer-supported collaborative learning: The basics". Zeitschrift für Berufs-und Wirtschaftspädagogik, 21, 2007, pp. 111-130.

[7] D. C. Geary, "Mathematics and learning disabilities", Journal of Learning Disabilities, 37(1), 2004, pp. 4-15.

[8] J. P. Gee, "What video games have to teach us about learning and literacy". New York: Palgrave Macmillian Publishing, 2014.

[9] S. R. Goldman. "Strategy instruction in mathematics." Learning Disabilities Quarterly, 12, 1989, pp. 43-55.

[10] E. Gray, D. Pitta, D. and D. Tall, "Objects, actions, and images: A perspective on early number development", The Journal of Mathematical Behavior, 18(4), 2000, pp. 401-413.

[11] K. Gravemeijer, "Local instruction theories as means of support for teachers in reform mathematics education. Mathematical thinking and learning", 6(2), 2004, pp. 105-128.

[12] D. Haylock, "Teaching mathematics to low attainers", SAGE, 1991, pp. 8-12.

[13] G. N. Karagiannakis and A. Cooreman, "Focused MLD intervention based on the classification of MLD subtypes", The Routledge international handbook of dyscalculia and mathematical learning difficulties, 2014, pp. 265-275.

[14] G. N. Karagiannakis, A. E. Baccaglini-Frank, and P. Roussos, "Detecting strengths and weaknesses in learning mathematics through a model classifying mathematical skills", Australian Journal of Learning Difficulties, 2017, pp. 1-27.

[15] R. Karsenty, A. Arcavi, and N. Hadas, "Exploring informal mathematical products of low achievers at the secondary school level". The Journal of Mathematical Behavior, 26(2), 2007, 156-177.

[16] K. E. Lewis and M. B. Fisher, "Taking stock of 40 years of research on mathematical learning disability: Methodological issues and future directions", Journal for Research in Mathematics Education, 47(4), 2016, pp. 338-371.

[17] M. A. Mariotti, "Artifacts and signs after a Vygotskian perspective: the role of the teacher", ZDM —The International Journal on Mathematics Education, 41(4), 2009, pp. 427-440.

[18] S. Michaels, C. O'Connor, and L. B. Resnick, "Deliberative discourse idealized and realized: Accountable talk in the classroom and in civic life". Studies in Philosophy and Education, 27(4), 2007, pp. 283-297.

[19] V. Morcom, "Scaffolding social and emotional learning in an elementary classroom community: A sociocultural perspective", International Journal of Educational Research, 67, 2014, pp. 18-29.

[20] M. Peltenburg, M. van den Heuvel-Panhuizen, and A. Robitzsch, "Special education students' use of indirect addition in solving subtraction problems up to 100—A proof of the didactical potential of an ignored procedure", Educational Studies in Mathematics, 79(3), 2012, pp. 351-369.

[21] A. B. Powell, J. M. Francisco, and C. A. Maher, "An analytical model for studying the development of learners' mathematical ideas and reasoning using videotape data", The Journal of Mathematical Behavior, 22(4), 2003, pp. 405-435.

[22] S. Puntambekar and J. L. Kolodner, "Toward implementing distributed scaffolding: Helping students learn science from design", Journal of research in science teaching, 42(2), 2005, pp. 185-217.

[23] K. Squire, "Video game-based learning: An emerging paradigm for instruction", Performance Improvement Quarterly, 21, 2008, pp. 7-36.

[24] I. Tabak, "Synergy: A complement to emerging patterns of distributed scaffolding", The Journal of the Learning Sciences, 13(3), 2004, pp. 305-335.

Scratch Introduction and Programming Education

Ruimeng Racic
Duquesne University
School of Education
yangr@duq.edu

***Abstract*— Scratch is a free visual programming language and online community for students between ages of 8 and 16, designed to help them learn and practice computer programming while working on personally meaningful projects such as animated stories and games. The goal of this article is to introduce the Scratch software program for children and demonstrate how it can be used for educators.**

Keywords- Scratch, programming language education, K-12.

I. WHAT IS SCRATCH?

Scratch is a free software program developed by the MIT Media Lab [1]. It is designed to help students between ages of 8 and 16 practice computer programming. Scratch has been accepted by many students, educators and parents to training children to create interactive stories, animations, games, apps etc. [2]. Scratch can help students to develop creative thinking and computational thinking skills for future math and science learning and projects, including simulations and visualizations of experiments, recording lectures with animated presentations, to social sciences animated stories, and interactive art [2].

II. HOW DOES SCRATCH WORK?

There are two main work screens from left to right on the home page of Scratch. The left screen is referred to as the Stage area, where images, such as animations, turtle graphics, etc. are displayed. This Stage area uses X and Y coordinates. Users can choose many ways to create sprites and stage background on the Stage area. For example, users can upload any figures or images from their computers or they can choose a sprite from the Scratch library. Users can also draw their own sprite manually using the Paint Editor, provided by Scratch. All sprites thumbnails are listed at the bottom of the Stage area (See Figure 1) [2].

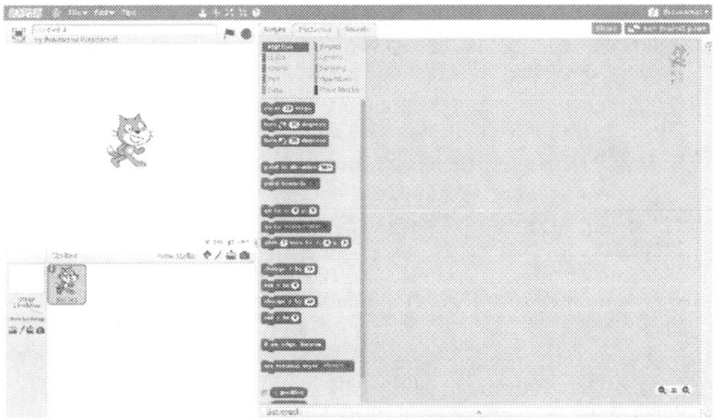

Figure 1. Main page of Scratch

Next, we address the area on the right in Figure 1, which is called Blocks area. Under the *Scripts* tab, all available scripts are listed and categorized in groups such as *Motion, Looks, Sound, Pen, Data, Events, Control, Sensing, and Operators* (see Figure 2). Those scripts can be applied by dragging them onto the Blocks Palette. Each script can also be tested individually by double-clicking the mouse (see Figure 3).

Category	Notes	Category	Notes
Motion	Moves sprites and changes angles and change X and Y values	Events	Contains event handlers placed on the top of each group of blocks
Looks	Controls the visuals of the sprite; attach speech or thought bubble, change of background, enlarge or shrink, transparency, shade	Control	Conditional if-else statement, "forever", "repeat", and "stop"
Sound	Plays audio files and programmable sequences	Sensing	Sprites can interact with the surroundings the user has created
Pen	Draw on the portrait by controlling pen width, color, and shade. Allows for turtle graphics.	Operators	Mathematical operators, random number generator, and-or statement that compares sprite positions
Data	Variable and List usage and assignment	More Blocks	Custom procedures (blocks) and external devices control and can import from PicoBoard or Lego WeDo 1.0/2.0

Figure 2. Introduction of Blocks 1 [4]

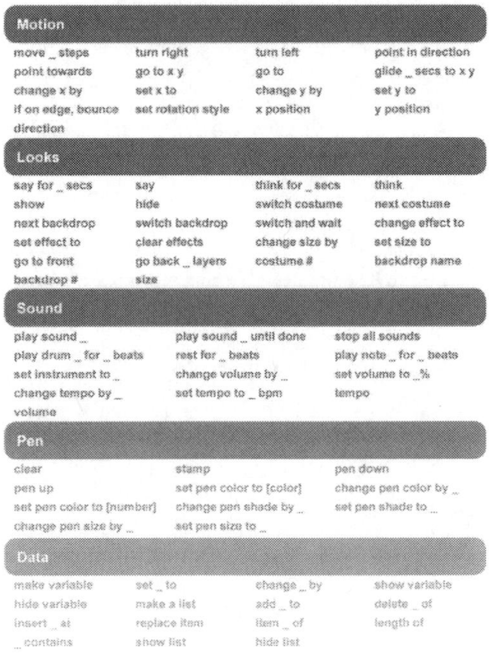

Figure 3. Introduction of Blocks 2 [5]

There are two additional tabs next to the *Scripts* tab, which are *Costumes* tab and *Sounds* tab (see Figure 4). The *Costumes* tab allows users to change the look of the sprite to create various effects, including animation. The *Sounds* tab (see Figure 5) allows users to insert/edit sounds and music to a *Sprite*.

Figure 4. *Costumes* tab [5]

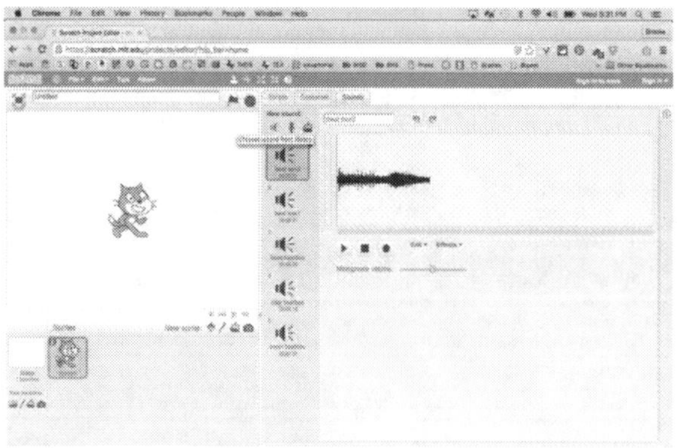

Figure 5. *Sounds* tab. [7]

III. SCRATCH IN EDUCATION

The Scratch programming environment is a computer programming language for children from 8 to 16 years old. Scratch can be integrated into the computer and technology curriculum so that students learn how to program and create multimedia applications and games with ease. Next, we discuss the use of Scratch in the educational curriculum.

Scratch has been widely introduced in after-school centers and other informal educational settings, and has broadened opportunities for children from under-represented groups who may eventually become designers and inventors [8]. Scratch allows students to create their own applications using their own creativity and imagination to create complex programming projects, even connecting with a simple robot used for a couple of sessions. The experience will help their own understanding of geometry, which will help reinforce learning as they are introduced more formally to the subject during mathematics lessons [8].

Creating a finished application involves many skills like the ones used by professional computer programmers, games designers, and multimedia producers, and the children learn the process of moving from the requirements of a desired application, though a design phase, to the engineering and testing of the finished application. Completed Scratch applications can be uploaded to a Web server to create a showcase for parents and other children to view [8].

It should be pointed out that introducing Scratch into classrooms will require teachers to spend additional effort preparing lesson plans for the technology sessions and ensuring that they had the programming knowledge to keep up with some of the more advanced young programmers who were working on projects at home and downloading projects from the Internet. Teachers and school districts need access to the resources and training required to give teachers the experience and confidence to incorporate Scratch into their lesson plans for computer/technology as well as other topics of the curriculum.

REFERENCES

[1] M. Marji, Learn to program with Scratch: a visual introduction to programming with games, art, science, and math. San Francisco, 2014.

[2] MIT, "About Scratch, " 2014, [Online] https://scratch.mit.edu/about/ [accessed March 2018]

[3] Scratch, "Research on Scratch, " 2014, [Online] https://scratch.mit.edu/info/research/ [accessed March 2018]

[4] Wikipedia, "Wikipedia.org.," 2017, [Online] Scratch.https://en.wikipedia.org/wiki/Scratch [accessed March 2018]

[5] Quizover.com, "1.7 Scr0370: the repeat loop in scratch 2.0.," 2017, [Online] https://goo.gl/images/xE4gZQ. [accessed March 2018]

[6] B. Derek, "Coding with Scratch Blocks and Scripts," 2015, [Online] http://www.dummies.com/programming/coding-with-scratch-blocks-and-scripts/ [accessed March 2018]

[7] Brookyntonia, "Interactive art with scratch and makey makey," instructables.com, 2016 [Online] http://www.instructables.com/id/Interactive-Art-With-Scratch-and-Makey-Makey/ [accessed March 2018]

[8] S. Crook, "Embedding Scratch in the Classroom," International Journal of Learning and Media, vol. 1, 2009, 17-21. doi:10.1162/ijlm_a_00035

An Introduction to Code.org

Bria Koch
Department of Instructional Technology and Leadership
Duquesne University
Pittsburgh, PA, USA
e-mail: kochb@duq.edu

Abstract—**Computational thinking and computer programming are permeating the landscape of today's schools. In order to prepare students for 21st-century careers, students of all ages need to learn fundamental skills in a developmentally appropriate way. How can that best be accomplished? What is Code.org? How can teachers use it in the classroom? This paper gives an introduction to the site, provides information about its free curriculum, and describes how teachers can begin using this in their classrooms.**

Keywords-computational thinking; coding; teaching; elementary education; 21st-century learning.

I. Introduction

In September 2017, the White House announced a $200 million per year commitment to implement computer science programs in America's schools. The funds were distributed immediately with the goal of increasing participation by all students but especially women and underrepresented minorities [4]. Currently, 20 US states have changed policy to support computer science education and ongoing work continues in 30 US states [1]. One of the organizations to spearhead this movement with prominent companies is Code.org.

Code.org is a non-profit organization dedicated to expanding access to computer science and increasing participation by women and underrepresented minorities. In Code.org's online courses, 45% of students are girls and 48% are underrepresented minorities, and in Code.org's high school classrooms, 37% are girls, and 56% African American or Hispanic. In partnership with corporations and foundations like Facebook, Amazon, Microsoft, and Google, Code.org is devoted to the vision that every student in every school should have the opportunity to learn computer science [2]. Code.org works to increase diversity in computer science because it is able to reach students of all backgrounds regardless of skill level or location. Its courses are available in over 50 languages and are used by students in over 180 countries [1]. Code.org can be used on any device with an Internet connection, and a specific app is not necessary to use it on a tablet or Smartphone.

This paper will provide a thorough introduction to the site Code.org and many of its offerings for students of all ages. Section 2 will take a look at the goals of Code.org and how teachers around the world are using this to help encourage learning in computer science. Section 3 takes a closer look at Code.org's curriculum and how teachers can best use the resources in their classrooms. Special consideration is given to teachers in Section 4. Lesson plans, professional development, and teacher accounts are all discussed. Finally, Section 5 concludes with some final thoughts about the future of this site and how it can continue impacting all learners.

II. Goals of Code.org

Code.org utilizes eight specific goals and metrics within its program. These goals include improving diversity in computer science, inspiring students, creating powerful courses, and reaching classrooms. Nearly 700,000 teachers have signed up to teach introductory courses using Code Studio, and over 21 million students have been enrolled, 9 million of which are female. The goal of preparing new computer science teachers is being met through professional development sessions conducted both online and in-person. Over 57,000 new teachers have been prepared to teach computer science across grades K-12 using Code.org's computer science curriculum. Code.org works to meet the goals of changing school district curriculums, setting up policies to support computer science, and implementing computer science programs on a global scale by partnering with 120 of the largest United States school districts to add computer science to their curriculum. These districts are far-reaching and teach almost 10% of all students in the United States, 15% of which are Hispanic and African American students [1].

Code.org can be used by students of all ages, including adults. Learners from any age group can be targeted, and the content is free. Creating an account provides teachers with an easy-to-understand key which allows them to see how students are progressing through each of the lessons. Assessments and surveys can be conducted for middle to high school students to help them prepare for the Advanced Placement (AP) test in computer science. Code.org has an entire curriculum for AP computer science in addition to courses that teach Java for older students [5].

III. Code.org Curriculum

Code Studio is where Code.org's full course catalog is housed. These courses take students through step-by-step modules independently, and the site automatically advances them to the next lesson upon completion. For each of the modules, there are videos and directions for students. The videos are also transcribed with still pictures to allow students to slow down the play or refer back to specific parts. Lessons are grouped for students in grades K-12, but using a tablet or touchscreen device can allow even younger students to experience Code.org [3].

For students in grades K-5, there are both "Express Courses" and fundamental courses for elementary schools. The "Express Courses" serve as great options for students getting started on their own because they are guided and have students using drag and drop blocks for coding. Pre-reader express, designed for children ages four to eight, combines the best of the kindergarten and first grade courses. The Express Course, for students ages nine to eighteen, provides an introduction to computer science and combines the best of the elementary school curriculum for older students [3]. Students start by learning the basics with simple directions like "move forward" or "move backward." Younger students can improve their understanding of positional words to make sure they are prepared for the following modules. As they move through the modules, they can program the characters to turn left or right, a great way to teach directional skills, and then eventually by number of degrees or even pixels.

Six courses are provided in the computer science fundamentals for elementary schools curriculum. Courses A and B are designed for pre-readers in elementary school classrooms. Course A provides an introduction for pre-readers aged four to seven, and while Course B is similar, it provides more variety for older students aged five to eight. Courses C through F are designed for older students in elementary classrooms. Course C, for students ages six to ten, teaches basics of computer science and allows students to create art, stories, and games. Course D, for ages seven through eleven, provides a review of Course C and then goes further with learning algorithms, nested loops, and conditionals. Course E introduces functions, and Course F, for ages nine through thirteen, combines all of the fundamentals to create more advanced art, stories, and games. All of these courses use themes that are relatable to the students including characters Angry Birds, Moana, Star Wars, Minecraft and Frozen [3].

Students in grades 6 to 12 have the opportunity to build real working apps, games, and websites using block coding, Java, Cascading Style Sheets (CSS), and HTML. The App Lab allows students to design and easily share apps using coding with blocks or Java. The Game Lab immerses students in a more complex programming environments with both animations and characters. Finally, the Web Lab allows students to make simple webpages using HTML and CSS. If students are able to successfully move through all of these courses and labs, Code.org provides links to third-party sites to teach even more difficult concepts [3].

IV. CODE.ORG FOR TEACHERS

Teachers can learn how to use Code.org from both the student-side and the teacher-side through Code.org's professional development opportunities that work to lower the level of "coding intimidation" for learners of all ages [5]. Code.org offers no cost teacher workshops both in person and online. Lesson plans are provided throughout each level to help teach the information, and current documents are supplied to show teachers the importance of computer science and computer science education. Because the site is so guided, especially the lessons on the computer, students can move through at their own pace, and it essentially teaches the students. This is especially helpful even if the teacher is not totally comfortable with the level of programming. There are also "Unplugged Activities" that have videos and full lesson plans for teachers to use in their classrooms. These activities do not require any type of technology or devices in the classroom but still teach the concepts of computational thinking [5].

V. CONCLUSIONS

Code.org is a non-profit organization was launched in 2013 with the goal of expanding access to computer science and increasing participation in computer science by girls and underrepresented students of color. They believe that all students should have the opportunity to learn computer science and that it should be part of the core curriculum within a school. The programs within Code.org meet students where they are at and enable all students the opportunity to learn about computer science and programming.

Currently, 20 percent of students in the United States have accounts on Code.org, and tens of millions have tried activities on the site [1]. Because of Code.org's dedication to diversity, in the future it could be beneficial to create even more opportunities for differentiation. While it is available in over 50 languages, it would be incredibly advantageous to take steps toward courses designed specifically for students with special needs. In the past two years using Code.org with K-4 students, the site is constantly evolving to best meet the needs of all 21st century learners.

ACKNOWLEDGMENTS

I would like to thank Dr. Joseph Kush for his encouragement to pursue this international endeavor and Dr. David Carbonara for his direction and reassurance throughout my graduate career.

REFERENCES

[1] About us. (2017). Retrieved October 13, 2017, from https://code.org/about

[2] Colby, J. (2015). 2,445 hours of code: What I Learned from Facilitating Hour of Code Events in High School Libraries. Knowledge Quest, 43(5), 12-17.

[3] Learn on Code Studio. (2017) Retrieved October 15, 2017, from https://studio.code.org/courses.

[4] Partovi, H. (2017, September 23). White House commits $200 million a year for computer science. Retrieved from https://medium.com/@codeorg/200-million-a-year-for-computer-science-6daf7e16fcc0

[5] Teach with Code Studio. (2017). Retrieved October 15, 2017, from https://studio.code.org/courses?view=teacher

Determining Pedagogically Sound Methods of Teaching and Learning Computational Skills

Cheryl Farren Tkacs
Instructional Designer
The Pennsylvania State University
University Park, PA, USA
Email: cft10@psu.edu

***Abstract*— If we assume even the youngest person can be guided and helped to become a computational thinker, is placing a computer or tablet in their hands the best way they will learn? This paper explores the literature to determine what computational skills learners need to function in the 21st century. Relying on sound pedagogical practices, it will also look at the types of technology and other non-computer devices that are currently being used and whether they are the most appropriate for the age level in developing computational thinking. Based on current research, a list of advantages and disadvantages of children using computers will be explored with recommendations for best practices offered for safe use.**

***Keywords-computational thinking*; *pedagogy*.**

I. What is Computational Thinkning?

The term computational thinking (CT) has become a popular term in recent years when Jeannette Wing used it to describe a fundamental skill that will be needed by everyone in the 21st century. Simply put at the time, she referred to it as "thinking like a computer scientist" [1]. She later refined the definition with input from colleagues to state: "Computational thinking is the thought processes involved in formulating a problem and expressing its solution(s) in such a way that a computer- human or machine- can effectively carry it out [2]. Computational thinking describes a cognitive approach that encompasses a list of abilities used in a problem solving process. For education, it allows the learner to move beyond tasks involving the lower order thinking skills and concentrate on developing more critical thinking and problem solving expertise that is based on concepts of computer science. The evolving definition of CT includes four cornerstones integral to the thought process. They include *decomposition* which is a breaking down of complex problems into smaller components, *pattern recognition* that looks for similarities within problems, *abstraction* that requires focus on the important information, and *algorithms* to develop a step by step solution to the problem [3]. These four skills are intertwined and separating them in the process would cause faulty outcomes in both programming for computer science and the thought processes in solving problems in other content areas.

In 2011, The International Society for Technology in Education (ISTE) and the Computer Science Teachers Association (CSTA) in partnership with leaders in education and industry, developed an operational definition of computational thinking [4]. It expands on the simpler definition first advanced by Wing and her colleagues. The operational definition states: Computational thinking (CT) is a problem-solving process that includes (but is not limited to) the following characteristics:

- Formulating problems in a way that enables us to use a computer and other tools to help solve them
- Logical organizing and analyzing data
- Representing data through abstractions such as models and simulations
- Automating solutions through algorithmic thinking
- Identifying, analyzing, and implementing possible solutions with the goal of achieving the most efficient and effective combination of steps and resources
- Generalizing and transferring the problem solving process to wide variety of problems

This operational definition includes the statement that the above skills are enhanced by attitudes that include:

- Confidence in dealing with complexity
- Persistence in working with difficult problems
- Tolerance for ambiguity
- The ability to deal with open-ended problems
- The ability to communicate and work with others to achieve a common goal or solution

Although its origins are in computer science, computational thinking has expanded and has application in other disciplines as well. Students use this logical approach to solving problems in many subject areas already. Whether it is math, language, the arts, or technology, there are complex problems to break down, steps created to accomplish the task, key components to be focused on, and research on how other projects with similar elements have been solved [5]. As Wing noted in her blog in 2016, great strides have been made in the 10 years since she first brought computational thinking to the forefront of computer science. We still need to look at how best we should be using computer technology in the classroom. More specifically, determining what is the most effective way to teach and learn computational thinking to all age and levels of learners [1].

Computational thinking is a process that allows us to tackle the solution of complex problems by implementing a process that breaks down the problem into a series of steps to develop solutions in a way that both humans and computers can understand. The primary focus is not programming but conceptualizing a method [6]. It is a combination of problem solving and critical thinking to create new ideas and solutions while using the higher level thinking skills. There are four main components to this process: decomposition, abstraction, analyzation, and algorithms.

Decomposition is the first step in the procedure and, as the term suggests, it is the process of deconstructing a complex problem into small parts. Being able to identify the important details is the first step in thinking abstractly thereby allowing learners to construct a solution that may be out of their normal area of expertise [7]. The ability to think critically is transferable to many disciplines both in K-12 and in higher education. Most problems are not isolated and being able to analyze relationships between problems is a matter of formulating a system of codes.

Thinking computationally requires the ability to think abstractly. Can the problem be explained or represented using a model or a simulation? Abstraction can be used to define patterns, make generalizations, or find properties that are common among the elements of a problem. It is ultimately the ability to transfer the scale and complexity to larger problems [8]. Abstraction hides the details. Direction must be on filtering only the key elements and being able to ignore extraneous details. Mastering the ability to sift through layers of information and get to the heart of the problem is a skill that is essential in all logical thinking processes leading to a confidence in dealing with more complex problems [4].

Computational thinking helps in analyzing possible solutions in the most effective method. Being able to review resources allotted and effectively use those resources can produce a cost-effective solution to the problem at hand often saving time and money in the process. Because computational thinking can be more tool oriented that other types of thinking, the combination of human thinking skills and computer technology can be a formidable solutions team [9].

Whether we realize it or not, we constantly use algorithms in making decisions or solving problems. An algorithm is nothing more than a series of steps to follow in completing a task or produce a solution. When using algorithms, the chances of making a mistake are minimalized while the chances for accuracy and success are maximized. Computational thinking is an extension of algorithmic thinking as it builds upon and incorporates many levels of abstractions in seeking solutions to problems. As such, it is an integral part of all school curriculums and, arguably, part of our everyday lives. Educators and employers assume that a learner has acquired some generic and personal skills through the process of education. These include areas of communication, problem solving, quantification, analytics, and synthesizing skills. An improvement or refinement of these skills enhances the academic work of the students and their employability [10] .

This paper explores the literature to determine what computational skills learners need to function in the 21st century. Section II covers a brief history of computational thinking and the first attempts to integrate into a school curriculum. Relying on sound pedagogical practices, Section III will look at the types of technology and other non-computer devices that are currently being used ascertaining whether they are the most appropriate for the age level in developing computational thinking. Studies detailing how children learn is the focus of Section IV. It offers suggestions and possible devices designed with the child's age level in mind to deliver age appropriate instruction on computational thinking. Finally, a list of advantages and disadvantages for children using computers will be explored with recommendations for best practices and safe use.

II. History of Computational Thinking

Computational thinking has had an influence in such areas as medicine, economics, law, and the humanities. It can be used to recommend online purchases, detect spam email in your Inbox and even personalize the coupons you receive at the local grocery store [11]. It is important to look at events that led to computational thinking being implemented across both educational curriculums and now becoming pervasive in our everyday thinking processes.

Computational thinking is not a new phenomenon. As early as the 1950s, computer experts were advocating the value of coding for deconstructing the components and using computer analysis to solve problems. Alan Perlis, along with his colleagues at Carnegie Institute of Technology (Carnegie Mellon University) coined the term *algorithmizing* to describe how humans do things arguing that it should become an integral part of our culture [12]. Eric Dijkstra, another forerunner in the field of computing, believed that the distinct nature of computing comes from its unique way of algorithmic thinking that could use natural language to connect problems and solutions [13]. The idea of algorithmic thinking becoming a multi-purpose tool was also being argued by many in the field as leading to higher order cognitive skills useful in multiple disciplines [14].

During the same era, the idea of computational thinking was gaining momentum in education with educators proposing these multi-purpose tools be implemented into the curriculum. Researchers expressed opinions on how computers could make teaching math, languages, music or any subject that require a proficiency of both mechanical and intellectual skills more dynamic using the frameworks provided by the computational thinking in computer science [15]. Seymour Papert was a great advocate of procedural thinking in the construction of knowledge and was one of the first to use the term computational thinking [16]. Papert's work was influential in the field of computers and education focusing his work on how children learn; encouraging student centered and project based discovery learning using technology. As a result of his work in *Mindstorms*, many people argued that learning to program developed cognitive skills that increased the ability to problem solve in many disciplines [16], [17]. His critics said there was no empirical evidence to support these claims of transfer and enhancement of cognitive skills to all domains [18]. The 1980s, with the invention of the supercomputers to aid in calculations and simulations, amplified the need for what was now being referred to as computational thinking in describing the mindset that was developed while using computational science [19]. Through the 1990s, computers began finding their way into schools and homes under the auspices of access to simulations, basic programming, preparation to enter Science, Technology, Engineering, and Math (STEM) fields and preparing students with 21st century skills [14].

Jeannette Wing entered the conversation when she reintroduced the term computational thinking back into academia. She followed the thinking of previous arguments that computational thinking was a tool that has its foundation in information processes and the ability divide a problem into its parts, concentrate on the important components, and develop a strategy for solving the problem thinking [1]. Wing's promotion of computational thinking was joined by such organizations such as Computer Science Teachers Association (CSTA), Computing at School (CAS) and Australian Curriculum Assessment and Reporting Authority (ANCARA) who outlined their own vision for computational thinking in the schools. They all included aspects of skills, attitudes, techniques, and lesson plans for developing logical reasoning, algorithmic thinking, decomposition, abstractions, and evaluation that schools are still trying to implement 10 years later [14].

Not all agree that computational thinking is the best method of problems solving including Papert who expresses his receptiveness to other approaches [16]. Other types of thinking have been considered indispensable in science and technology and have also been supported by educators including engineering thinking, logical thinking, systems thinking, rational thinking, and ethical thinking to name just a few [14]. Nevertheless, computational thinking is establishing itself in the K-12 environments where students are learning programming by exploring and practicing; building on Papert's vision of constructivism.

Making computational thinking an integral part of any curriculum still has many obstacles to overcome. Discussions and research on pedagogical issues, assessment of CT learning objectives, and the most important issue of deciding what should be taught and when it should be taught is just part of the work that must be done to support the belief that CT has a place in all disciplines not just computer science.

III. Children and Computers

There is no doubt that computers have transformed the lives of people all over the world. In order to compete in this world, it has become necessary to have a level of competence using technology and this particularly includes our children as they prepare for a world not even invented as yet. Computers are shaping children's lives both at home and in school. They play games, use social media to connect with friends and family, attend class online, do homework, access the Internet, and watch videos. As early as 1994, Congress decided that technology can aid students in meeting a higher standard of learning and enacted the *Goals 200 Educate America Act* and the *Improving America's Schools Act*. As a result, the percentage of schools with computer access to the Internet increased from 35% to 95% (U.S. Department of Education, 2000). In the *Current Population Survey* conducted in 2001, several key findings were noted about computer usage among children ages 5 to 17 [19].

- 90% of children and adolescents use computers. (47 million persons).
- Computer usage starts early. 75% of five years olds use computers and about 25% of them use the Internet.
- Computer and Internet usage is divided along demographic and socioeconomic lines with children of more highly educated parents having the higher use rate.
- There was no difference in sexes in overall computer usage as compared to earlier statistics where boys had a higher rate of usage.
- More children and adolescents use computers at school (81%) than at home (65%).

Comparing those statistics to the 2012 U.S. Census Bureau, the age span has changed to include 3 to 17 year olds with a 70% access to the Internet from inside and outside the home. In 2012, with nearly every school having computers and two-thirds of children having Internet and computer access in their homes, it is apparent that computers had become an integral part of children's lives in a short span of time. The number of children having access to computers and the Internet is growing exponentially every year. It is also important to note that these are statistics for only the United States [20].

If we look beyond the U.S. borders, approximately one-third of the world's population is under the age of 18. In third world countries they make up half of the population while they are less than 25% in industrialized nations. Around the world, children face many challenges from basic survival to discrimination and exploitation. In recent years, due to the greater availability of media through satellites, more and more young people in third world countries have access to computers, TV, and the Internet and are exposed to information from around the world. It is that access to technology that can give them the chance at education and being able to make a difference in their world [21].

With computers engrained in children's lives, it is important to understand how computers can both enrich and benefit students as well as how it hinders their growth and development.

A. Disadvantages of Computer Use by Children and Adolescents

Opponents of young children using computers feel that parents, educators, and psychologists should take a more in-depth look at the risks of supplying computers at too early of an age. Their criticism includes children having access to violent games, inappropriate content, and aggressive advertising which can adversely affect their relationships with other children and the adults in their lives. They cite a 1998 National Science Board report that overuse of computers by children can create individuals that will not be able to cope with reality and the demands of personal commitments [22].

Research has shown that there are a number of physical and emotional concerns that can arise from prolonged use of computers by children and adolescents. For toddlers, too many "bells and whistles", bold colors, and flashing lights can overstimulate and the child becomes irritable and cranky [15]. Smaller children need to have more human interaction in order to learn social skills to communicate effectively (verbally and non-verbally). Without these social skills, children find it difficult to read subtle signals through reading body language and personal appearance [23].

An important side effect of prolonged computer use is that there is too much sedentary time involved. Children's posture and bone growth can be stunted and the lack of physical play can result in week muscles and obesity [24] [11]. Results can range from injuries to backs, wrists, and legs to seizures in children suffering from photosensitive epilepsy. Children with computers in their rooms get two to five hours less of sleep that their parents did at the same age [25]–[27]. Behavioral problems, including aggressive behavior, have been reported in children that engage in online game playing for long intervals [28], [39]. While older children can improve their visual spatial skills when using or playing computer games, too much on-screen time can negatively impact a toddler's eyesight. The nerves and eye muscles are not sufficiently developed and computer vision syndrome can result [29].

The disadvantages of computer use among children and adolescents is not insurmountable. Practical suggestions, common sense usage, and monitoring by parents can ensure that children can safely and effectively use computers to increase their intellectual and physical development so they can succeed in whatever world they find themselves in the future.

B. Recommendations for Children Using Computers

In order to provide the safe and intellectually engaging experiences for children using the computer at home and in educational situations, The Future of Children organization offered some guidelines to protect children's physical and mental development while still allowing them the freedom to explore, communicate, and learn with technology. Their recommendations were published in the journal *Children and Computer Technology* and the main suggestions include:

- More public and private research to assess the effects of extended computer use on children's physical, intellectual, social and psychological development.
- Parents, teachers, and other adults that work with children should limit time spent with computers and supervise the content they are accessing.
- Dialog among researchers, software developers, and government agencies should be encouraged and supported to create high quality content for children.
- Education agencies should research, refine, and adopt age appropriate guidelines for children's computer fluency.
- Teachers both in education technology programs as well as classroom teachers should be provided with professional development workshops that are focused on the training and skills they need to use age appropriate technology in the classrooms.

In addition to the above list, *The Future of Children* organization also made recommendations to help narrow the disparity of computer and Internet access between socio-economic groups and they addressed the need for universal design to be included so children with special needs will have the same advantages in using computers to learn, discover, participate, and compete in the world.

IV. TEACHING COMPUTATIONAL SKILLS

If we accept the premise that children should be taught computational thinking, the next step would be to decide the most effective way to teach and learn CT. Parents and educators have a responsibility to use the research to determine what concepts students can best learn and when in their developmental stage. What should we teach and when? Toddlers are handed iPads and they explore by pressing icons to see what will happen. As the child enters teen years, the dependence on electronic devices is evident as you watch them hunched over staring at the screen, texting rather than interacting face to face with their friends rarely being farther than a hand's reach away from their phones. This is not necessarily learning computational thinking. In addition, research conducted by health care professionals remind us of the benefits and hazards that can result from overuse and misuse of technology in both children and adolescents.

With the knowledge gained from studies on how children learn and focusing on using devices, software, and STEM toys that are age appropriate, this next section will look at options for teaching and reinforcing the understanding of computational thinking concepts for children and adolescents. The idea of coding is the element that most of these devices and software have in common. They teach children to think logically by applying the method of analyzation, decomposition, application of solutions and then generalizing those solutions to new situations are key objectives in these lessons.

A. Toddlers

Today's parents want to give their child an intellectual head start by placing electronic devices in the child's hands to strengthen their computer and problem solving skills. And yet, research supports the fact that children under the age of two do not have the hand-eye coordination to hold a device, move a mouse, tap an icon, follow the action on the screen or have the attention span to understand what is happening. Experts believe that toddlers are more in need a more hands-on relationship with the world and people around them.

This does not mean children as young as three years old can't learn to think critically and or will fall behind their peers if not given access to computer devices. Children at this age are learning creativity and developing their motor skills. There are many STEM toys available on the market that foster computational thinking

through tactile play. A few of these STEM toys that fulfill both the intellectual and physical needs of 3 to 5-year-old children promoting discovery and problem solving skills that are key in computational thinking include manipulative robots that can be programmed in a variety of ways.

Think & Learn Code-a-Pillar teaches the basics of coding. The segments of the *Code-a-Pillar* contain chips that area embedded with the commands turn right, turn left, make a sound, and more. Children can separate and reconnect them in any order and the toy will carry out the sequence. *Cubetto* is a small square smiling robot that, like the *Code-a-Pillar*, will follow a series of commands. Colored blocks represent the commands that *Cubetto* will follow as they are placed in the sequence that the child want the robot to follow. The *Kibo* robot is made of blocks fitted together in a variety of configurations. Once it is built, the robot's body is scanned and pushing a start button carries out the program.

Ozobots are another robot version that area only 1-inch-tall which making them more suitable for age 5 and up. These small robots can move on different types of surfaces including a tablet screen. Paths are programmed using color and the robot follows the colored lines drawn on paper or a screen. Colors correspond to different commands. As the child becomes more advanced, pro-set blocks of code from *Google Blockly*, a library that adds a code editor to web and Android apps using interlocking, graphical blocks , can be used to program the *Ozobots'* movements. *Dash and Dot* are a team of mobile robots that children can use a suite of apps to control. *Dash* is the mobile robot of the duo while *Dot* is stationary. Apps vary in the range of complexity and are run by *Google Blockly*. Puzzles and challenges can be solved by programming *Dash and Dot*.

Engaging in construction-based robotics, even toddlers are learning a wide range of concepts and demonstrate the mastering of various learning outcomes involving computational thinking, robotics, problem-solving, and programming [30]. This list contains just some toys that can provide the opportunity to move through the cornerstones of CT while providing a tactile approach that is not taxing on growing bodies.

B. K-12

As children enter school, they have more options and opportunities to learn and engage in computational thinking both in and out of the classroom. At this stage, learning tools such as toys, puzzles, and games continue to be active means of employing computational thinking. Some board games new to the market including *Robot Turtle Game* and *Code Monkey Island* are designed to teach logic and development and programming skills by using conditional statements, looping, and other operators to move players around the board. *Puzzlet* is another board game that links the student's programming to the way characters move in an app-based world on a tablet. Bringing girls into the world of coding is the focus of items such as *Jewelbots*, the latest incarnation of friendship bracelets. They can be programmed through if/then statements to light up when a friend is near, vibrate if they get a text or a "like" on Instagram, and any number of other programs they can write themselves.

Following progressive steps that are found in board games, such as the ones listed, the student is using increasingly more difficult algorithms in these thinking activities. This type of instructional strategy capitalizes on children's interest and skills [31]. Teachers can add these types of activities to their lessons to connect abstract thinking patterns to real-life situations.

When teaching computational thinking through coding programs, one of the guiding principles is the "low floor, high ceiling" concept. Simply stated, the programming environment being used should be easy enough for a beginners to have success in creating a working program but powerful and complex enough to keep a more advance user engaged [32]. Some of the more popular graphical programming environments include: *Scratch*, *Alice*, *Game Maker*, *Kodu*, and *Greenfoot*. These examples use three stage progression, use-modify-create, to help the learner progress from novice to expert. Older students can use programs like *Snap*, robotic kits, *Arduino*, and *Gogo Boards* as a jumping off point to learning high level programming languages such as Java (a general-purpose computer programming language based on C++), Python (a purpose programming language that emphasizes code readability and a syntax which allows programmers to express directions in fewer lines of code), or Scheme a (programming language that follows a minimalist design philosophy).

For teachers looking to include non-computer lessons to teach computational thinking, there are a host of sites that have pedagogically based lessons to incorporate into almost any discipline for the K-12 environment. A good first stop is Code.org, a non-profit organization whose vision is to have every student have the opportunity to study computer science and especially advocates for women and minorities. They promote computer science and learning computational skills each year through the *Hour of Code* campaign. They provide curriculum guidance with lessons available for elementary, middle, and high school on their website.

Other resources available to teachers looking to include computational and critical thinking skills in their classrooms include Global Digital Citizen Foundation, Barefoot Computing, Computer Science Teachers Association, Exploring Computational Thinking (Google for Education), and CS Unplugged. These sites contain lesson plans and links to additional resources that help teachers incorporate the elements of coding and computational thinking into their courses.

As children grow and develop, parents and educators still need to monitor device use to prevent vision and other stresses that can occur from overuse. It is also important to keep in mind that the computational tools and games that are currently on the market vary in their effectiveness of teaching and addressing engagement with all the components of computational thinking. If we are employing these tools in a K-12 environment, developers need to create additional components to present programs or create new ones that guide the learner through all the competencies of computational thinking and be guided by research strategies on how children learn to problem solve [33].

C. *Higher Education*

This paper did not look at research that involved computational thinking and computer use in higher education, however, in a few short years students that have been exposed to computational thinking as they progressed through grade school, junior high, and high school will already have those higher order thinking skills and will be expecting universities to continue fostering deeper learning approaches in courses where students will be expected to think critically, conduct problem solving research, collaborate face-to-face or online with their classmates, and participate in more self-paced and directed learning in the courses they take. Some of these students have already arrived on the university's doorstep. Faculty in higher education should be using technology tools in creating course materials and assignments that have real-life application. Some universities are leading the way in using Problem Based Learning (a student centered approach with the teacher facilitating problem solving scenarios), design thinking (teaching students that the best solutions are those that are empathy-driven and end-user-centric), and gaming (where the interface is designed to learn about subject content in order to promote the algorithmic method to solve problems encouraging higher-order thinking). *Makerspaces* are another way of providing the experiences for people of all ages to experiment, iterate, and create in an area that is equipped with technology and other types of tools they can use. The time is now to prepare to meet the needs of the next generation of learners in higher education.

V. CONCLUSION

Computers are tools and how they help or hinder children is dependent on our guidance. In the classroom, it is the responsibility of educators to explore and develop new structural approaches of using technology in ways that support the curriculum goals and learning objectives of the various disciplines. Computers are one way to enhance the traditional curriculum and engage students providing them with a systematic procedure that utilizes computational thinking to solve complex problems. The design practices that are involved with computational thinking does not solely apply to using computers or software programs. These processes, specifically ones involving experimenting, testing and debugging, reusing and remixing, and abstracting can also be applied to the STEM toys discussed in this paper. Once mastered, students will be able to apply the method in all aspects of their lives.

Before children can be introduced to computational thinking, their teachers need to learn how CT fits into core curriculum courses and expand their understanding of how it can be applied. Changes and expansion of programs to include the elements of computational thinking requires vision, planning, and cooperation among administration, teachers, and parents. It also requires a pedagogical knowledge of the mental learning processes that children need to succeed without overtaxing their physical, mental, and emotional well-being. The question of assessment should be addressed as well. If students are part of a curriculum designed to include computational thinking, decisions must be made by educators and administrators detailing what students should be able to do or know and how they will be assessed upon mastering computational skills.

ISTE, CSTA, and the National Science Foundation (NSF) have proposed a Model for Systematic Change for K-12 educators and administrators to use in implementing computational thinking into the curriculums. The strategies' guide includes plans that range from short term (Year 1), mid-term (Years 2 – 5), and long-term (years 6 – 11). These strategies map activities for stakeholders to follow, suggestions for partnerships with national groups, and goals that will help direct and become the agents of change in our schools.

Computational thinking has gone far beyond teaching computer science since its inception in the 20th century. While much of what we are teaching in our schools today will be obsolete in 5 to 10 years, the ability to think critically and creatively are the skills that are, and will be, valued as students move from academia and into the workforce.

REFERENCES

[1] J. M. Wing, "Computational thinking," *Communications of the ACM*, vol. 49, no. 3. pp. 33–35, 2006.

[2] J. Cuny, L. Snyder, and J. M. Wing, "Demystifying computational thinking for non-computer scientists," *Unpubl. Manuscr. progress, 2010. [Online]. Available: http//www.cs.cmu.edu/~CompThink/resources/TheLinkWing.pdf.* [Accessed on Sept. 12, 2017].

[3] C. C. Selby and J. Wollard, "Computational thinking: The developing definition," *ITiCSE Conf. 2013*, pp. 5–8, 2013.

[4] ISTE and CSTA, "Operational definition of computational thinking," *Report*, p. 1030054, 2011.

[5] Barefoot Computing, "Computational thinking: How do we think about problems so that computers can help?," 2014. [Online]. Available: http://barefootcas.org.uk/barefoot-primary-computing-resources/concepts/computational-thinking/. [Accessed on Sept. 28, 2017].

[6] A. Yadav, "Computational thinking and 21st century problem solving," 2011.

[7] H. S. Sarjoughian and B. P. Zeigler, "Abstraction mechanisms in discrete-event inductive modeling," in *Winter Simulation Conference Proceedings*, 1996, pp. 748–755.

[8] J. Uhlman and A. Aho, "Foundations of computer science in C," *Found. Comput. Sci.*, pp. 776–786, 1994.

[9] D. Barr, J. Harrison, and L. Conery, "Computational thinking: A digital age skill for everyone," *Learn. Lead. with Technol.*, vol. 38, no. 6, pp. 20–23, 2011.

[10] D. Bradshaw, "Transferable intellectual and personal skills," *Oxford Rev. Educ.*, vol. 11, no. 2, pp. 201–216, 1985.

[11] J. M. Wing, "Computational thinking benefits society," *J. Comput. Sci. Coll.*, vol. 24, no. 6, pp. 6–7, 2014.

[12] A. Newell, A. J. Perlis, and H. A. Simon, "Computer science," *Science (80-.).*, vol. 157, no. 3795, pp. 1373–1374, 1967.

[13] E. W. Dijkstra, "Programming as a discipline of mathematical nature," *Am. Math. Mon.*, vol. 81, no. 6, p. 608, Jun. 1974.

[14] M. Tedre and P. J. Denning, "The long quest for computational thinking," *Koli Call. Conf. Comput. Educ. Res.*, pp. 120–129, 2016.

[15] W. Feurzeig, "Computer systems for teaching complex concepts," Cambridge, MA, 1969.

[16] S. Papert, *Mindstorms: Children, computers and powerful ideas*, vol. 1. 1983.

[17] R. E. Mayer, J. L. Dyck, and W. Vilberg, "Learning to program and learning to think: What's the connection?," *Commun. ACM*, vol. 29, no. 7, pp. 605–610, 1986.

[18] M. Guzdial, "Education paving the way for computational thinking," *Commun. ACM*, vol. 51, no. 8, p. 25, 2008.

[19] M. Debell and C. Chapman, "Computer and internet use by children and adolescents in 2001: Statistical analysis report," Jessup, MD, 2004.

[20] M. K. Shields and R. E. Behrman, "Children and computer technology: Analysis and recommendations," vol. 10, no. 2, pp. 4–30, 2000.

[21] S. Gigli, "Children, youth and media around the world: An overview of trends & issues," Washington, D.C., 2004.

[22] "Computers and children," *Alliance Child.*, pp. 1–8, 2000.

[23] K. Subrahmanyam, P. Greenfield, R. Kraut, and E. Gross, "The impact of computer use on children's and adolescents' development," *J. Appl. Dev. Psychol.*, vol. 22, no. 1, pp. 7–30, Jan. 2001.

[24] E. de Jong, T. L. S. Visscher, R. a HiraSing, M. W. Heymans, J. C. Seidell, and C. M. Renders, "Association between TV viewing, computer use and overweight, determinants and competing activities of screen time in 4 to 13-year-old children," *Int. J. Obes. (Lond).*, vol. 37, no. 1, pp. 47–53, 2013.

[25] L. Straker, B. Maslen, R. Burgess-Limerick, P. Johnson, and J. Dennerlein, "Evidence-based guidelines for the wise use of computers by children: Physical development guidelines," *Ergonomics*, vol. 53, no. 4, pp. 458–477, 2010.

[26] P. C. Kendall, M. S. Khanna, A. Edson, C. Cummings, and M. S. Harris, "Computers and psychosocial treatment for child anxiety: Recent advances and ongoing efforts," *Depression and Anxiety*, vol. 28, no. 1. pp. 58–66, 2011.

[27] L. Straker, C. Pollock, and B. Maslen, "Principles for the wise use of computers by children," *Ergonomics*, vol. 52, no. 11, pp. 1386–1401, 2009.

[28] R. B. Williams and C. A. Clippinger, "Aggression, competition and computer games: Computer and human opponents," *Comput. Human Behav.*, vol. 18, no. 5, pp. 495–506, 2002.

[29] N. Kozeis, "Impact of computer use on children's vision," *Hippokratia*, vol. 13, no. 4, pp. 230–231, 2009.

[30] M. U. Bers, L. Flannery, E. R. Kazakoff, and A. Sullivan, "Computational thinking and tinkering: Exploration of an early childhood robotics curriculum," *Comput. Educ.*, vol. 72, pp. 145–157, 2014.

[31] S. Y. Lye and J. H. L. Koh, "Review on teaching and learning of computational thinking through programming: What is next for K-12?," *Computers in Human Behavior*, vol. 41. pp. 51–61, 2014.

[32] S. Grover and R. D. Pea, "Computational thinking in K-12: A review of the state of the field," *Educ. Res.*, vol. 42, no. 1, pp. 38–43, 2013.

[33] B. Simon, T. Y. Chen, G. Lewandowski, R. McCartney, and K. Sanders, "Commonsense computing: what students know before we teach," *Proc. Second Int. Work. Comput. Educ. Res.*, pp. 29–40, 2006.

Hybrid Learning: A Summary of Current Models and Research

Stefanie Graban
Department of Instructional Technology and Leadership
Duquesne University
Pittsburgh, PA, USA
e-mail: grabans@duq.edu

Abstract—**Hybrid learning is quickly becoming more popular in schools across the United States. What exactly is hybrid learning? How is it different from other teaching methods? And what does research say about hybrid learning? This paper summarizes the current knowledge on hybrid learning, along with pros and cons of each type of hybrid learning.**

Keywords-hybrid learning; technology in the classroom; blended classroom; flipped classroom.

I. Introduction

Hybrid learning is a classroom orientation that combines traditional, online, and collaborative methods [5] [6]. In some literature, it is also called "blended" learning. According to Crawford, Barker, and Seyam, "[h]ybrid classes are a mix of online and face-to-face instruction. Generally, the online portion is between 30 and 79 percent of the total class schedule" [2]. There are many different definitions of hybrid learning and of what it includes. There is no one correct way to do it. Hybrid learning can and should be tailored to the specific needs of a classroom [8].

The rest of the paper is structured as follows. In section 2, different methods of hybrid learning are described. In section 3, current research on hybrid learning is summarized. Finally, the conclusions are in section 4.

II. What Does Hybrid Look Like?

Hybrid learning is different from other types of instruction. First, hybrid learning is different from classrooms that use technology because hybrid does not need to involve technology at all [3] [6]. Hybrid enables transformative uses of technology, and does not just use technology for technology's sake [3]. As said by Lin, "simply putting materials on the Web will not guarantee that students engage with and learn from them" [3]. Second, hybrid learning is not merely an online course. Hybrid can have online components, but it also incorporates different teaching and learning techniques. Asynchronous learning is usually an individual learning effort. Hybrid can have individual parts, but it is not 100% independent [3].

What does hybrid look like? Hybrid learning can be done in many ways and can involve a lot of different multimedia [3]. One way that hybrid learning can happen is in a traditional classroom, where only some students get hybrid lessons [6]. This would work well for students who are gifted and need an extra challenge, or for students who need remediation [3] [6]. "The first important strength of hybrid learning was that it provided multiple modes of delivery that were more focused on meeting the diverse needs of the learners" [3]. Those students get their individual differentiation, while others continue with the lesson. This method can be difficult because it involves more work for the teacher. "The workload associated with designing and implementing hybrid courses may seem overwhelming, especially for less experienced hybrid instructors" [3]. Also, students may not be willing or able to complete assignments that are different from what their peers are doing.

Another example of what hybrid looks like could be a flipped classroom. In a flipped classroom, the students learn the content on their own as "homework", while activities are done in class [6]. Many students struggle with traditional homework, and they may have a better chance of succeeding if they complete those assignments in class with the assistance of peers and teachers. Removing lecture time from the classroom allows for more authentic experiences. Also, it can train students to be independent learners at home [3]. The downsides for this method include availability of technology. Students without technology at home would have difficulty completing online notes or watching videos [3]. Students who do not have a computer at home would be unable to complete any computer-based assignment. Students have to be self-directed enough to complete their work at home. "Well-designed online learning... demands that learners accept increased responsibility for their learning" [3]. Without that work at home, the classwork would be useless. Teachers would have to re-teach the lesson, taking away the benefit of flipping the classroom in the first place. Students must be motivated and organized enough to complete their content lessons at home.

A third example of hybrid learning is blended lessons. This is where traditional classroom practices are blended with newer technology applications [6]. With all of the resources available online, classroom materials can be extremely flexible. Students can learn the same content in many ways. Note that blended lessons must use technology when it fits, and teachers should not force technology into a lesson [6]. The major downside to this is when technology does not work. If a part of the lesson relies on technology, faulty devices or malfunctioning Internet can disrupt the entire classroom. "Issues such as lack of technology skills and lack of high-speed access for online components of the course could negatively impact student attitudes toward learning" [3]. An example of this is Flash simulations that are common in science classrooms. Flash does not work well with Apple products, so schools that use iPads or Mac computers may not be able to use those resources.

A fourth example of hybrid learning is the hybrid rotation model. This is similar to what elementary teachers have done for a long time, but adapted for older students. There are three stations – direct, independent, and collaborative. In the direct station, teachers work directly with the students [6]. This is a good chance to work one-on-one with students who need some individual attention. In the independent station, students work independently on an assignment [6]. This would be an opportunity to incorporate technology such as educational videos. In the collaborative station, students work in small groups to complete an assignment [6]. Collaborative can involve technology, traditional paper work, or both. The station names and functions may change a bit depending on what version of this model is used, but the underlying concept is the same. The major advantage of the rotational model is that students learn the same topic in three ways. Additionally, students get to work with both teachers and peers, which makes the lesson more social and student centered. Difficulties in this model include timing and work completion. The teacher has to determine how quickly or slowly to move students through each station. Moving too quickly will cause the students to rush and not really learn much from their stations. Moving too slowly risks students misbehaving or distracting others if they get done early. "It seems that instructors need to be more sensitive to the course goals when deciding the amount of time required for the online component, and to design online activities that are in full alignment with course goals" [3]. Another downfall is the students' ability to work together. Some students do not understand exactly how to collaborate, and may need to be explicitly taught how to collaborate with peers.

III. RESEARCH ON HYBRID

Researchers agree that blended or hybrid learning can have benefits for students. According to Alducin-Ochoa and Vázquez-Martínez, who studied university students using blended learning, "the BL [blended learning] modality enabled students to control their learning process and received constant feedback, which provided them with better opportunities to understand and to broaden their knowledge" [1]. The U.S. Department of Education released a meta-analysis in 2010 that agrees. "The overall finding of the meta-analysis is that classes with online learning (whether taught completely online or blended) on average produce stronger student learning outcomes than do classes with solely face-to-face instruction" [4]. Blends of online and face-to-face instruction showed stronger learning outcomes, with a significant effect size of +0.35 [4]. From the perspective of the educational institution, hybrid can be an effective way to offer more classes while reducing the overall load on the school. "Research at the University of Central Florida found that hybrid courses allowed the university to offer more classes at peak demand times of the day" [2]. There is a lot more research available for specific classrooms and hybrid learning, and there is still much more that can be learned as technology changes over time [6].

IV. CONCLUSIONS

In conclusion, technology is a part of all of our lives and should naturally be a part of our classrooms. Integrating technology into classrooms has proven to be effective in multiple studies. However, what is actually effective in any one classroom depends on the students [6]. There are multiple ways for teachers to use technology in the classroom. Teachers should use what is best for their students to achieve the best instructional outcomes. Do not use technology just for the sake of using technology. Find what works for the students, and know that what works might change from class to class [6]. Teachers have always been able to adapt to new learning conditions. The advances in hybrid learning can definitely increase learning for all students.

ACKNOWLEDGMENT

S. Graban would like to thank Dr. Joseph Kush for providing assistance with this paper.

REFERENCES

[1] J. Alducin-Ochoa, and A. Vázquez-Martínez, "Hybrid learning: An effective resource in university education?," International Education Studies, vol. 9, no. 8, pp. 1-14, 2016. DOI: 10.5539/ies.v9n8p1.

[2] C. Crawford, J. Barker, and A. Seyam, "The promising role of hybrid learning in community colleges: Looking towards the future," Contemporary Issues in Education Research, vol. 7, no. 3, pp. 237-242, 2014 DOI: 10.19030/cier.v7i3.8645.

[3] Q. Lin, "Student views of hybrid learning: A one-year exploratory study," Journal of Computing in Teacher Education, vol. 25, no. 2, pp. 57-66, 2009. Available from http://www.tandfonline.com/toc/ujdl20/current, 2018/1/26.

[4] B. Means, Y. Toyama, R, Murphy, M. Bakia, and K. Jones. Evaluation of evidence-based practices in online learning: A meta-analysis and review of online learning studies, Washington, D.C.: U.S. Department of Education, Office of Planning, Evaluation, and Policy Development, 2010.

[5] M. B. Pinto and W. Anderson, "A little knowledge goes a long way: Student expectation and satisfaction with hybrid learning," Journal of Instructional Pedagogies. Available from http://www.aabri.com/jip.html, 2018/1/26.

[6] H. Staker and M. B. Horn, "Classifying K-12 blended learning", Innosite Institute, 2012.

[7] J. Thompson, "6 blended learning models: When blended learning is what's up for student success," eLearning Industry, 2016. Available from https://elearningindustry.com/6-blended-learning-models-blended-learning-successful-students, 2018/1/26.

A Review of the Importance of Computational Thinking in K-12

Katharine McClelland and Lori Grata Instructional
Technology and Leadership doctoral student Duquesne
University
Pittsburgh, PA USA
mcclellandk@duq.edu
gratal@duq.edu

***Abstract*—In the K-12 setting, it is important for students and teachers to recognize that computational thinking is more than just using technology or computer science. It is a mindset, a way of approaching difficult problems. Approaching all content areas through this lens will help ensure all learners are exposed to these valuable skills and are able to be successful in our ever-evolving global society. This paper reviews computational thinking in a K-12 setting, considering all content areas and inclusive practices.**

Keywords-computational thinking, K-12.

I. INTRODUCTION

Computational thinking opens doors for more than just students of technology. It is a way of thinking through problems and processing the steps which can lead to a solution, helping develop the capacity and limits of computing [12]. In the K-12 setting, it is important for students and teachers to recognize that computational thinking is more than just using technology or computer science. It is a mindset, a way of approaching difficult problems. Yadav, Hong, and Stephenson state that "the essence of computational thinking involves breaking down complex problems into more familiar/manageable sub-problems (problem decomposition), using a sequence of steps (algorithms) to solve problems, reviewing how the solution transfers to similar problems (abstraction), and finally determining if a computer can help us more efficiently solve those problems (automation)" [13].

With the constant evolution of technology, it is imperative that teachers empower their students to become digital citizens and encourage them to take ownership of their learning. Students may be born with technology in hand, but they must be guided so that they know how to use it appropriately. Yadav, Hong and Stephenson stress that computer science plays a large role in our current society and helps to keep it connected [13]. Therefore, by introducing computing ideas like computational thinking to students early, we can help children become more than just consumers of technology; they can use the tools to someday make an impact on the world.

Computational thinking can be defined as the process of taking a difficult problem and breaking it apart into multiple little problems which we know how to solve. Wing states that computational thinking "involves solving problems, designing systems, and understanding human behavior, by drawing on the concepts fundamental to computer science" [12]. As computational thinking has continued to evolve, the International Society for Technology in Education (ISTE) and the Computer Science Teachers Association (CSTA) collaborated with members of K-12, higher education, and members of industry to develop an operational definition of computational thinking [5]. From this collaboration, we can define computational thinking as a problem-solving process that includes the characteristics of formulating problems in a way that enables one to use a computer and other tools to help solve them, logically organizing data, analyzing data, representing data through abstractions, and automating solutions through algorithmic thinking. Additionally, computational thinking is identifying, analyzing, and implementing possible solutions with the goal of achieving the most efficient and effective combination of steps and resources. Computational thinking can generalize and transfer the problem-solving process to a wide variety of situations, such as confidence in dealing with complexity, persistence in working with difficult problems, tolerance for ambiguity, the ability to deal with open-ended problems, and the ability to communicate and work with others to achieve a common goal or solution [5].

When applied across different content areas, computational thinking influences how students approach and solve problems. In providing various ways to approach problems, computational thinking helps to ensure success for the problem-solver [11]

Providing students with the tools and supports to find new or unique methods to solve problems will also strengthen students' confidence in their ability to problem-solve. Educators should continually work towards instilling this sense of agency within their students, directly affecting their ability to take control of their lives both in and out of the classroom and into the future [7]. Sneider, Stephenson, Schafer and Flick point out that when students approach a problem with a background of computational thinking, their knowledge can help them see the systems that are before them and develop new problem-solving skills within any content area [11].

In the sections to follow, we will cover the significance of computational thinking in mathematics and science in Section II, Section III will discuss computational thinking in special education, English and history will be discussed in Section IV and electives will be covered in Section V with our conclusion being found in Section VI.

II. MATHEMATICS AND SCIENCE

In K-12 learning, especially within the mathematics and sciences, embedding computational thinking ideas aids students as they work to expand their understanding of concepts and processes. It is important to recognize that this is not a new idea or fad, but rather a foundational concept that has recently earned the attention of educators and researchers. In fact, some of the same skills that are classified as computational thinking are woven throughout the Mathematical Practices (MP) and the Science and Engineering Practices (SEP) found within the Common Core State Standards (CCSS), as shown in Figure 1 [8]. These practices are designed to support students' learning and understanding of mathematical, scientific, and engineering practices throughout their entire education, starting in kindergarten. In fact, most teaching resources, including textbooks and online resources integrate real world applications of these practices and computational thinking skill sets throughout their lessons, activities, and explorations. A few examples include Google for Education, Code.org, and ISTE.

Alignment between mathematical practices and scientific and engineering practices.

Mathematical Practices (MP)	Science and Engineering Practices (SEP)
1. Making sense of problems and persevering in solving them	1. Asking questions and defining problems 3. Planning and carrying out investigations
2. Reason abstractly and quantitatively	2. Developing and using models 3. Planning and carrying out investigations 5. Using mathematics and computational thinking
3. Construct viable arguments and critique the reasoning of others	5. Using mathematics and computational thinking 6. Constructing explanations and designing solutions 7. Engaging in argument from evidence 8. Obtaining, evaluating, and communicating information
4. Model with mathematics	2. Developing and using models 3. Planning and carrying out investigations
5. Use appropriate tools strategically	2. Developing and using models 3. Planning and carrying out investigations 4. Analyzing and interpreting data
6. Attend to precision	3. Planning and carrying out investigations 8. Obtaining, evaluating, and communicating information
7. Look for and make use of structure	4. Analyzing and interpreting data 6. Constructing explanations and designing solutions 7. Engaging in argument from evidence
8. Looking for and expressing regularity in repeated reasoning	5. Using mathematics and computational thinking 6. Constructing explanations and designing solutions

Figure 1. Alignment between mathematical practices and scientific and engineering practices.

Although mathematics and science are assumed to be the most natural areas for computational thinking, it spans across all other curricula as well. Czerkawski explains that this is because computational thinking is merely a problem-solving skill for all disciplines and can be taught through integration in the content area or exclusively teaching the skills [3]. Barr, Harrison, and Conery explained that by integrating computational thinking in the K-12 curriculum across content areas, students are able to learn these important skills in a non-traditional way that enables students to internalize them, thus making it natural for students to connect the knowledge across content and apply the skills in different situations [1]. Figure 2 provides a visual representation which supports Barr, Harrison and Conery's point that every student should be learning computational thinking as it affects core subjects like reading writing and math; it is a way of thinking, processing, and problem-solving [1] [2].

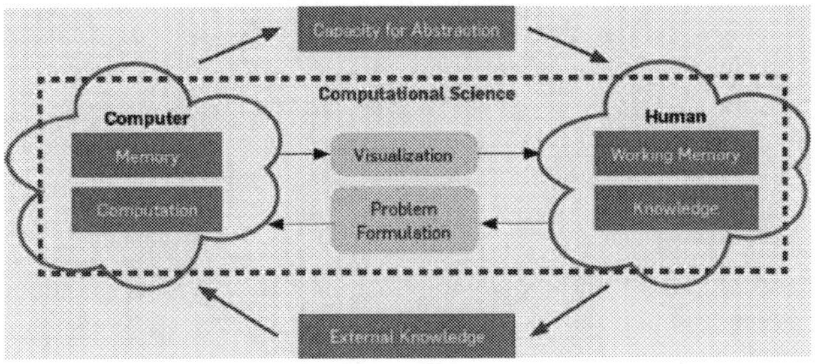

Figure 2. Connecting Computational Thinking to Life

Computation thinking helps build skills that all levels of learner need, including "confidence in dealing with complexity, persistence in working with difficult problems, tolerance of ambiguity, the ability to deal with open-ended problems, and the ability to communicate and work with others to achieve a common goal or solution" [1]. In fact, Deschryver and Yadav take this point one step further as they argue for the need of both "new literacies and computational thinking to promote creative thinking" across disciplines in an attempt to bridge the divide between traditionally creative content areas (music, art, and writing) and scientific areas (math, science, engineering) [4]. By embedding learning activities using collaboratively defined literacies and the incorporation of computational thinking skills, foundational skills can be developed to help scaffold learning and foster creative thinking amongst learners, helping to avoid narrow interpretations and approaches to learning.

III. SPECIAL EDUCATION

Teachers of special education use computational thinking in their day-to-day work; they are trained to see patterns between students and behaviors. Special education teachers use this skill set to teach students to look at complex problems in different ways, applying the content and computational thinking skills as they problem-solve. This is particularly important as Israel, Wherfel, Pearson, Shehab, and Tapia point out that students with disabilities are underrepresented in the fields of science, technology, engineering, and mathematics (STEM) [6]. So, by including computational thinking skills within the K-12 curriculum, students both with and without learning disabilities will grow more through their exposure to these skills and approaches to problem-solving. One integral element of computational thinking is a collaborative learning experience, highlighting students' attributes and showcasing their respective strengths [6].

IV. ENGLISH AND HISTORY

In the areas of English and history, it is natural to collaborate to build students' communication, writing, and reading skills, which align nicely with the concepts of computational thinking, including conceptualization (of the problem), abstraction (of important details), and creativity (when developing the solution/outcome). Shaikh explains that in the English language arts, history, and social studies classrooms computational thinking can be used to teach students how to use a piece of software to create a product [10]. Through this collaboration, the lesson can be extended to include computational thinking skills, allowing the students to be challenged. An example that highlights the integration of computational thinking in a history class is an assignment where the student compares events of ancient times with a his/her current life in a blog [1].

As an alternative example, when discovering problems within literature or history, students could be encouraged to expand a problem and find new ways of looking at it [9]. Computational thinking can aid K-12 educators in their classroom by linking the current educational objectives to classroom practices [1].

V. ELECTIVE CLASSES

Elective classes in a K-12 setting are often overlooked but can be instrumental in teaching computational thinking within a K-12 setting. Computer programing is a common elective that students can take to learn computational thinking when offered, but computational thinking does not need to be limited to just one elective. Like in the core subjects, electives can be useful for engaging students in a new way of thinking. According to the Department of Labor, there are an estimated 1.4 million computer-related jobs that will be available by 2020. Therefore, encouraging students to peruse electives in computing will help build early interest which will help fulfil these estimated jobs (as cited in [6]). Music is another elective area in which computational thinking can be taught and used. One example is having students use scratch.com to create musical instruments to study pitch. Using scratch, the students learning pitch are using computational thinking through abstractions [1].

VI. CONCLUSION

By integrating computational thinking in a variety of disciplines in K-12, students will learn computational thinking throughout the school day, having the opportunity to use and combine their skills within different subject matter [1]. According to Sanford and Naidu, a student can use computational thinking to extend his/her thinking beyond the obvious solution, regardless of the class, as it encourages student initiative and innovation [9]. Through this approach, students become prepared and excited to answer the "what if" questions that are proposed in class, which is necessary when developing students as life-long learners.

REFERENCES

[1] D. Barr, J. Harrison, and L. Conery, "Computational thinking: A digital age skill for everyone," in Learning & Leading With Technology, 2011, vol. 38 issue 6, pp. 20-23.

[2] S. Cooper, L.C. Pérez, and D. Rainey, "Education K-12 computational learning," in Communications of the ACM, 2010, vol. 53, issue 11, p. 27

[3] B.C. Czerkawski, "Classroom implementations of computational thinking: Examples from education majors," in Proceedings of the World Conference on E-Learning, USA, 2016, pp. 151-156.

[4] M.D. Deschryver, and A. Yadav, "Creative and computational thinking in the context of new literacies: Working with teachers to scaffold complex technology-mediated approaches to teaching and learning," in Journal of Technology and Teacher Education, 2015, vol. 23, issue 3, pp. 441-431.

[5] International Society for Technology in Education, and Computer Science Teachers Association, "Operational definition of computational thinking for K–12 education." (2011).

[6] M. Israel, Q.M. Wherfel, J. Pearson, S. Shehab, and T. Tapia, "Empowering K-12 students with disabilities to learn computational thinking and computer programming," in Teaching Exceptional Children, 2015, vol. 48, issue 1, pp. 45-53. doi: 10.117/00400599155594790.

[7] J. Malyn-Smith, B. Coulter, J. Denner, I. Lee, J. Stiles, and L. Werner, "Computational thinking in K-12: Defining the space," in Proceedings of the Society for Information Technology & Teacher Education International Conference, USA, D. Gibson & B. Dodge, Eds., 2010, pp. 3479-3484.

[8] R. Mayes, and T.R. Koballa, "Exploring the science framework: Making connections in math with the common core state standards," in Science Scope, 2012, vol. 36, issue 4, pp. 15-22.

[9] J.F. Sanford, and J.T. Naidu, "Computational thinking concepts for grade school," in Contemporary Issues in Education Research (Online), 2016, vol. 9, issue 1, p. 23.

[10] S. Shaikh, "Should we be teaching computational thinking in schools?," in Fractus Learning, 2016.

[11] C. Sneider, C. Stephenson, B. Schafer, and L. Flick, "Computational thinking in high school science classrooms," in The Science Teacher, 2014, vol. 81, issue 5, pp. 53-59.

[12] J.M. Wing, "Computational thinking," in Communications of the AMC, 2016, vol. 49, issue 3, pp. 33-35.

[13] A. Yadav, H. Hong, and C. Stephenson, "Computational thinking for all: Pedagogical approaches to embedding 21st century problem solving in K-12 classrooms," in Tech Trends, 2016, vol. 60, pp. 565-568, doi: 10.1007/s11528-016-0087-7.

Teaching ESL and Instruction Design with Computational Thinking and Robot-Assisted Language Learning

Jianan Zhou
School of Education, Duquesne University
Pittsburgh, United States
E-mail: zhouj4@duq.edu

Abstract—Living in the 21st century, it seems impossible for everything to develop without technology, critical thinking, and computational thinking. This paper is to address the application of computational thinking on English as Second Language (ESL) teaching and robot-assisted language learning. After illustrating that computational thinking is a process to solve problems, while computational linguistics is a field concerned with the statistical or rule-based modeling of natural language, this paper gives a brief introduction of the Language Acquisition Device theory and how ESL teachers design the instructions and teach English by following the computational thinking process. Robots, however, can also be used to interact with English language learners and to help them with their speaking skills in the 21st-century classroom.

Keywords-Computational Thinking; Computational linguistics; ESL instruction; Robot-assisted language learning.

I. INTRODUCTION

Computational thinking (CT) is a problem solving process that includes a number of characteristics, such as logically ordering, analyzing data and creating solutions using a series of ordered steps; and dispositions, such as the ability to confidently deal with complexity and open-ended problems. CT is essential to the development of computer applications, but it can also be used to support problem solving across all disciplines, including math, science, and the second language learning.

Currently, CT is broadly defined as a set of cognitive skills and problem solving processes that include (but are not limited to) the following characteristics [8][9]:

- Using abstractions and pattern recognition to represent the problem in new and different ways.
- Logically organizing and analyzing data.
- Breaking the problem down into smaller parts.
- Approaching the problem using programmatic thinking techniques such as iteration, symbolic representation, and logical operations.
- Reformulating the problem into a series of ordered steps (algorithmic thinking).
- Identifying, analyzing, and implementing possible solutions with the goal of achieving the most efficient and effective combination of steps and resources.
- Generalizing this problem-solving process to a wide variety of problems.

Computational linguistics (CL) is an interdisciplinary field concerned with the statistical or rule-based modeling of natural language from a computational perspective, as well as the study of appropriate computational approaches to linguistic questions. The theoretical goals of CL include the formulation of grammatical and semantic frameworks for characterizing languages in ways enabling computationally tractable implementations of syntactic and semantic analysis; the discovery of processing techniques and learning principles that exploit both the structural and statistical properties of language; and the development of cognitively and neuroscientifically plausible computational models of how language processing and learning might occur in the brain [7]. Today, CL often works as a member of interdisciplinary teams, which can include regular linguists, experts in the target language, and computer scientists.

In this paper, we are going to address the application of computational thinking on English as Second Language (ESL) teaching and robot-assisted language learning. In Section II, the Language Acquisition Device theory shows how the human mind processes language acquisition of children's innate predisposition. Additionally, Section III gives a brief introduction of how ESL teachers design the instructions and teach English by following the computational thinking process. Robots are discussed in Section IV that they can also be useful in interacting with English language learners and to help them with their speaking skills in the 21st-century classroom.

II. UNIVERSAL GRAMMAR (UG) IN LINGUISTICS

The theory of universal grammar proposes that if human beings are brought up under normal conditions, then they will always develop language with certain properties. For instance, our brains can distinguish nouns from verbs, or distinguish the function words from the content words. The Language Acquisition Device (LAD) is a hypothetical module of the human mind posited to account for children's innate predisposition for language acquisition [1], and is a concept of an instinctive mental capacity that enables children to acquire and produce language, same as the process of how computers classify different documents. For example, we put verbs in the "verb" folder, or distinguish the Microsoft Word document by ending of ".doc". The theory proposes that there is an innate, genetically determined language faculty that knows these rules, making it easier and faster for children to learn to speak than it otherwise would be.

Chomsky [1] states that the development of language in the individual must involve three factors: (1) genetic endowment, which sets limits on the attainable languages, thereby making language acquisition possible; (2) external data, converted to the experience that selects one or another language within a narrow range; (3) principles not specific to the Faculty of Language.

As an interesting side note of historical importance, Chomsky made a number of important advances in the field of computer programming languages. He is credited with the development of the Chomsky hierarchy, a rigorous mathematical model of grammar [5]. Both of the mathematical model of grammar and universal grammar theories are vital and a great advance to the field of computer science and programming language theory.

III. Computational Thinking is Applied to English Language Teaching/Learning

Teachers in Science, Technology, Engineering, and Mathematics (STEM) focused classrooms that include computational thinking, allow students to practice problem-solving skills, such as trial and error [10]. Basically, computational thinking is an iterative process based on three stages:

1. Problem formulation (abstraction);
2. Solution expression (automation);
3. Solution execution and evaluation (analyses).

However, why can we not apply the computational thinking process to the English as a Second Language (ESL) teaching in the classrooms? Therefore, this will be how ESL teachers structure the language teaching or design the instructions by following the computational thinking process [3]:

- Exploration

During the exploration phase, teachers can let ESL students watch some movie clips in English, whose contents should be related to what grammar or vocabularies they are current learning, such as the simple past tense, or vocabularies of different colors or animals. After watching the materials, students will be given a series of structured activities to engage in the production writing and speaking skills.

- Analysis and breakdown

This phase focuses on the analysis of the student's comprehension of the materials and the elements they have found, such as new vocabularies, grammar features, etc. Particular attention should be drawn on certain elements. For example, the present progressive tense has been used whole time in the story that they watch. Then, the students will be encouraged to use the present progressive tense make sentence to talk about what things are happening in their real life. Also, as part of this analysis, students will be asked to write down the sentences they thought could best express the meaning of the story. Each student will choose the most important sentences for the whole class brainstormed, and then they will come up the main line of the story they read or the video they watched.

- Identification of language patterns and theme

Identification of language patterns and theme is the process of the study of the grammar, which focuses on how language elements are ralted to each other and the rules are established. A parse tree, as an example shown in Figure 1, models the grammar of a language and expresses the grammar in a way that clarifies the meaning of the elements in the language [5]. The word "thinking" is classified as a noun as a lower level of the parse tree. Meanwhile, the three-word "the educated student" is classified as a noun phrase at the higher level of the parse tree.

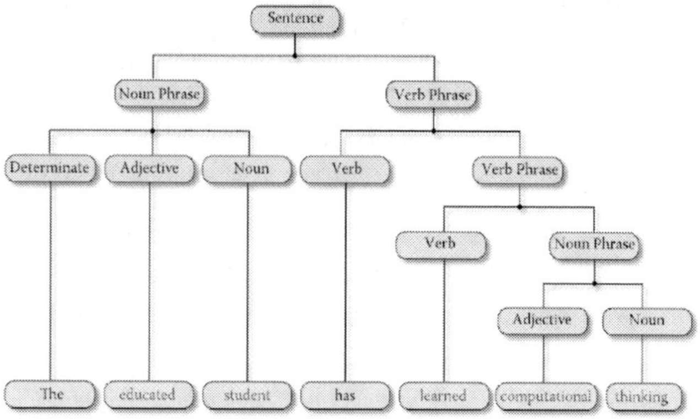

Figure 1. The structure of an English sentence is shown in this parse tree.

- Abstraction

If the previous stage is to let students generate a complete sentence by following the structure of the parse tree, then this step is to ask them to organize a short story following the five "wh-" question and one "how" question shown as TABLE 1.

TABLE 1. THE FIVE "WH-" QUESTIONS AND ONE "HOW" QUESTION.

WHAT	Describe the story you want to present.
WHO	What are the characters in the story?
WHEN	When does this story happen?
WHERE	Where does this story take place?
WHY	Why you want to write a story like this?
HOW	What does each character interact?

- Implementation: coding with "Scratch"

This is the phase in which students use Scracth.mit.edu to code the movements of the cats, make the scenery based on their own stories. With Scratch, students can program their own interactive stories, games, and animations. Also, they can share their creations with others in the online community. Scratch helps students, including English language leaners learn to think creatively, reason systematically, and work collaboratively, which are the essential skills for life in the 21st century. At this stage each student can works in groups in order to get all together to discuss progress, they help each other with not only the technology problems, but also the language problems. The meetings among group members were very important because they allowed to involve all class members and everyone could contribute to the show with his/her point of view. On one hand, it improves students speaking proficiency; on the other hand, it encourages student's teamwork spirit.

- Assessment and improvement

In addition to the checks and adjustments made during the learning process, instead of using tests or quizzes, the students are encouraged to use blogs to share stories or their writing assignments with others online where has more of an authentic writing experience. Since they can get feedbacks from a wider audience typically has access to read posted entries, students will get less anxiety and more motivations to do that, which means students tend to put more effort on it. Also, I believed that language is a communication tool, so students are encouraged to talk about what they have learned and what they did in the classroom in English with their parents and some digital device (e.g., robots, which we will discuss in the next section), in order to build an English-speaking environment outside of the classroom.

IV. Robot-Assisted Language Learning

It is effective when second language learners directly interact with a native speaker in a class, and researcher believed that autonomous robots embedded voice recognition technology could perform the role of native speakers to interact with learners [2]. Also, research study has confirmed that this type of interaction between robots and humans not only improves teaching effectiveness but also learning motivation, because students are less anxious and more cheerful [4].

Given the fact that computers cannot conduct open ended dialogues and cannot give feedback to open ended questions [6], these problems can demonstrate that while technology could have much to offer for the learners for its high efficiency in delivering materials and interations. The robot teachers, which enhance English laguage learners' learning process, could fix the difficulties of addressing the complex learner needs and inability to answer open-ended question in real time.

Despite the great benefits of using robots in second/foreign language learning, the current application may be limited because of the two major reasons: autonomous robots have complex artificial intelligence and are so expensive that normally schools cannot afford them. Therefore, an alternative to solving the above problems is to buy robots with simple autonomous functions (e.g., Amazon's Echo, Jibo, Google Home, etc.). These robots are mostly developed in a small size and at a lower cost. Meanwhile, they could be simply controlled by instructors to perform pedagogical missions and teaching materials in the classroom activities for facilitating learner's engagement and oral interaction.

V. Conclusion and Future Work

With the number of courses steadily increasing to meet students' needs and demands, ESL students are getting more frequently encouraged or required to take English language courses to complete their study in English-speaking countries, or even non-English-speaking countries. Although the development of technology has made language-learning opportunities increasingly more accessible to a growing number of people, there is not too much research about learning English with computational thinking or robots. This paper is aim to call the attention of English language teacher to the use of the computational thinking and technology tools like robots. Future research needs to focus on the pedagogy and instruction design of using the computational thinking process and technology tool (e.g. robots) in the 21st-century ESL classroom.

References

[1] N. Chomsky, Approaching UG from below. In Interfaces + Recursion = Language? Chomsky's Minimalism and the View from Semantics, eds. Uli Sauerland and Hans–Martin Gärtner. Berlin: Mouton de Gruyter, 2007.

[2] J. Han, "Emerging technologies – Robot assisted language learning," Language Learning & Technology, vol. 16, pp. 1-9, 2012.

[3] M. Lonigro, "ESL, computational thinking and robotics," Retrieved from: https://marilina63.wordpress.com/ December, 2017

[4] S. Papert, Mindstorms: Children, computers, and powerful ideas (2nd ed.). New York, NY: Basic Books, 1993.

[5] D. D. Riley, and K. A. Hunt, Computational Thinking for the Modern Problem Solver. Chapman and Hall. London, 2014.

[6] A. Seileek, A. Farhan, and A. O. A. Sa'aleek, "Computer assisted language learning: Merits and demerits," Language in India, vol. 12, pp. 31-44, 2012. Retrieved from: http://www.languageinindia.com/april2012/v12i4april2012.pdf December, 2017

[7] L. Schubert, "Computational Linguistics, The Stanford Encyclopedia of Philosophy," Retrieved from: https://plato.stanford.edu/archives/spr2015/entries/computational-linguistics December, 2017

[8] S. Grover, and R. Pea, "Computational thinking in K–12: A Review of the State of the Field," Educational Researcher, vol. 42, pp. 38–43, 2013. doi: 10.3102/0013189X12463051

[9] C. Stephenson, and B. Valerie, "Defining computational thinking for K-12," CSTA Voice, vol. 7, pp.3–4, 2011.

[10] D. Barr, J. Harrison, and L. Conery, "Computational thinking: A digital age skill for everyone," Learning & Leading with Technology, vol. 38, pp. 20–23, 2011.

Conversation: Loose Parts - A Pathway from Play to Technology

Julia Williams, David D. Carbonara, Rose Mary Mautino
School of Education, Duquesne University, USA
williamsj@duq.edu, carbonara@duq.edu, mautino@duq.edu

***Abstract*--Computational thinking was defined as a way humans solve problems. It is not trying to get humans to think like computers. There has been a lack of interest for computational thinking in higher education. This presentation is calling for an innovative approach that starts with the identification of a discipline specific problem space within a higher education student's program of study.**

Keywords- loose parts; imaginative behavior; instructional design; computational thinking.

I. INTRODUCTION

This presentation is designed to engage participants in an active discussion of critical thinking, computational thinking [18], creativity, imagination and loose parts. Imagination is a life-long cognitive endeavor and acts as the catalyst for all creative functions. If we believe that experiences expand imagination and that imaginative acts expand our reality, we consider how we can create meaningful and creative experiences for students of all ages. As educators, we create meaningful experiences for our students. Some of these experiences take the form of STEM-based technology actions [7]. However, at the higher education level, we sometimes forget the fundamental nature of meaningful play experiences. The concept of loose parts provides the vehicle for higher education faculty and students to practice problem-solving strategies in discipline-specific situations. The practice is often considered 'risky' because solutions are not always known. However, the success/failure cycle that often occurs in 'risky' problems acts as a catalyst to create and enhance problem-solving schemas. The process starts with parts that can be moved, carried, combined, redesigned, lined up, and taken apart and put back together. These actions can be repeated in coding, in STEM activities and in any discipline-specific content that encounters problems and dilemmas. After all, computational thinking is about the schema we form to create workable heuristics and algorithms. The nature of playing with loose parts shows the user that designing and redesigning is a welcome practice. Loose parts form the basis for future problem-solving schemas. This discussion will provide loose parts with which the participants can play.

II. LITERATURE REVIEW

Imagination is a life-long cognitive and affective act. It serves as the catalyst for all creative actions [10] [17]. This essential dynamic serves both our cultural and scientific lives. Vygotsky [17] stated, and was later re-interpreted by Moore [11], that imagination is the link between emotion and thought and between reality and imagination. Piaget [14] makes a connection between the initial stage of imaginative autistic thought, which later develops into a stage of realistic thinking. This notion of imagination and play is later found in Hewes [6] discussion of play as essential for optimal development. Our notion of introducing play at an early age supports the development of students' cognition to perform coding and to build robots later in life.

Imaginative behavior is based on the brain's ability to draw upon and combine elements from our previous experiences. These experiences are cumulative and are based on both informal and informal learning processes that shape our future behavior. As teachers, we can structure these experiences so that we are infusing imaginative thinking into the curriculum. Our curriculum becomes experiences that promote imagination and we welcome imaginative behavior. Vygotsky [17] states that the brain not only stores and retrieves our experiences but also combines those experiences into new meaning and permits our behavior to change. Thus, when we learn to code or to build robots, we often combine parts together in unique ways to form new mindful structures.

Loose Parts is a term that was created by Nicholson [12] in the 1970's. This term is defined as providing children with "loose" materials that can be carried, moved, revised, taken apart and put back together. Loose parts not only develops all areas of the domains of child development but also encourages creativity and develops problem solving skills [1][11][13]. Loose parts can be the use of natural materials such as stones, bark, sand, but also can include construction materials such as wood, wire, plastic and so on. When children manipulate such materials, they are expanding their ideas and are often collaborative with others in order to make meaning from their creations [5].

As we use these loose parts in our imaginative behavior, we often find ourselves repeating processes that serve our purpose at the time. Our purpose could be solving problems that have known solutions as in learning environments or as problems that do not have known solutions as in authentic living. Jonassen [8] discussed the process of solving well-structure and ill-structured problems. He wrote that novice problem-solvers often rely on listed heuristics while experienced problem-solvers use analogical stories that are similar to a current problem situation. He posited how a problem-solver moves from listing the discrete parts of a solution to telling a story about the problem so as to solicit a solution. We find that our experiences change our behavior over time and if we are permitted to experience loose parts at the beginning of our learning, then we can use our imagination to alter our behavior. Thus, we can use our imaginative behavior during the building of code and the construction of robots or any other task that requires computational thinking. As teachers, we need to acknowledge the importance of imagination in the process of creating products [2].

Instructional design principles are used to create the Loose Parts curriculum. An awareness of the barriers [3] to learning new techniques begins the process. Some of these barriers are internal doubts about our ability to solve a problem or the external barriers of insufficient time or materials to solve a problem. The internal and external barriers are considered by the instructors who start the process to learn about the students. The design begins with the instructors talking with the students to identify their internal fears about performing in a Loose Parts environment. The design phase continues in the construction of the learning environment so that time and resources and support are readily available to the students [16]. An empathetic atmosphere is presented to alleviate fears and to create a warm and welcoming environment.

Social connectedness is designed into the process as influenced by Slagter van Tryon and Bishop [15]. People often work well together to solve problems. The sharing of ideas helps to build heuristics and algorithms. Students are encouraged to discuss the process of Loose Parts with each other and to build on the sharing of ideas. Additionally, the concept of Loose Parts could be considered as an ill-structured problem. However, the awareness of this phenomenon could provide a catalyst to design the learning environment to embrace the problem-solving strategy where the complete solution is unknown [4]. Drag and drop programming is a visual programming language that requires low reading levels and almost is absent of syntactical structure [9]. The low reading level is important so that we can show children in grade 1 or even in Kindergarten how to program in code. The process starts with an avatar on a screen and our desire to make it move. Movements such as left, right, up and down are easily understood by most students between the ages of five and eight. It is a powerful tool for students to effectuate action such as sequential movements and loops [9]. We may be familiar with the Logo turtle robot created by Seymour Papert in the 1960's. This same programming environment was converted to drag and drop programming in apps such as Hopscotch, Scratch and Alice.

III. OBJECTIVES

1. Participants will be introduced to the concept of loose parts.
2. Participants will discuss how imagination, computational thinking is integral in engaging the use of technology.
3. Participants will create structures using loose parts
4. Participants will transfer created structures into technology pieces.

IV. CONCLUSION AND FUTURE WORK

It is important to learn problem solving skills and higher order thinking and creativity early. Student can progress into computational thinking as part of their second nature and not as a new skill to acquire in upper grades or at the university. Students will spend a lifetime of learning in the realm of solving problems. They will learn the power of imagination to develop habits of mind to think of new ways to solve problems. This practice permits them to constantly build on their learning.

REFERNCES

[1] S. Bredekamp and C. Copple. (Eds.) *Developmentally appropriate practice in early childhood programs serving children from birth to age 8*. Washington, DC: NAEYC. 1997.

[2] A. Echhoff and J. Urbach. Understanding imaginative thinking during childhood: Sociocultural conceptions of creativity and imaginative thought. *Early Childhood Education Journal, 36*(2). pp. 179-185. 2008.

[3] P. Ertmer. Addressing first- and second-order barriers to change: Strategies for technology integration. *Educational Technology research and Development, 47*(4). pp.47-61. December 1999.

[4] P. A. Ertmer, D.A. Stepich, C.S. York, A. Stickman, X.L. Wu, S. Zurek, and Y. Goktas. How instructional design experts use knowledge and experience to solve ill-structured problems. *Performance Improvement Quarterly, 21*(1), pp.17–42. 2008.

[5] J. L. Frost. *Play and playscapes*. Albany, NY: Delmar. 1992.

[6] J. Hewes. *Let the children play: Nature's answer to early learning*. Early Childhood Learning Knowledge Centre. 2006.

[7] P. Hopkinson and P. James. Practical pedagogy for embedding ESD in science, technology, engineering and mathematics curricula. *International Journal of Sustainability in Higher Education, 11* (4). pp. 65-379. 2010. https://doi.org/10.1108/14676371011077586 [Retrieved: January, 2018].

[8] D. H., Jonassen. Instructional design models for well-structures and ill-structure problem-solving learning outcomes. *Educational Technology Research and Development, 45*(1). pp. 65-94. 1997.

[9] C. Kelleher and R. Pausch. Lowering the barriers to programming: A taxonomy of programming environments and languages for novice programmers. *ACM Computing Surveys (CSUR), 37*(2), 83-137. 2005. [Retrieved April 2016]

[10] G. Lindqvist. Vygotsky's theory of creativity. *Creativity Research Journal, 15*(4). pp. 245-251. 2003.

[11] R. Moore. *Childhood's domain: Play and place in child development*. Berkeley: MIG Communications. 1990. [Retreived May 2015].

[12] S. Nicholson. The theory of loose parts: An important principle for design methodology. *Studies in Design Education Craft & Technology, 4*(2). 5-14. 1972. [Retrieved May 2015].

[13] S. Nicolson and S.G. Shipstead. *Through the looking glass* (3rd edition). Columbus, OH: Merrill Prentice Hall. 2002.

[14] J. Piaget. *Play, Dreams and Imitation in Childhood.* London: Routledge and Kegan Paul Ltd. 1951.

[15] P. J. Slagter van Tryon and M. J. Bishop. Theoretical foundations for enhancing social connectedness in online learning environments. *Distance Education, 30*(3), pp. 291–315. 2009. [Retrieved April, 2014].

[16] J. J. G. van Merriënboer and P. A. Kirschner. Ten steps to complex learning: A systematic approach to four-component instructional design (2nd ed.). New York, NY: Routledge. 2013.

[17] L. S. Vygotsky. *Mind in society:The development of higher psychological processes* (M. Cole, V. John-Steiner, S. Scribner & E. Souberman., Eds.) (A. R. Luria, M. Lopez-Morillas & M. Cole [with J. V. Wertsch], Trans.) Cambridge, Mass.: Harvard University Press. (Original manuscripts [ca. 1930-1934]) 1978. [Retrieved August 2014]

[18] J. Wing. Computational thinking. *Communications ACM, 49*(3). 33-35. doi: 10.1145/1118178.1118215. 2006. [Retrieved October 2014].

Proposal for a Lesson Support System using Computer Virtualization Technology

Yuto Terao
Graduate School of Information and Telecommunication Engineering
Tokai University
Tokyo, Japan
e-mail: 2bjt1224@gmail.com

Kenta Morita
Graduate School of Engineering
Mie University
Mie, Japan
e-mail: morita.k@star.tokai-u.jp

Naoki Morita
Graduate School of Information and Telecommunication Engineering
Tokai University
Tokyo, Japan
e-mail: morita@tokai.ac.jp

***Abstract*—To understand how software operates, it is necessary to repeat an operation many times with the software. However, carrying out a repeat operation that involves settings is not easy. In this study, we use a snapshot of VirtualBox to restore a personal computers (PC) to any previous settings state. As a result, we developed a system that allows students to continue exercises by restoring their PC to an earlier state or by copying the state of an instructor PC.**

Keywords-computer virtualization technology; compute-assisted instruction.

I. INTRODUCTION

Recently, classes in which students use PC or tablet devices have become more commonplace [1]. Students are more accustomed to typing rather than performing operations using software [2]. It is important that students be able to repeat an operation several times in order to master the use of the software. However, students are often only required to imitate an instructor's operation in actual classes. In this study, we propose a system whereby students can repeat operations during a lecture.

In this paper, Section II introduces the problems students face when acquiring a new skill, Section III describes our proposal, Section Ⅳ explains the developed system, Section V evaluates of our system and presents a review by instructors and Section VI summarizes our work.

II. PROBLEMS

Instructors project their desktop display onto a screen which is used to demonstrate how to use the software, and show students how to perform the operations. Students need to perform an operation repeatedly in order to master the use of the software. However, students must restore settings by themselves when performing a specific operation.

For example, we use “Data Analysis Tools” when performing statistical processing with Excel [3]. When we want to add “Data Analysis Tools” to the ribbon, we need to check “File”> “Options”> “Add-ins”, “Manage:”, “Excel Add-ins”, “Go…”, “Analysis ToolPak”. If the instructor makes the students repeat the operation, the students must restore the ribbon to its original state when “Data Analysis Tools” was not added. Otherwise, any changes in add-ons

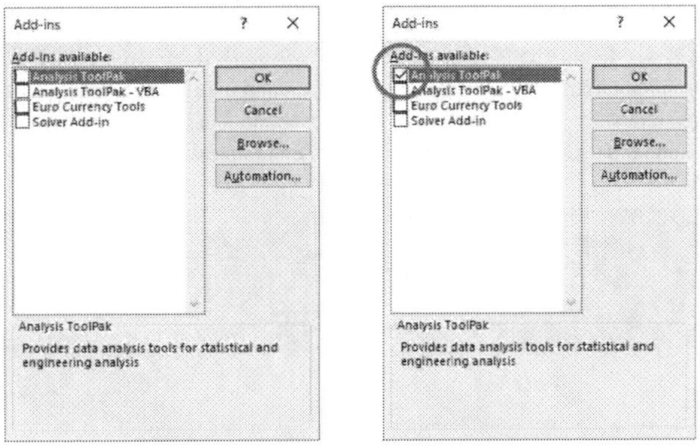

Default The state added to the ribbon

Figure 1. Dialog windows for add-ins settings.

are kept when repeating exercises (Figure 1). Some actions, such as the "Empty Recycle Bin" operation cannot be undone, and if the registry is rewritten by installing an application, it cannot be restored.

Students who are not skilled at performing operations with software need to practice the same operation many times. Therefore, even after some students have finished practicing an operation, others may take more time. Even in cases where all students have not finished practicing, the instructor may have to move on to the next exercise and end the practice session. As a result, the next explanation about how to use the software may not be understood by all students, forcing the instructor to delay future sessions until all students have finished their work in the previous session.

III. PURPOSE

The purpose of this research is to setup each student's PC to easily perform repeat operations. Specifically, when the students are instructed to repeat an operation, the new system would restore the student's PC to its original state. Or, when the instructor explains the contents of the next lecture to the students, the system prepares the student's PC by loading a state where it can perform the next operation. We propose the introduction of virtualization technology to realize this system. The snapshot function of virtualization technology can preserve the state of a PC. Students can perform operations from a preserved state by restoration, even after performing different operations.

For example, snapshots S1, S2 are taken before and after performing an operation in Excel (Figure 2). When snapshot S1 is restored, the PC can return to a state prior to activation of Excel, thereby allowing the student to repeat the same operation. Even if the desired operation has not been completed on Excel, the PC can revert to the state after the Excel operation was performed by restoring snapshot S2.

Students can use snapshots on Guest PC. Guest PC is a software function that emulates the working environment of one PC on a Host PC (Figure 3). Students can use the Guest PC without having to actively think about the Host PC when using the Guest PC with full screen. However, restoration of a state in the Guest PC can only be controlled by the Host PC. Therefore, the student not only operates the Guest PC, but also operates the Host PC to perform further operations during lessons and exercises (Figure 4). Additionally, if the snapshot was not properly taken, the state of the Guest PC cannot be restored.

The purpose of this study is to facilitate the restoration of a snapshot with 1 click on the Guest PC without the Host PC control of the Host PC. Furthermore, restoration of a state on a student's Guest PC based on a snapshot operation demonstrated by the instructor will be examined.

IV. Developed System

The system developed in the study is shown in Figure 5. This system is constructed from five modules. We used VirtualBox [4] provided by Oracle as virtualization technology software. Modules were designed for this study using Java. A snapshot for the model operation to be performed by students during lectures was prepared by the instructor before the lecture.

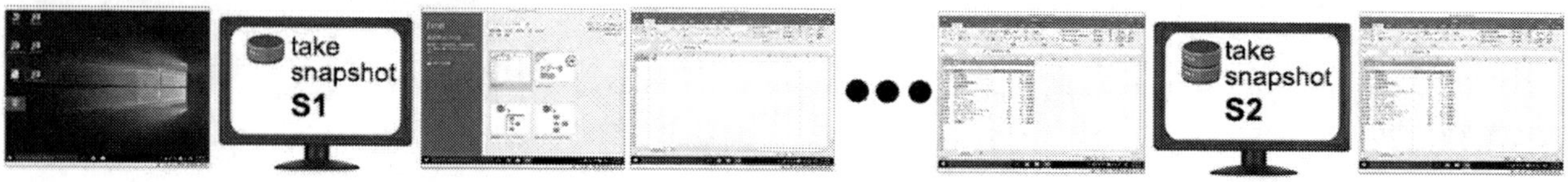

Figure 2. Example of taking a snapshot at different times.

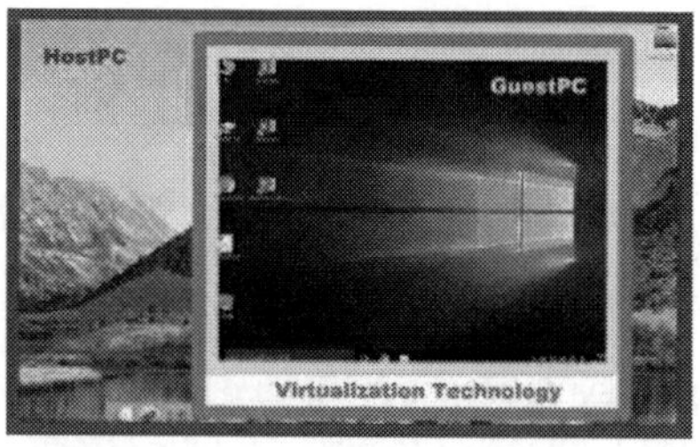

Figure 3. Virtualization PC on Real PC.

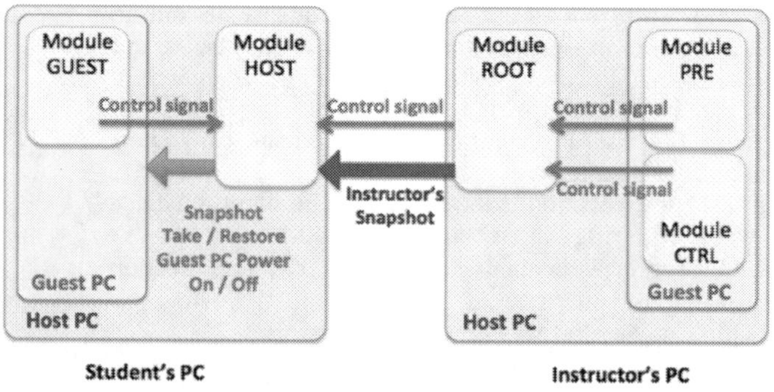

Figure 5. System structure.

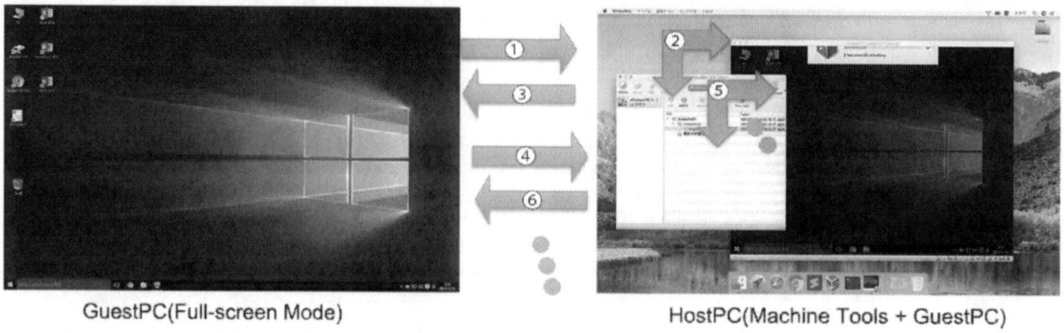

Figure 4. Traditional practice.

A. *Student PC*

Module HOST performs an operation on the student PC's Host PC, and Module GUEST performs an operation on the student PC's Guest PC.

Module HOST imports snapshots by lecturers onto student PCs. Then, Module HOST displays the Guest PC screen in full screen mode. Depending on the control signal of Module GUEST, a snapshot is either saved / restored for the student or the instructor's snapshot is restored on the Guest PC. These processes correspond to Table I when they are performed by existing functions of VirtualBox.

Figure 6 (A) shows the operation screen of Module GUEST, and the sending of a control signal from Module GUEST to Module HOST. The 'Import' button sends a signal to restore the Guest PC based on a snapshot from the instructor and the load button sends a signal to restore the Guest PC based on the snapshot of the student. The 'Save as' button sends a signal to take a snapshot of the state of the PC at that time. After progressing to the next session, the saved snapshot becomes restoration point information available by the 'Load' button.

Thus, students can use the Guest PC without having to actively think about the Host PC. They can perform the repeat operation or synchronize to the lesson with only one click of Module GUEST.

B. *Instructor PC*

Module ROOT operates on the Host PC for the instructor PC; Module PRE and Module CTRL operate on the Guest PC for the instructor PC.

Module ROOT has three functions. First, it performs the function of preserving snapshots of the instructor based on the control signal from Module PRE. Second, the function of transmitting the control signal that determines which snapshot is to be restored by Module HOST on the student PC is performed by Module CTRL Third, the transfer of the snapshot from the instructor PC to the Host PC of the student PC is performed with cooperation from Module HOST.

Figure 6 (B) shows the operation screen of Module CTRL, and the restore points from all snapshots are displayed as a list. The snapshot of the selected thumbnail image becomes the restoration information of the 'Import' button of Module HOST.

TABLE I. TRADISIONAL SNAPSHOT OPERATION

Take snapshot process
(1) Click "Machine" (2) Click "Take Snapshot…" (3) Insert Snapshot name (4) Click "OK"
Snapshot restore process
<< Guest OS Power off >> (1) Click "File" (2) Click "Close" (3) Click "Power off the machine" (4) Click "OK" << Snapshot restore >> (5) Select target snapshot (6) Click "Restore" (7) Click off "Create a snapshot of the current machine state" (8) Click "Restore" << Guest OS restart >> (9) Click "Start"

V. EVALUATION

We verified the effectiveness of the developed system. For the purposes of verification, we researched possible factors that could affect the actual operation, such as disk capacity and transfer time, and asked several instructors to review our research.

A. *Performance*

The snapshot stores all the information needed to restore the state of the computer. The information includes not only operations by the user, but also background operations run by the operating system. The larger the size of the snapshot, the more time it takes to save and restore a state. Tables II and III show the size, the saving time, and the restoring time of a snapshot.

Figure 7 and Figure 8 show the contents of Word [5] and Excel exercises, and the operations described are included in the Microsoft Office Specialist Study Guide [6][7]. From these results, we confirmed that snapshots can be saved and restored in as long as 10 seconds.

Although it depends on the work content, when performing the exercise during basic experimental class without using our system, it was necessary for the instructor to wait about 15 minutes for the students to re-do an exercise. The instructor was able to restore the previous state even in one minute by using our system.

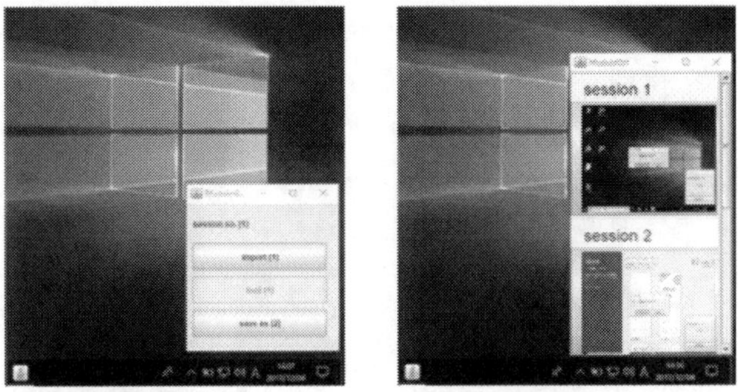

(A) (B)

Figure 6. Module window figure caption: (A) Module GUEST (B) Module CTRL

TABLE II. SPEC OF PC THAT WAS USED

	Windows10 Pro (Lenovo Yoga2 Pro)		Mac OS Sierra (MacBook Pro 2012)	
	Real	Virtual	Real	Virtual
CPU	i7 (1.8GHz)	2CPU	i7 (2.3GHz)	2CPU
Memory	8GB	3GB	8GB	4GB
Storage	256GB	80GB	251GB	120GB
Used Space	–	24.8GB	–	29.8GB

TABLE III. SNAPSHOT SIZE AND RESTORE TIME

	Windows		Mac	
	Restore time	Snapshot size	Restore time	Snapshot size
Word	20sec	168MB	18sec	140MB
Excel	20sec	204MB	18sec	180MB
Idle	–	45MB	–	71MB

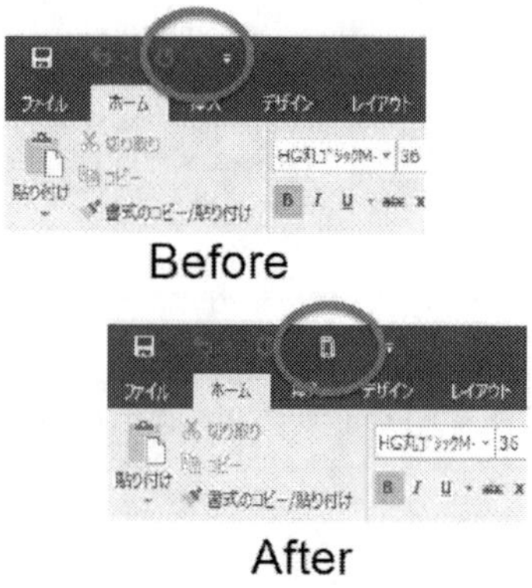

Figure 7. Before and after exercise of Word

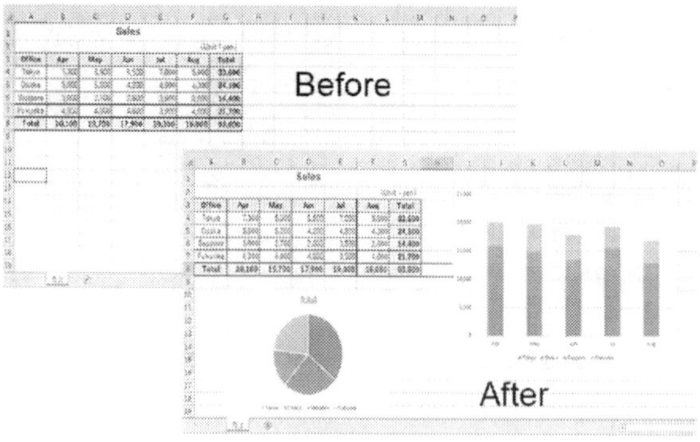

Figure 8. Before and after exercize of Excel

B. Review

Here are some of the comments from instructors:

1) Mr. Murayama (Information Technology):

- I think that it can be used at the time of class that students need to accumulate basic knowledge to advance to the next session.
- I would like to use it for debugging and verification of the system.

2) Mr. Fujino (Computer science):

- This tool will bring a lot of benefit to my computer science courses, such as operating systems and databases.
- Considering the situation of exercise, it will very convenient for students when they make mistakes in exercises if they can reset the states of the computer.

We got a favorable impression from instructors.

VI. CONCLUSION

In a conventional computer class environment, it is difficult for students to learn how to repeat an operation demonstrated by an instructor as the instructor has time constraints and must wait for each student to complete the operation.

In this paper, we introduce the possibility of a new classroom approach by using computer virtualization technology, and thereby demonstrated the performance of this system.

In the future, we are planning to confirm the system's effectiveness by using it in other instructional classes.

ACKNOWLEDGMENT

This work was supported by JSPS KAKENHI Grant Number 16K16324.

REFERENCES

[1] G. Thavamalar, "Successful implementation of e-learning: Pedagogical considerations", The internet and higher education, Vol.4 No.3, pp.287-299, 2001.

[2] D. Grant, "A Comparison of Student Perceptions of their Computer Skills to their Actual Abilities", Journal of Information Technology Education, Vol.8, pp.141-160, 2009.

[3] Excel 2016 by Microsoft. [Online]. Available from: https://products.office.com/en-us/excel, 2017.12.05

[4] Oracle VM VirtualBox. [Online]. Available from: http://www.oracle.com/technetwork/server-storage/virtualbox/overview/index.html, 2017.12.05

[5] Microsoft Word 2016. [Online]. Available from: https://products.office.com/en-us/word, 2017.12.05

[6] K. Sato, "Microsoft Office Specialist Taisaku Text Word 2016", Nikkei Business Publications, Inc., ISBN978-4-8222-5321-9 (in Japanese)

[7] J. Toki, "Microsoft Office Specialist Taisaku Text Excel 2016", Nikkei Business Publications, Inc., ISBN978-4-8222-5322-6 (in Japanese)

Using Deep Learning Methods to Automate Collaborative Learning Process Coding Based on Multi-Dimensional Coding Scheme

Takahiro Kanayama
Graduate School of Bionics, Computer and Media Sciences
Tokyo University of Technology
Tokyo, Japan
email:g211701051@edu.teu.ac.jp

Kimihiko Ando
Cloud Service Center
Tokyo University of Technology
Tokyo, Japan
email:ando@stf.teu.ac.jp

Chihiro Shibata
Graduate School of Bionics, Computer and Media Sciences
Tokyo University of Technology
Tokyo, Japan
email:shibatachh@stf.teu.ac.jp

Taketoshi Inaba
Graduate School of Bionics, Computer and Media Sciences
Tokyo University of Technology
Tokyo, Japan
email:inaba@stf.teu.ac.jp

***Abstract*—In computer-supported collaborative learning research, it may be a significantly important task to figure out guidelines for carrying out an appropriate scaffolding by extracting indicators for distinguishing groups with poor progress in collaborative process upon analyzing the mechanism of interactive activation. And for this collaborative process analysis, coding and statistical analysis are often adopted as a method. But as far as our project is concerned, we are trying to automate this huge laborious coding work with deep learning technology. In our previous research, supervised data was prepared for deep learning based on a coding scheme consisting of 16 labels according to speech acts. In this paper, with a multi-dimensional coding scheme with five dimensions newly designed aiming at analyzing collaborative learning process more comprehensively and multilaterally, an automatic coding is performed by deep learning methods and its accuracy is verified.**

Keywords-CSCL; coding scheme; deep learning methods, automatic coding

I. Introduction

A. Analysis on Collaborative Process

One of the greatest research topics in the actual Computer Supported Collaborative Learning (CSCL) research is to analyze its social and cognitive processes in detail in order to clarify what kinds of knowledge and meanings were shared within a group as well as how and by what arguments knowledge construction was performed. In addition, it is also required to develop CSCL system and tools with scaffolding function which may activate collaborative process by utilizing such knowledge.

However, because main data for the collaborative process analysis include contributions over chatting, images and voices on tools such as Skype, and various outputs prepared in the course of collaborative learning, it is totally inadequate to perform just quantitative analysis in order to analyze such data. Therefore, CSCL research changed direction more or less to qualitative research [1] -[4].

As these qualitative studies often result in in-depth case study, however, they have a downside that it is not easy at all to derive guidelines with generality, which are applicable also to other contexts. Therefore, studies have been conducted in recent years based on an approach of verbal analysis in which labeling for appropriately representing properties (hereinafter referred to as coding) is performed to each contribution in linguistic data of certain volume generated over the collaborative learning from perspectives of linguistics and collaborative learning activities [5]. On the other hand, an advantage of the approach is its capability of quantitative processing for significantly large scale data while keeping qualitative perspective. However, it is a task requiring significant time and labor to perform coding manually and it is expected to become impossible to perform coding manually in a case that data becomes further bigger in size.

In our research project, we have achieved certain results in a series of previous studies reported last year in eLmL 2017 and the like, using deep learning technique for automatic coding of vast amount of collaborative learning data [6]-[8]. In this paper, while verification is performed for accuracy of the automatic coding based on deep learning technique similarly to last year, supervised data has been constructed by conducting coding manually depending on adopted multi-dimensional coding scheme in order to newly analyze collaborative learning process in a more multilateral and comprehensive manner.

B. Purpose of This Study

The final goal of our research project is to implement support at authentic learning and educational settings such as real time monitoring of collaborative process and scaffolding for inactive groups based on analyses of large scale collaborative learning data as mentioned above.

As a further development of our previous research, a technique for automatizing coding of chat data is developed based on a multi-dimensional coding scheme capable of expressing collaborative learning process more comprehensively and its accuracy is verified in this paper.

Specifically, after newly performing coding manually for substantial amount of the same chat data, which was used in the previous studies, a part of it is learned as training data by deep learning methods and then automatic coding is conducted for the test data. For accuracy verification, we try to verify the accuracy of automatic coding by calculating precision and recall of automatic coding of test data in each dimension. We also evaluate what type of misclassification occurred frequently in each dimension.

C. *Structure of This Paper*

In this paper, the outline and results of our previous work are shown in Section II. Our coding scheme newly developed this time is described in Section III. Section IV presents the dataset with the statistics of the new coding labels assigned by the human coders. Our experiments and results of the study are shown in subsequent Section V. Finally, in Section VI, we present the conclusion and future work to complete the paper.

II. PREVIOUS WORK

Outline of our previous work [6] is shown below.

A. *Conversation Dataset*

Conversation dataset for the study conducted last year is based on conversations among students obtained from chat function within the system performing online collaborative learning by using CSCL originally developed by the authors for lectures in the university [9]. By the way, we will add that this data is also used in the research of this paper. Usage situation of CSCL as the source of the dataset is shown in Table I. Since students participated in multiple classes, number of participant students is less than the number obtained by multiplying number of groups and that of group members.

B. *Coding Scheme*

According to a manual for coding prepared by the authors, a label was assigned to each contribution of chat. Any of the 16 types of labels as shown in Table II was assigned. The ratio of each label is shown in Figure 1.

C. *Automatic Coding Approach Based on Deep Learning*

In the previous study, we adopted three types of Deep Neural Network (DNN) structures: 1) Convolutional Neural Networks (CNN), 2) Long-Short Term Memory (LSTM) and 3) Sequence to Sequence (Seq2Seq). Of the three models, Seq2Seq model is a deep neural network consisting of two LSTM units called encoder and decoder, and learning of classification problem and sentence generation is performed by entering pairs of strings of words to each part [10][11]. For example, the pair corresponds to a sentence in certain language and its translated sentence in case of translation system as well as to question sentence and response sentence in case of question and answer system, respectively.

In addition, a model based on Support Vector Machine (SVM), which is a traditional machine learning approach is used as a baseline. Accuracy of each model is verified by comparing automatic coding concordance rate and Kappa coefficient. About technology and experiment results in detail for each classification model, please refer to existing literatures of the authors [6]-[8].

TABLE I. CONTRIBUTIONS DATA USED IN THIS STUDY

Number of Lectures	7 Lectures
Member of Groups	3-4 people
Learning Time	45-90 mintutes
Number of Groups	202 groups
Number of Students	426 students
Dataset	11504 contributions

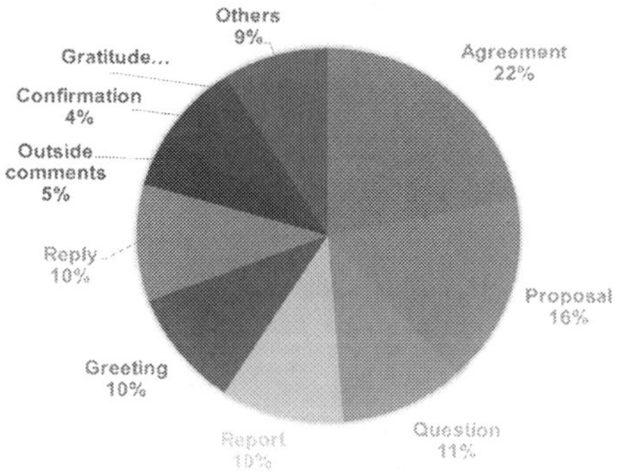

Figure 1. Ratio of each conversational coding labels

TABLE II. LIST OF LABELS

Label	Meaning of label	Contribution example
Agreement	Affirmative reply	I think that's good
Proposal	Conveying opinion, or yes/no question	How about five of us here make the submission?
Question	Other than yes/no question	What shall we do with the title?
Report	Reporting own status	I corrected the complicated one
Greeting	Greeting to other members	I'm looking forward to working with you
Reply	Other replies	It looks that way!
Outside comments	Contribution on matters other than assignment contents / Opinions on systems and such	My contribution is disappearing already; so fast! / A bug
Confirmation	Confirm the assignment and how to proceed	Would you like to submit it now?
Gratitude	Gratitude to other members	Thanks!
Complaint	Dissatisfactions towards assignments or systems	I must say the theme isn't great
Noise	Contribution that does not make sense	?meet? day???
Request	Requesting somebody to do some task	Can either of you reply?
Correction	Correcting past contribution	Sorry, I meant children
Disagreement	Negative reply	I think 30 minute is too long
Switchover	A contribution to change event being handled, such as moving on to the next assignment	Shall we give it a try?
Joke	Joke to other members	You should, like, learn it physically? :)

D. Experiment and Assessment

1) Outline of experiment

For the data set with manually prepared coding labels as described above, we compared the prediction accuracy of automatic coding for each model.

With separation of sentences into morpheme using MeCab conducted at first as a preprocessing of data, words with low use frequency were substituted by "unknown". Subsequently, just 8,015 contributions were extracted and 90% and 10% of them were sorted into data for training and test, respectively.

Naive Bayes, Linear SVM, and SVM based on RBF Kernel were applied as baseline approaches.

2) Experiment Results

Table III shows prediction accuracy (concordance rate) of models proposed in the previous study and those adopted as baseline for test data. The concordance rate here refers to a proportion that manually assigned label conforms with predicted label output by a model. It is proved, as Table III shows, that accuracy of the proposed model's result is higher than that of baseline model. Among the three models as described above, it is found that there is almost no difference in concordance rate between the approaches based on CNN and LSTM (0.67-0.68). These approaches show concordance rates a little bit higher (around 2 to 3%) compared with SMV as a baseline approach (0.64-0.66).

On the other hand, a model based on Seq2Seq showed the highest concordance rate among all of the models (0.718), higher by 5 to 7% and 3 to 4% compared with SVM and other models, respectively.

TABLE III. PREDICTIVE ACCURACIES FOR BASELINES AND DEEP-NEURAL-NETWORK MODELS

Naïve Bayes		SVM(Linear)		SVM(RBF Kernel)	
unigram	uni+bigram	unigram	uni+bigram	unigram	uni+bigram
0.554	0.598	0.642	0.659	**0.664**	0.659

CNN		LSTM		Seq2Seq	
with wikipedia	w.o. wikipedia	single-direction	bidirection	bidirection	bidir. w. interm.
0.686	0.677	0.676	0.678	**0.718**	0.717

Then, results as described above are discussed using Kappa coefficient, which means concordance rate excluding accidental ones. At first, it may be said that LSTM model has achieved sufficiently higher result as the Kappa coefficient for the model shows 0.63. In general, Kappa coefficient of 0.8 or higher is believed to be preferable for utilizing automatic coding discrimination result by a machine in a reliable manner, however, further higher concordance rate is required. In case of Seq2Seq model, on the other hand, Kappa coefficient is 0.723 with great improvement, if not reaching 0.8.

The experiment results above have suggested that Seq2Seq model is superior to other approaches due to consideration for context information. Since Seq2Seq is a model with reply sources entered, it is believed that the improvement in the accuracy has been partly caused by not separate capturing of each contribution but consideration of the context information.

III. NEW CODING SCHEME

As our previous studies mentioned some cases that Replay may include a meaning of Agree in the coding scheme, the fact that the definition of one label may sometimes overlap the definition of another label has become a factor making it difficult to assign a label always with accuracy and reliability. In addition to these technical problems, more importantly, labels based on speech acts, which express the linguistic characteristics of the conversation are insufficient for the analysis of the learning process. With this single linguistic scheme, it is almost impossible to realize whether members of a group engage in activities to solve the task, how members coordinate each other in terms of task division, time management, etc. during their collaboration, how each member constructs his argument, how members discuss and negotiate each other. From those described above, we propose a new coding scheme so that the automated coding accuracy will improve and that we may understand more accurately and globally collaborative process.

Our new coding scheme is constructed based on the multi-dimensional coding scheme proposed by Weinberger et Fischer [12]. As shown in Table V, our scheme consists of five dimensions, while Weinberger and Fischer's one has four dimensions without Coordination dimension. We provide labels basically regarding a contribution as a unit similarly to way we used in the previous studies. In addition, while such values as number of contributions are provided as Participation dimension labels, those in other four dimensions are provided by selecting one label from among multiple labels. In other words, since one label is given for each dimension for one contribution, a plurality of labels will be assigned to one contribution. Therefore, the coding work with this scheme is extremely complicated and takes a lot of time, but the merit of automated coding is even greater. Each dimension is described in detail below.

TABLE V. NEW CODING SCHEME

Dimension	Description
Participation	Frequency of participation in argumentation
Epistemic	How to be directly involved in problem solving
Argumentation	Ideal assertion in argumentation
Social	How to cope with others' statements
Coordination	How to coordinate to advance discussion smoothly

A. Participation Dimension

Participation dimension is for measuring degree of participation in arguments. As this dimension is defined as quantitative data including mainly number of contributions and its letters, time of contributions, and interval of contributions, coding is performed by statistical processing on the database while requiring neither manual nor artificial intelligent coding. The list is shown in Table VI.

Since Participation dimension labels handle number of specific contributions, it is possible to analyze quantitatively different aspects of participation in conversations but impossible to perform qualitative analysis such as whether the conversation contributed to problem solving.

TABLE VI. PARTICIPATION DIMENSION

Category	Description
Number of contributions	Number of contributions of each member during sessions
Number of letters of a contribution	Number of letters during a single speech
Time for contribution	Time used for a contribution
Interval of contributions	Time elapsed since last contribution
contributions distribution	Standard deviation of each member within a group

B. Epistemic Dimension

This dimension shows whether each contribution is directly associated with problem solving as a task and the labels are classified depending on contents of the contributions as shown in Table VII. This dimension's labels are assigned to all contributions.

Weinberger and Fischer's scheme has 6 categories to code epistemic activities, which consist in applying the theoretical concepts to case information. But, as shown in Table VII, we set only two categories here, because we want to give generality by which we can handle as many problem-solving types as possible. "0n Task" here refers to contributions directly related to and such contributions with contents as shown below belong to "Off Trask".

- Contributions to ask meaning of problems and how to proceed with them
- Contributions to allocate different tasks to members
- Contributions regarding the system

Since Epistemic dimension represents whether directly related to problem solving, it works as the most basic code for qualitative analysis. In case of less "On Task" labels, for example, it is believed that almost no effort has been made for the task.

Besides, labels of Argument and Social dimensions are assigned when Epistemic dimension is "On Task", whereas those of Coordination dimension are assigned only when it is "Off Task".

TABLE VII. LABELS IN EPISTEMIC DIMENSION

Label	Description
On Task	contributions directly related to problm solving
Off Task	contributions without any relationship with problem solving
No Sense	contributions with nonsensical contents

C. Coordination Dimension

Coordination dimension code is assigned only when Epistemic code is "Off Task" and it is also assigned to such contributions that relate to problem solving not directly but indirectly. A list of Coordination dimension labels is shown in Table VIII but the labels are assigned not to all contributions of "Off Task" but just one label is assigned to such contributions that correspond to these labels. In addition, in case of replies to contributions with Coordination dimension labels assigned, labels of the same Coordination dimension are assigned.

"Task division" here refers to a contribution to decide who to work on which task requiring division of tasks for advancing problem solving. "Time management" is a contribution to coordinate degree of progress in problem solving, and for example, such contributions fall under the definition that "let's check it until 13 o'clock," and "how has it been in progress?" "Meta contribution" refers to a contribution for clarifying what the problem is when intention and meaning of the problem is not understood. "Technical coordination" refers to questions and opinions about how to use the CSCL System. "Proceedings" refer to contributions for coordinating the progress of the discussion.

Since Coordination dimension labels are assigned to such contributions that intend to problems smoothly, it is believed to be possible to predict progress in arguments by analyzing timing when the code was assigned. Further, in case of less labels of Coordination dimension, it may be predicted that smooth relationship has not been created within the group.

On the other hand, if a large number of these labels were assigned in many groups, it may be understood that there exists any defect in contents of the task or system.

TABLE VIII. LABELS OF COORDINATION DIMENSION

Label	Description
Task division	Splitting work among members
Time management	Check of temporal and degree of progress
Technical coordination	How to use the system, etc.
Proceedings	Coordinating the progress of the discussion.

D. Argument Dimension

Labels of Argument dimension are provided to all contributions, indicating attributes such as whether each contribution includes the speaker's opinion and whether the opinion is based on any ground. Labels of this dimension are provided to just one contribution content without considering whether any ground was described in other contribution.

A list of Argument dimension labels is shown in Table IX. Here, presence/absence of grounds is determined whether any ground to support the opinion is presented or not but it does not matter whether the presented ground is reliable or not. A qualified claim represents whether it is asserted that presented opinion is applied to all or part of situations to be worked on as a task. "Non-Argumentative moves" refer to contributions without including any opinion and simple questions are also included in this tag. Also, as a logical consequence, this label is assigned to all off-task contribution in the Epistemic dimension.

Labels in Argument dimension are capable of analyzing the logical consistency of contribution contents. For example, if a contribution is filled just with "Simple Claim" it is assumed as a superficial argument.

In comparison with Weinberger and Fischer's scheme, we do not set for now the categories of macro-level dimension in which single arguments are arranged in a line of argumentation such as arguments, counterarguments, reply, for the reason that it seems difficult that the automatic coding by deep learning methods for this macro dimension works correctly.

TABLE IX. LABELS IN ARGUMENT DIMENSION

Label	Description
Simple Claim	Simple opinion without any ground
Qualified Claim	Opinion based on a limiting condition without any ground
Grounded Claim	Opinion based on grounds
Grounded and Qualified claim	Opinion with limitation based on grounds
Non-argumentative moves	contribution without containing opinion (including questions)

E. Social Dimension

Labels in Social dimension are provided when Epistemic code is "On task" but they are provided not to all contributions "On task" but to a contribution which conforms to Epistemic code. This dimension represents how each contribution is related to those of other members within the group. Therefore, it is required to understand not only a contribution but also the previous context. Table X shows a list of labels of the dimension.

"Externalization" refers to contributions without reference to other's contributions and it is assigned to contributions to be an origin of arguments mainly at the start of argument on a topic. "Elicitation" is assigned to such contributions that request others for extracting information including question. "Consensus building" refers to contributions that express certain opinion in response to other's contribution and they are classified into the three labels below. "Quick consensus building" is assigned to such contributions that aim to form prompt consensus with other's opinion. It is assigned to a case to give consent without any specific opinion. "Integration-oriented consensus building" is assigned to such contributions that intend to form consensus with other's opinion while adding one's own opinion. "Conflict-oriented consensus building" is assigned to such contributions that confront with other's opinion or request revision of the opinion. "Summary" is assigned to contributions that list or quote contributions that have been posted.

Since Social dimension code represents involvement with others, it may be understood how actively the argument was developed or whose opinion within the group was respected by analyzing Social dimension labels. For example, it may be assumed that arguments with frequent "Quick consensus building" result in accepting all opinions provided with almost no deep discussion.

F. Learning for each code granting and artificial intelligence

In the new coding scheme, "Participation" dimension labels are automatically generated from contribution logs, whereas other labels require manual coding by human coders in order to build up training data for deep learning and test data. Further, labels to be provided are decided by selecting from any of the dimensions of "Argument", "Social" and "Coordination" depending on a result of "Epistemic" labels. "Argument" and "Social" dimension labels are provided if the "Epistemic labels are "On task." In a case that "Epistemic" labels are "Off task", those in "Coordination" dimension are provided.

TABLE X. CODE OF SOCIAL DIMENSION

Label	Description
Externalization	No reference to other's opinion
Elicitation	Questionning the learning parner or proviking a reacion from the learning partner
Quick consensus building	Prompt consensus formation
Integration-oriented consensus building	Consensus formation in an integrated manner
Conflict-oriented consensus building	Consensus forming based on a confrontational stance
Summary	Statment listing or quoting contributions

IV. DATASET AND STATISTICS

A. Target Dataset

The raw dataset is taken from the real conversation log of the CSCL system, which is the same one as that of previous study (Table I). On this dataset, the coding labels were newly annotated based on the new coding scheme. Labeling was manually carried out by several people in parallel. The human coders were lectured about the new coding scheme by a professional in advance in order to code labels as accurately as possible. To evaluate the accuracy of the manual coding, we had each contribution annotated by two annotators and measured the coincidence rate for each dimension of the new coding scheme.

B. Manual Coding and Preprocessing

While 9,962 contributions were manually coded in all, some contributions do not make sense as a text of CLSL. For instance, the duplicated posts, the blank posts, and the contributions that consist of only ASCII art can be mentioned. Such kinds of contributions were marked as "non-sense" when the annotators labeled, and removed or simplify ignored when the computer read them. After that, 9,197 contributions were remained as the useful data, on which the substantial jobs such as learning and classification are feasible.

The coincidence rates of the coding labels given by two human coders are significant for understanding the difficulty of the prediction, as well as to see the correctness of the manually coded labels. Table XI shows the coincidence rate, the number of the valid contributions, and that of the coincidence contributions for each dimension. For the Epistemic dimension, since the coincidence rate is high for human coders, we can expect that it is also easy for machines to classify them. On the other hand, for the Social dimension, since the coincidence rate is low for human coders and the valid samples are sparse, the opposite result is expected.

TABLE XI. THE VALID CONTRIBUTIONS AND THE COINCIDENT CONTRIBUTIONS

	# of valid contributions	# of coincidence contributions	Rate
Epistemic	9,197	8,460	0.92
Argumentation	9,083	7,765	0.85
Coodination	4,543	3,510	0.77
Social	3,917	2,619	0.67

C. Statistics of the New Coding Lables

In this subsection, we describe the statistics of the new coding labels assigned by the human coders with respect to each dimension. As we have multiple coders classify them, the statistics depend on the coders. When making a dataset for machines, we limit the contributions so as to have the same label assigned by the human coders. Thus, we describe the statistics of such contributions.

The ratios of "On task" and "Off task" in the Epistemic dimension are shown in Figure 2. In our dataset, the 'On task' contributions were a bit fewer than the 'Off task.' This implies that, at least from the view point of the conversation log, the cost of the communication was more than the cost of discussion in group work. Although this result is just an instance obtained by applying our CLCS system to the actual group works for limited lectures, we can at least conclude that the communication cost is not small in a group work.

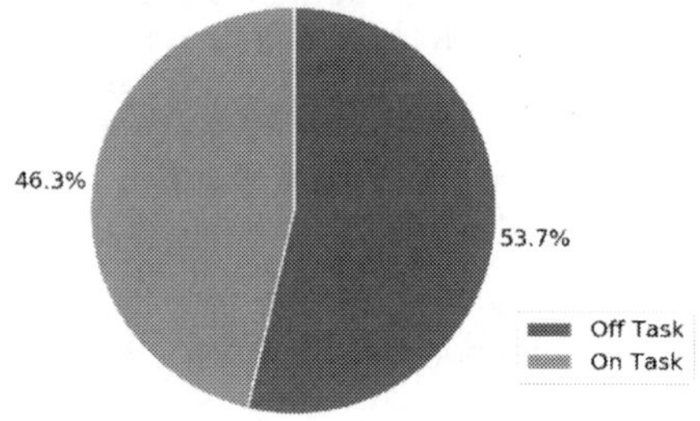

Figure 2. Ratio in the Epistemic dimension

Figure 3 shows the ratios of the labels in the Social dimension. Recall that its domain is On-task contributions. The label "Externalization" accounted half of the On-task contributions. The "Quick consensus building" followed it. Meanwhile, the ratios of the "Summary" and the "Consensus Buildings" except for the "Quick" one were small. These statistics show that the actual discussion mainly consisted of expressions of their opinions. Although we found that the contributions building consensus rarely come up in a real group work, we believe that they are the important keys for the discussion. Thus, we may can weight them when we assess the contribution to the discussion by students.

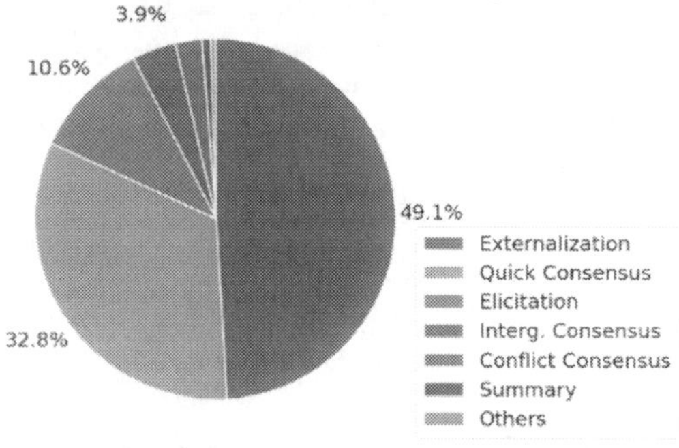

Figure 3. Ratio in the Social dimension

With respect to the "Coordination" dimension, the domain of which is the Off-task contributions, the most of them are assigned to "Other" as Figure 4 shows. The contributions labeled "Other" consist of short sentences that are not significant for neither discussion nor coordination of the group work. The representative examples are greetings and kidding. Meanwhile, the statistics show that the contributions except for "Other" also occupies more than a quarter. Since these kinds of contributions are related to coordinating tasks in the group work, they can be thought as important contributions for the assessment.

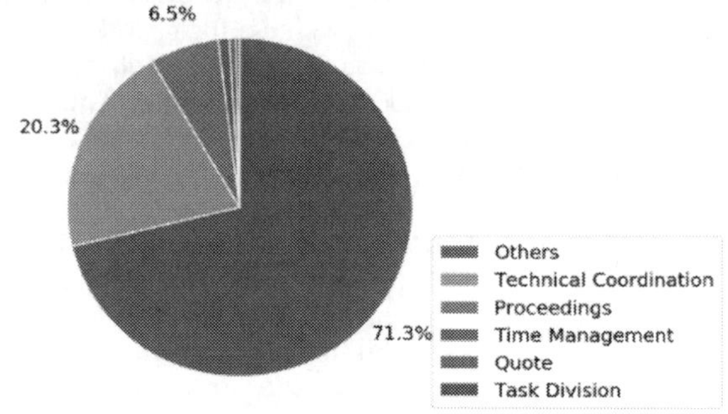

Figure 4. Ratio in the Coodination dimension

The labels in the "Argument" dimension are assigned independently of other dimensions. Thus, its domain spans both the On-task and the Off-task contributions. As shown in Figure 5, the label "Non-Argumentative moves" occupied more than 60 % of all. The label "Simple Claim" occupied the second percentage. To assess the discussion of the group work, at least it is necessary to remove the "Non-Argumentative" contributions and pay attention to which kind of claim is presented, even if almost every claim can be classified into the "Simple Claim". Therefore, the automatic coding for this dimension is as valuable as for the other three dimensions.

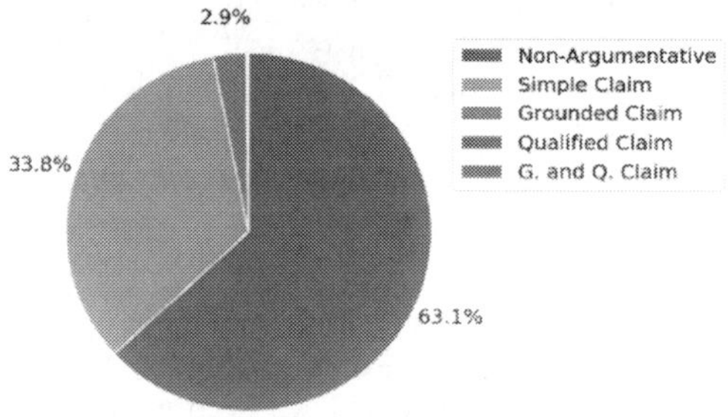

Figure 5. Ratio in the Argument dimension

V. EXPERIMENTS

A. Approach to Learing and Classifcation

As described in Section II, deep neural networks (DNNs) outperform other machine learning methods significantly at least for the coding labels proposed by our previous studies [6]-[8]. Their results of the experiments show that the Seq2Seq-based model achieves the highest accuracy among several DNN structures. Thus, we apply the Seq2seq-based model to classify our new coding labels in this paper.

The new coding scheme has four axes to be labeled as discussed in Section III; the Epistemic, the Coordination, the Argument, and the Social dimension. In the following experiments, the labels in each axis, or the dimensions, are learned and classified. There are solid dependencies among the Epistemic, the Coordination and the Social dimensions, while the Augment dimension is independent of the other dimensions. As shown in Figure 6, there is a dependency tree among the former three dimensions. For instance, the label of the Social dimension is assigned only if that of the Epistemic is "On task." Therefore, the number of available contributions for learning is different for each classification task. In the following experiments, since we use the samples that have the coincidence labels only, the number of the available contribution was 8,460 for the Epistemic, 7,795 for the Augmentation, 3,510 for the Coordination, and 2,619 for the Social.

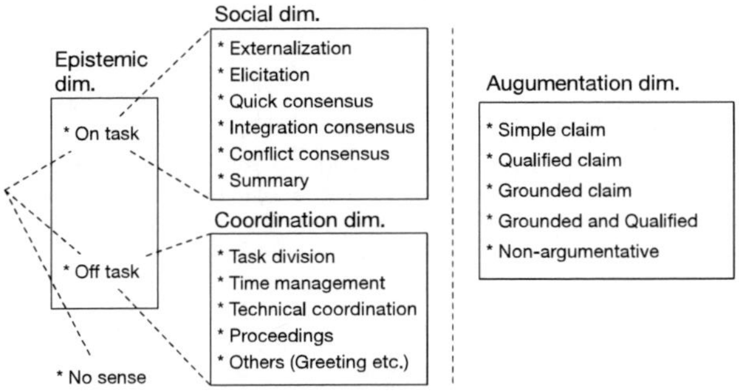

Figure 6. Dependency of Dimentions

B. Parameter Settings

We set the parameters for learning to the same values as in our previous study. They include the various kinds of the parameters such as the number of layers, the vector sizes of layers, the option of the optimization algorithms, learning rate, etc. The details can be referred to our previous studies [6]-[8].

C. Results for the Epistemic Dimension

The results of the experiments show that the On and Off tasks can be classified correctly with sufficiently high accuracy (Figure 7). The Seq2seq-based model achieves more than 90 % in both precision and recall (Table XII). Since the coincidence ratio by two human coders is 91%, we can say that the accuracy of automatic coding, which is comparable to human beings was obtained for the Epistemic dimension.

TABLE XII. PRECISION AND RECALL FOR THE EPSTEMIC DIMENTION

	Precision	Recall	F1-Score	Support
On Task	0.90	0.91	0.90	390
Off Task	0.92	0.91	0.91	456
Average(Micro) / Total	0.91	0.91	0.91	846

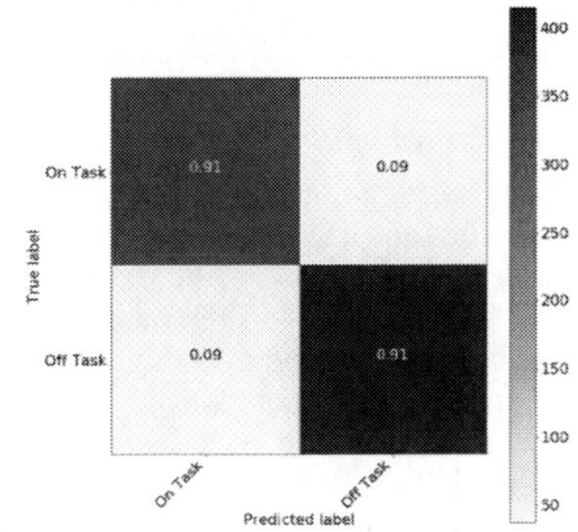

Figure 7. Confusion matrix for the Epstemic dimension

D. Results for the Argument Dimension

The classification accuracy is also high for the Argument dimension. The micro-averaged F1 score is 87 % (Table XIII). Especially, the F1 score for the label "Non-argumentative Moves" is high sufficiently (92 %), which means that our model can surely recognize whether the contribution has any substantial meaning as a claim or not. On the other hand, while the precision for the "Simple Claim" is high (89 %), the recall for it is low (72 %). According to the confusion matrix shown in Figure 8, a quarter of the Simple Claim is misclassified into the Non-argumentative. This is because it is difficult to distinguish contributions that have a very small opinion from that have no opinions.

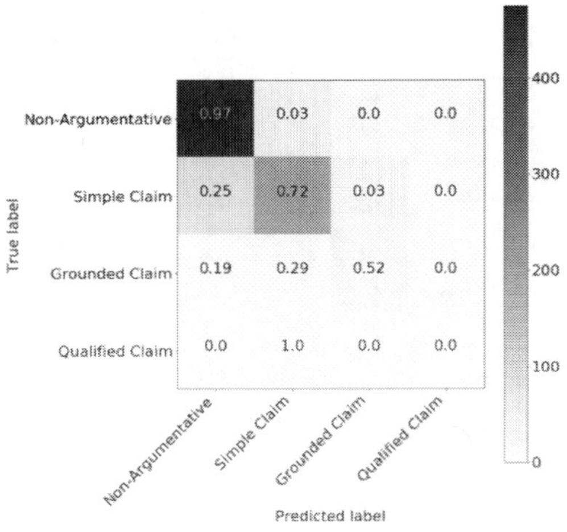

Figure 8. Confusion matrix for the Argument dimension

TABLE XIII. PRECISION AND RECALL FOR THE ARGUMENT DEMENTIONFFIGU

	Precision	Recall	F1-Score	Support
Non-Argumentative	0.87	0.97	0.92	491
Simple Claim	0.89	0.72	0.80	264
Grounded Claim	0.58	0.52	0.55	21
Qualified Claim	0.00	0.00	0.00	1
Average(Micro) / Total	0.87	0.87	0.87	777

E. Results for the Coordination Dimension

Regarding the Coordination dimension, our model also achieved high classification accuracy. Seeing that the number of supports varies greatly among the labels, we should evaluate the classification ability of the model by the micro-averaged accuracies over all coding labels. As Table XIV shows, the micro-averaged F1 score was 85 %.

According to the results for each label (Figure 9), the following is observed. The major labels such as "Other" and "Technical coordination" are classified correctly with high precisions, while the minor labels such as "Time Management", "Quote" and "Task Division" are not. Because the data for those miner labels are very limited, which have less than 50 contributions, it is quite difficult to learn them accurately. One of our future issues is to find some way to deal with those sparse labels.

TABLE XIV. PRECISION AND RECALL FOR THE COORDINATION DIMENTION

	Precision	Recall	F1-Score	Support
Others	0.91	0.91	0.91	242
Technical Coordination	0.81	0.80	0.81	82
Proceedings	0.58	0.70	0.64	20
Time Management	0.33	0.25	0.29	4
Quote	0.00	0.00	0.00	1
Task Division	0.00	0.00	0.00	2
Average(Micro) / Total	0.85	0.86	0.85	351

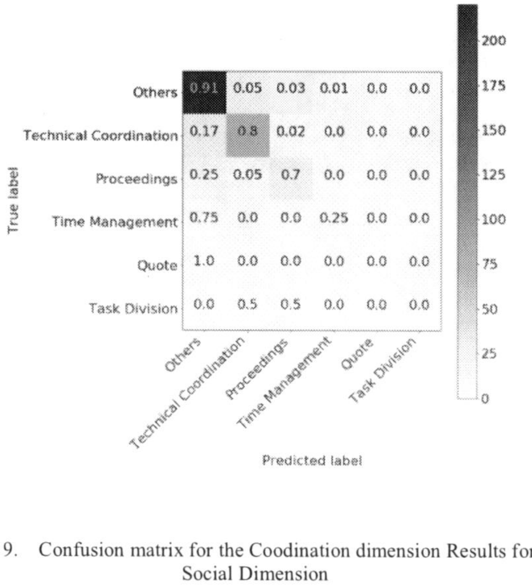

Figure 9. Confusion matrix for the Coodination dimension Results for the Social Dimension

F. Results for the Social Dimension

Comparing to the other dimensions, the accuracy was relatively low for the Social dimension. The F1 score was 70 % (Table XV). Since labeling the Social sometimes needs understanding the deep meaning of the contribution and the background story of the discussion, it seems to be difficult for machines to learn them correctly with limited data.

According to Figure 10, the recall of the label "Externalization" is especially low (61 %), while those of "Quick Consensus" and "Elicitation" are high sufficiently (93 % and 97 %, respectively). According to the confusion matrix in Figure 10, there is a major reason that worsen the accuracy; the Externalization labels are easily misclassified to the Quick Consensus and to the Elicitation, but not vice versa. This fact also explains the reason why the precisions for the Quick Consensus and the Elicitation are low though the recalls for them are high. To improve the result, it is necessary to pursue the causes of these two types.

TABLE XV. PRESCISION AND RECALL FOR THE SOCIAL DIMENTION

	Precision	Recall	F1-Score	Support
Externalization	0.86	0.61	0.72	127
Quick	0.71	0.93	0.81	88
Elicitation	0.56	0.97	0.71	29
Interg. Consensus	0.17	0.14	0.15	7
Conflict Consensus	0.00	0.00	0.00	6
Summary	0.00	0.00	0.00	3
Others	0.00	0.00	0.00	2
Average(Micro) / Total	0.72	0.72	0.70	262

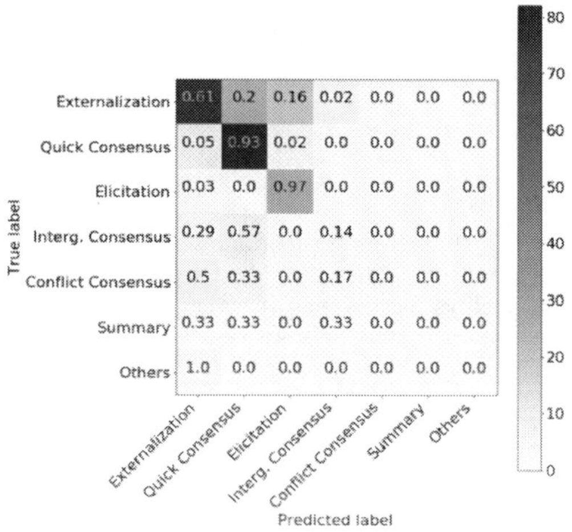

Figure 10. Confusion matrix for the Social dimension

VI. SUMMARY AND FUTRE WORK

A. Summary

In this study, we proposed a newly designed coding scheme with which we tried to automate time-consuming coding task by using deep learning technology.

We have constructed a new coding scheme with five dimensions to analyze different aspects of the collaboration process. After manually coding a large volume dataset, we proceeded to the machine learning of this dataset using Seq2seq model. Then, we evaluated the accuracy of this automatic coding in each dimension. Except some typical types of the misclassifications, the results were overall very good. These results indicate with certainty that we can introduce this model to authentic educational settings and that even for large classes that have many students, we can perform real-time monitoring of learning process or ex-post analysis of big educational data.

B. *Future Work*

As for the future research directions, we may have two approaches to pursue.

The first approach is about some typical misclassifications in the Social Dimension. To improve prediction accuracy, one could make more explicit and comprehensible the referential relation between a contribution and others even for the machines, if one indicates contributions to which a contribution refers. For example, with regard to the typical misclassification mentioned above between "Externalization" and "Quick Consensus" or "Elicitation", since contributions labeled "Externalization" have no reference to other contributions, we can hope to effectively reduce these misclassifications with this kind of indicator. In addition, as the next step of this paper, it seems to be worth trying to compare the accuracy using DNN models other than Seq2seq and other network structures such as memory networks [13].

The second approach concerns the intrinsic structure of our coding scheme. Since the scheme contains different dimensions and under each dimension different labels are hierarchically organized, it is very interesting to discover not only correlations among dimensions, but also among labels belonging to different dimensions [14]. If we can input the information about the correlation between such labels in some form at the time of automatic classification, the accuracy of automatic coding can be further improved.

ACKNOWLEDGMENT

This work was supported by JSPS KAKENHI Grant Number 26350289, 17H02004 and 16K01134.

REFERENCES

[1] G. Stahl, T. Koschmann, and D. Suthers, "Computer-supported collaborative learning," In The Cambridge handbook of the learning science, K. Sawyer, Eds. Cambridge university press, pp. 479-500, 2014.

[2] P. Dillenbourg, P. Baker, A. Blaye, and C. O'Malley, "The evolution of research on collaborative learning," In Learning in humans and machines: Towards an interdisciplinary learning science, P. Reimann and H. Spada, Eds. Oxford: Elservier, pp. 189-211, 1996.

[3] T. Koschmann, "Understanding understanding in action," Journal of Pragmatics, 43, pp. 435-437, 2011.

[4] T. Koschmann, G. Stahl, and A. Zemel, "The video analyst's manifesto (or The implications of Garfinkel's policies for the development of a program of video analysis research within the learning science)," In Video reseach in the learning sciences, R. Goldman, R. Pea, B. Barron and S. Derry, Eds. Routledge, pp. 133-144, 2007.

[5] M. Chi, "Quantifying qualitative analyses of verbal data : A pratical gauide ," Journal of the Learning Science, 6(3), pp. 271-315, 1997.

[6] C. Shibata, K. Ando, and T. Inaba, "Towards automatic coding of collaborative learning data with deep learning technology", The Ninth International Conference on Mobile, Hybrid, and On-line Learning, 2017, pp. 65-71.

[7] K. Ando, C. Shibata, and T. Inaba, "Analysis of collaborative learning processes by automatic coding using deep learning technology", Computer & Education, 43, pp.79-84, 2017.

[8] K. Ando, C. Shibata, and T. Inaba, "Coding collaborative learning data automatically with deep learning methods", JSi SE Research Report, 32, 2017.

[9] T. Inaba and K. Ando, "Development and evaluation of CSCL system for large classrooms using question-posing script," International Journal on Advances in Software, 7(3&4),pp. 590-600, 2014.

[10] D. Bahdanau, K. Cho, and Y. Bengio, "Neural machine translation by jointly learning to align and translate," arXiv preprint arXiv, pp.1409.0473, 2014.

[11] O. Vinyals and Q. V. Le, " A Neural Conversational Mode," arXiv preprint arXiv:1506.05869, (ICML Deep Learning Workshop 2015), 2015.

[12] A. Weinberger and F. Fischer, "A frame work to analyze arugmetative knowledge construciton in computer-supported learning," Computer & Education, 46(1), pp. 71-95, 2006.

[13] S. Sukhbaatar, A. Szlam, J. Weston and R. Fergus, "End-to-end Memory Networks," Proceedings of the 28th International Conference on Neural Information Processing Systems, pp. 2440-2448, 2015.

[14] F. Scafino, G. Pio, M. Ceci, and D. Moro, "Hierarichical multi-dimensional classification of web documents with MultiWebClass," International Conference on Discovery Science, pp.236-250, 2015.

SmarTTeaching in Pharmacology

J. Pieter H. van Wyk
Department of Pharmacology and Therapeutics
Sefako Makgatho Health Sciences University (SMU)
South Africa
e-mail: e.pharmacology.smu@gmail.com

***Abstract*—The state of education is changing mainly due to developments in the electronic media. SmarTTeaching in Pharmacology at Sefako Makgatho Health Sciences University (SMU) has been developed to introduce the principle of the flipped classroom to students using electronic lectures and social media platforms. This was done by reducing face to face lecture time, providing downloadable PowerPoint slideshows and worksheets, offering potential test and examination questions on Instagram and introducing applications of basic pharmacology concepts on Twitter. Completed worksheets are photographed with smartphones by students and these are emailed to the lecturer for e-filing. Important to note with this approach is that it can also be completely used for e-learning where students are mostly not in classrooms.**

Keywords - SmarTTeaching; e-learning; e-pharmacology; flipped classroom; social media.

I. Introduction

The flipped classroom concept was in practice for a number of years before Bergmann and Sams in their published book, titled "Flip Your Classroom: Reach Every Student in Every Class Every Day" established it as a teaching model in 2012 [1]. The aim of this newly introduced model is to transform dated teaching methods that are ineffective and often fail to engage students in the classroom [2]. The flipped classroom aims to give students the opportunity to prepare themselves on a specific topic, with the aid of technology. Classes are then structured for problem solving and guided by the lecturer [1].

Globally, students can be divided into two studying clusters. The first group is characterized by passive learning and relies extensively on the lecturer as the leading source of information. The second group highly values independent learning and will readily make use of new sources of information. The flipped classroom is ideally suited to students who learn autonomously and will use online teaching materials for example slide shows or videos.

The role of the lecturer differs greatly in these two teaching methods. Previously lecturers were required to be present during classes while in flipped classroom lecturers are now facilitators working alongside prepared students, guiding them as groups or on individual level.

Section 2 discusses the features and challenges of smarTTeaching in a flipped classroom. Section 3 looks at various components used in the smarTTeaching model and Section 4 briefly shows the e-learning cycle. In Section 5, the conclusion is that smarTTeaching in conjunction with electronic and social media is the future of education.

II. The Future of Medical Education: Smart-Teaching in a Flipped Classroom

A. *Features of the Flipped Classroom*

Technology will play a huge role in the future of medical education [3]. While there is not much literature as yet regarding the relatively new concept of the flipped classroom approach, the limited data has shown the following:

- An analysis of 62 articles indicated that flipped learning gained popularity amongst engineering educators after 2012 [4]. This could point to a more positive attitude regarding flipped classrooms.
- One of the most commonly cited benefits of flipped learning is its flexibility, which allows students to work at their own pace. This includes being able to pause or re-watch videos [5].
- The rationale behind flipped learning is for students to prepare for lectures, while face to face class time is used for exercises and interaction between students and lecturers [6].
- Several authors argue that flipped learning contributes to students' professional skills such as life-long learning [7], learner autonomy [8], critical thinking [9] and interpersonal skills [10].
- It was also observed that class attendance improved [11], students were better prepared for lectures and information better retained [12]. In the case of flipped classrooms more time was devoted to studies and better study habits developed when compared to traditional teaching [13].

B. Challenges of Flipped Learning

As with any new initiative, flipped learning offers a few challenges for both instructor and student.

The most challenging for lecturers is the input in converting a course from a traditional teaching approach to a flipped format. Challenges for students include uninteresting online material [14] while Ossman and Warren indicated that rather than watching the videos, students prefer reading slides [15]. This increases the workload of the lecturer who has to create the slides.

It was also reported that class attendance for certain courses was made not compulsory but students had no excess to high speed internet connectivity [16]. Student resistance was another challenge that flipped learning instructors faced. This was due to the traditional approach throughout their educational career and students feeling overwhelmed with a new class format requiring active participation in the learning process.

III. SMARTTEACHING PHARMACOLOGY AT THE SEFAKO MAKGATHO HEALTH SCIENCES UNIVERSITY, SOUTH AFRICA

Pharmacology is unique due to the fact that medicine is crucial in the practice of almost all medical disciplines. To be in line with global educational trends the Department of Pharmacology and Therapeutics at the Sefako Makgatho Health Sciences University (SMU) has in recent years developed an e-learning pharmacology course called SmarTTeaching. Many components of social media are applied in conjunction with the flipped classroom approach in this blended learning model. The focus is to encourage studying independent of classroom attendance yet supported with high quality electronic learning resources.

A. e-Lectures: PowerPoint Slides

Microsoft PowerPoint is used to create e-lectures in which a topic is composed of various slides. Such a slideshow consists of a title slide (slide 1), a slide showing the index (slide 2), and slides with sub-topics each followed by slides with the content. The final slide indicates the topic of the next slideshow. For best results the majority of slides should reflect content and contain keywords regarding the subject of that particular slide. Slides should also be dynamic with movement and colour, graphs and diagrams that clearly illustrate lecturing content.

B. Worksheets: Content-based Worksheets and their Submission

Each e-lecture has a worksheet that must be printed and completed by students as they progress through a slideshow. The questions of a worksheet are based on the content of the slideshow and completed worksheets are photographed with students' smartphones. These photographs are then emailed to the lecturer and all submissions are stored in a dedicated e-file for future reference ad as proof of the completion of both the e-classes and their worksheets.

C. Instagram: Example Questions

Instagram is used to provide students with examples of typical test and examination questions as well as related information concerning topics in the pharmacology syllabi. This platform is well visited and constantly assists students with revision of lectures and by providing additional information on topics [17].

D. Twitter: Application of Basic Concepts

This account is mostly used for short courses to support the theoretical aspect of topics covered in e-learning or flipped classroom lectures. For example, the potential changes which medicines undergo in the body are explained and discussed in a slideshow. The Twitter account is then used to inform students of changes which specific medicines would undergo. These discussions are not limited to a time frame but carries throughout the academic year. Students are examined on information presented on this platform [18].

E. Facebook: Global Research

The Pharmacology Facebook page is used very effectively to inform students regarding the latest global research developments in all fields of medicine. This Facebook page has also become a well-recognized international pharmacology vehicle and is followed by many medical students, pharmacologists, pharmacists, scientists and practitioners in different fields of medicine [19].

F. Website: Central Platform

A web-site dedicated to SmarTTeaching in Pharmacology is used as the central platform for interaction between students and lecturers. e-Lectures can be studied online or downloaded from the site. Worksheets are available for download in pdf-format or can be printed directly from the website. The site is designed to supply information regarding various aspects of the Pharmacology Department's teaching content and research [20].

G. Slides: Additional Features

Figure 1 is an example of an e-slide dealing with subject content. On the top right hand of the slide are icons for direct access to social media (WhatsApp, email, website, Facebook, Twitter and Instagram) as well as the last three icons for learning objects, the index and to exit the slideshow. Page numbers are indicated to the right of the slide which, when clicked on, will take the student to slides with additional information.

IV. E-LEARNING CYCLE

The aim of smarTTeaching is to establish and place in practice an e-learning program for Pharmacology teaching based on information supported by social media. The e-learning cycle is represented in the figure 3. During this e-learning cycle the study material is made available to the students on a website from where the content can be downloaded or printed.

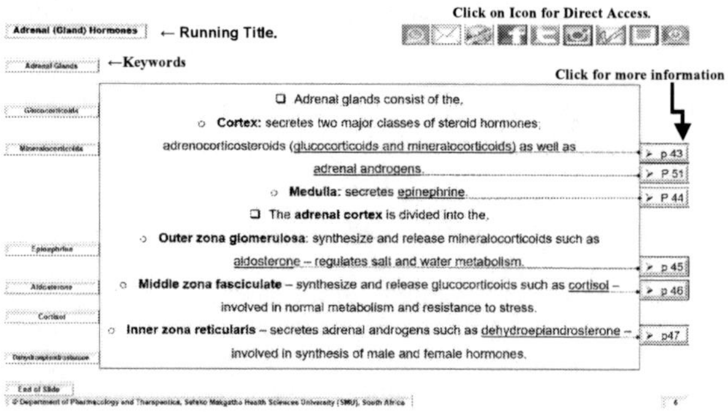

Figure 1. Example of an e-slide dealing with subject content.

Figure 2 is an example of a worksheet also containing the various social media platforms.

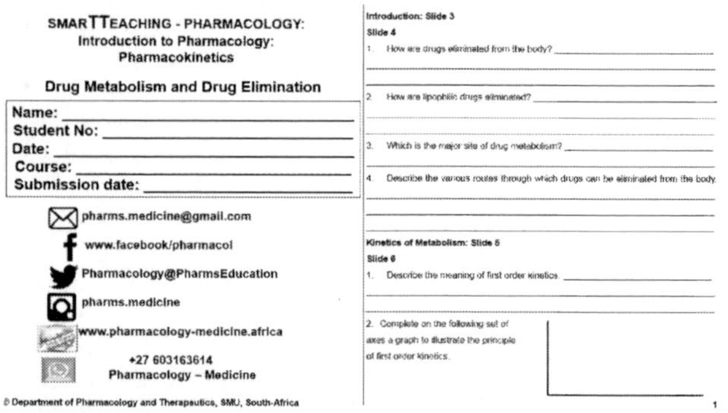

Figure 2. Example of a worksheet used to answer questions related to information on e-slides.

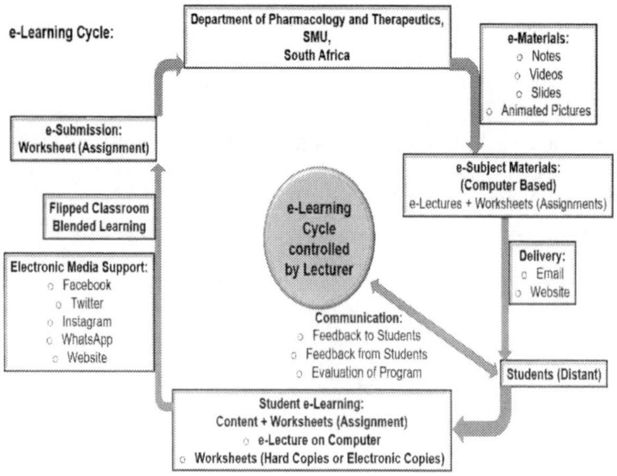

Figure 3: The e-learning cycle as modelled by the smarTTeaching approach.

It is however important that the online delivery system is reliable to ensure effective use of electronic media. Social media can be used to different extents and purposes to make the learning process effective. Worksheets need to be submitted electronically on a date and time determined by a lecturer.

V. CONCLUSIONS

The impact of electronic and social media on education is permanent and irreversible. It should therefore be a logical move for lecturers and students to apply electronic devices and applications towards the improvement of academic performance. SmarTTeaching as an initiative not only focuses on students, but also provides opportunities for lecturers to be creative to a level not previously possible without electronics.

Due to their previous exposure to only a face to face classroom approach, students were initially resistant to the flipped classroom concept. Once the benefits of using electronic devices such as smartphones, tablets, laptops and desktop computers were realized, appreciation of the smarTTeaching classroom method greatly escalated.

Participation amongst Pharmacology students at SMU has become the norm and the various social media platforms are well utilized. This is especially true for Instagram where potential test and examination questions are shared. Besides the students of SMU the information shared on social media also attracts international attention especially the Facebook page as it is focused on both students and practitioners of various medical disciplines.

The compulsory completion and email submission of worksheets is very effective as studying is immediate and continuous and not postponed until the first test or examination.

The introduction of the SmarTTeaching concept to lecturers has been met with some resistance regarding the transition from the old way of doing things to the new. Although the initial input in developing such an e-learning concept is time-consuming and demanding, the process when implemented is extremely dynamic for both lecturers and students. Updates of content are immediately available and new information can easily be introduced into an e-lecture. Supporting data such as graphs, figures and videos can also easily be added. The future and success of such an electronic teaching intervention requires a mind-shift, mostly by the teaching staff as students are more susceptible to alternatives, especially as it utilizes electronic and social media.

REFERENCES

[1] J. Bergmann and A. Sams, "Flip Your Classroom: Reach Every Student in Every Class Every Day," ISTE/ASCD; 2012.

[2] N. B. Mehta, A. L. Hull, J. B. Young, and J. K. Stoller, "Just imagine: new paradigms for medical education." Academic Medicine, vol. 88, 10, 2013, pp. 1418-1423.
[3] E. Dustyn, M. Williams, and M. Ochsner, "The Future of Medical Education: Flipping the Classroom" Education Technology Journal, vol. 16, 2016, pp. 14–15.
[4] A. Karabulut-Ilgu, N. J. Cherrez, and C. T. Jahren, "A systematic review of research on the flipped learning method in engineering education". British Journal of Educational Technology, doi: 10.1111/bjet.12548, 2017.
[5] D. N. Buechler, P. J. Sealy, and J. Goomey, "Three pilot studies with a focus on asynchronous distance education". Paper presented at Proceedings of 121st ASEE Annual Conference & Exposition, Indianapolis, IN, 2014.
[6] R. Bailey and M. C. Smith, "Implementation and assessment of a blended learning environment as an approach to better engage students in a large systems design class". Paper presented at Proceedings of 120th ASEE Annual Conference & Exposition, Atlanta, 2013.
[7] S. Luster-Teasley, S. C. Hargrove-Leak, and C. Waters, "Transforming undergraduate environmental engineering laborato-ries for sustainable engineering using the case studies in the sciences instructional method". Proceedings of the 121st ASEE Annual Conference & Exposition, Indianapolis, IN, 2014.
[8] M. K. Kim, S. M. Kim, O. Khera, and J. Getman, "The experience of three flipped classrooms in an urban university: An exploration of design principles". Internet and Higher Education, vol. 22, 2014, pp. 37–50.
[9] S. C. Chetcuti, J. T. Hans, and J. P. Brent, "Flipping the engineering classroom: Results and observations with non-engineering students". Proceedings of 121st ASEE Annual Conference & Exposition, Indianapolis, IN, 2014.
[10] K. Yelamarthi, S. Member, and E. Drake, "A flipped first-year digital circuits course for engineering and technology students". IEEE Transactions on Education, vol. 58, 2015, pp. 179–186.
[11] J. Rutkowski, "Flipped classroom—from experiment to practice". Proceedings of the 1st International KES Conference on Smart Technology Based Education and Training, Chania, Greece: Springer, 2014, pp. 565 – 574.
[12] B. Love, A. Hodge, N. Grandgenett and A. W. Swift, "Student learning and perceptions in a flipped linear algebra course. International Journal of Mathematical Education in Science and Technology, vol. 45, 2014, pp. 317–324.
[13] C. Papadopoulos and A. S. Roman, "Implementing an inverted classroom model in engineering statics: Initial results." Proceedings of the 117th ASEE Annual Conference & Exposition, Louisville, KY, 2010.
[14] R. Olson, "Flipping engineering probability and statistics—Lessons learned for faculty considering the switch." Proceedings of the 121st ASEE Annual Conference & Exposition, Indianapolis, IN, 2014.
[15] K. A. Ossman and G. Warren. "Effect of flipping the classroom on student performance in first year engineering courses". Proceedings of the 121st ASEE Annual Conference & Exposition, Indianapolis, 2014.
[16] A. Amresh, A. R. Carberry, and J. Femiani, "Evaluating the effectiveness of flipped classrooms for teaching CS1". Proceedings of Frontiers in Education Conference, FIE (pp. 733–735). Oklahama City, OK: IEEE Xplore Digital Library. 2013, pp 733 – 735.
[17] https://www.instagram.com/pharms.medicine. [Accessed: March 2018].
[18] https://twitter.com/PharmsEducation [Accessed: March 2018].
[19] https://www.facebook.com/pharmacol. [Accessed: March 2018].
[20] https://www.pharmacology-medicine.africa [Accessed: March 2018].

Tracking Verb Phrases for Formative Feedback in Foreign Language Writing

Shuai Shao, Kazuhiro Ohtsuki, Hidenari Kiyomitsu, Min Kang
Graduate School of Intercultural Studies
Kobe University
Kobe, Japan
e-mail: samveldf@stu.kobe-u.ac.jp, ohtsuki@kobe-u.ac.jp,
kiyomitsu@carp.kobe-u.ac.jp, kang@kobe-u.ac.jp

***Abstract*—Providing feedback is crucial in the language learning process. In time, formative feedback can help both learners and teachers confirm the ongoing acquisition of language. However, as of today, there is still little research not only on manual formative feedback but also on automated formative feedback. Thus, in this paper, we elaborate on how to track learners' acquisition for formative feedback by developing a system for foreign language writing. The system is implemented based on the results of an analysis of data collected from conventional face-to-face classrooms in Chinese learning.**

Keywords-foreign language writing; automated formative feedback; phrase extraction; dependency relation; change detection.

I. INTRODUCTION

Feedback plays an important role in foreign language learning [1]. The effectiveness of corrective feedback has been clarified by a number of researchers [2]-[4]. Meanwhile, formative feedback became an indispensable component as well [5]. Because providing feedback can be time consuming and costly, automated feedback has also drawn much attention [6].

Previous research has shown the advantage of the automated feedback system over the paper-based feedback [7]. Educational Testing Service (ETS) has developed a Web-based writing evaluation service, *Criterion*, and Vantage Learning has created *My Access*, which are both programs that combine a scoring engine with a separate editing tool, which provides grammar, spelling and mechanical feedback [8]. On the other hand, Warschauer and Grimes [8] conducted a mixed-methods case study to evaluate the use of those programs in classrooms. They pointed out that although the programs saved teachers' grading time and learners tended to edit their writings more, the editing was usually superficial and no iterative process was observed. These automated systems are just designed to improve the writing quality in the current document by finding errors, which is different from a teacher's goal which is to improve the learners' writing ability to produce better new documents [9]. Thus, research on the long-term usage of automated systems becomes a necessity.

Simone and Christian implemented a Web-based feedback system in their lectures and analyzed the effects of the system which provided automated formative feedback throughout the semester [10]. They found that students who received feedback achieved higher scores and became more motivated and confident. Formative feedback can not only help learners but also help teachers improve their instructional strategies [11]. Nevertheless, additional research on automated formative feedback in foreign language writing is still rare.

The aim of our research is to design an automated formative feedback environment to facilitate the writing process. In this paper, we report the partial results concerning the on-going research. We focus on the writing process in Chinese for Japanese learners, especially on Japanese-Chinese translation process. Furthermore, verb-object (V-O) phrases are chosen as the targets of providing feedback because V-O phrases are basic sentence structures expressing the meanings of sentences and appear frequently in teaching materials for beginners.

In Section 2, we look at the V-O phrases in several translation exercises conducted in face-to-face classrooms and first analyze the translations manually to observe how learners translate the corresponding Japanese phrases to the Chinese phrases in time-series. In Section 3, based on the results of the analysis, we build a prototype system to track changes of learners' translations concerning the phrases and provide this to learners to help them confirm their progression in the learning process. The tracking results will also be provided to teachers to give them an overview of the learners' acquisition of the material. The conclusion will be given in Section 4.

II. ANALYZING LEARNING LOG DATA

A. *Data from Classrooms*

68 sophomore students (2 classes of 34 students) taking "Intermediate Chinese" at Kobe University, Japan, whose overall Chinese proficiency level was empirically considered to be intermediate were subjects for this research. The students were asked to translate Japanese sentences into Chinese as a class exercise every week. One specific word "花見" (hanami or cherry-blossom viewing) is chosen as the target to providing feedback. We designed three Japanese sentences containing the word "花見" (hanami or cherry-blossom viewing) and put them respectively into three exercises over eight weeks: the interval between the first two exercises was one week, and the interval after the 2nd exercise was six weeks. In the 1st week, the Chinese translation of the phrase "花見に行く" (go to see cherry blossoms) was presented as a hint along with the exercise paper for Class 1 while not Class 2. In the following week,

the students from both classes did the 2nd exercise without any hint. Then in the interim, in the 3rd week, the teacher thoroughly explained about the various translations of "cherry-blossom viewing" and told the students of both classes that "看樱花" (see cherry blossoms) was the most appropriate answer. Five weeks later, the 3rd exercise containing "cherry-blossom viewing" was conducted. The three Japanese sentences are listed below.

S1. "もし明日雨が降らなければ，私たちは花見に行くつもりです．"

(If it doesn't rain tomorrow, we are going to see cherry blossoms.)

S2. "もし花見に行くなら，京都が一番いい．"

(If you go to see cherry blossoms, Kyoto is the best place.)

S3. "来年 3 月末に私は神戸に来る予定だが，花見に来るのではなく，出張に来るのだ．"

(I plan to come to Kobe at the end of March next year for business trip not for cherry blossom viewing.)

B. Analysis and Results

TABLE I. CORRECT ANSWER RATE OF "花見" (CHERRY-BLOSSOM VIEWING)

	Week 1	Week 2	Week 8
Class 1	100%	94.1%	94.1%
Class 2	73.5%	88.2%	100%

TABLE II. PERCENTAGE OF STUDENTSCHANGING ANSWERS BETWEEN EXERCISES

	Week 1- 2	Week 2- 8	Week 2- 8(G2-G1)
Class 1	85.3%	64.7%	23.5%
Class 2	52.9%	64.7%	23.5%

Our analysis focuses on the changes of translation of the specific word "cherry-blossom viewing" found in all three exercises. There were four main translations, "看樱花" (see cherry blossoms), "看花" (see flowers), "赏花" (admire flowers), and "观赏樱花" (admire cherry blossoms). Although "cherry-blossom viewing" is a word in Japanese, it should be translated as a verb phrase in Chinese, with one verb and one noun. The Japanese word "花見" (cherry-blossom viewing) refers to the tradition of sitting under blooming cherry trees to appreciate the beauty of the cherry blossoms. Thus, even though the kanji/Chinese character "花" (flower) exists in both Japanese and Chinese, in the original Japanese word it specifically refers to cherry blossoms. However, in translations such as "看花" (see flowers), "赏花" (admire flowers), "花" (flower) means flowers without explicitly referring to cherry blossoms. Hence "樱花" (cherry blossoms) is considered as a more appropriate translation. In addition, all three sentences come from everyday conversations, "观赏樱花" (admire cherry blossoms) seems too formal in this context. Therefore, we divided the different translations into three groups: Group 1 (G1: most appropriate): "看樱花" (see cherry blossoms); Group 2 (G2: correct but flawed): "看花" (see flowers), "赏花" (admire flowers), and "观赏樱花" (admire cherry blossoms), as well as Group 3 (G3: mistakes). We then calculated the percentage of correct answers for each exercise and also the percentage of students changing answers overtime according to descriptive statistics methods.

Table 1 shows the percentage of correct answers (G1 & G2) of the word "花見" (cherry-blossom viewing) in the three exercises. As we can see, students in Class 1 achieved 100% accuracy because of the hint, however, Class 2 only achieved 73.5%. However, it is noteworthy that in the following week, the accuracy of Class 1 fell while that of Class 2 increased. In week 3, the teacher explained about the exercises conducted previously and emphasized the most appropriate translation. In week 8, the accuracy of Class 2 exceeded that of Class 1, which suggested that giving students answers without any explanation was not as effective as one might think. This kind of input may lead students to just use the answer without any active thinking or reflection involved.

Table 2 shows the percentage of students who changed answers between the exercises. In week 1, all students in Class 1 used the most appropriate translation owing to the hint. However, 85.3% of Class 1 changed their answers in week 2, which indicated that the hint had not been properly memorized. In week 2, the percentage of G1 was 14.7% in Class 1 and 8.8% in Class 2. The percentage of students changing answers in both classes between exercise 2 and 3 were identical, and there were over 20% of students in each class who changed their answers from G2 to G1. These percentages reveal that students' self-reflection can improve their accuracy but explanations by a teacher can further facilitate the learning process.

Based on the above results, it is revealed that by tracking the changes of translation, teachers could confirm the effects of the provided hint and explanation; students may benefit from the formative feedback to find out the weak points in the learning process.

III. SYSTEM DESIGN AND OUTPUT ANALYSIS

A. Formative Feedback System

We propose an approach to provide feedback for learners' time-serial data in Japanese-Chinese translation process, with a focus on tracking changes on V-O phrases. The key idea in the approach is the utilization of the dependency relation between two words that consist of a phrase for tracking. By using a dependency parser, we can obtain the structural information of input sentences in which the phrase should be contained; based on that information we can extract the phrase within and then detect whether a learner has changed the phrase or not by comparing the extracted phrase with that from the sentences in previous translation exercises. If the phrase cannot be extracted, there are two possible reasons. One is that the learner used an incorrect phrase. The other is that the learner used a different correct phrase with different dependency relation.

Currently, the approach is presented for the simple sentences with one V-O phrase. The approach can be divided into two phases, as shown below.

1) The preparation for, and extraction of verb phrase:

a) A teacher or a learner chooses the V-O phrase (We call it intended phrase or IP.) to which he/she wants to confirm the acquisition.

b) Learners' translations which should contain the IP (based on the source language sentence) will be processed by a Chinese parser and the V-O phrase (We call it learner's phrase or LP.) will be extracted based on the dependency parser's result.

2) The formative feedback:

a) The LP will be extracted along with the information of the time when it was submitted (timestamp). As a result, extracted LPs will be in time series, and LP submitted later can be compared with the previous LP.

b) The extraction and comparison will provide not only the information of the phrases but also the detection of whether the learners have changed their translations or not. Subsequently, the results of all the exercises will be presented to both learners and teachers.

B. Algorithm for Prototype System

Following the above approach, we built a prototype system. In this system, we utilized the Stanford Parser [12] through Python NLTK (Natural Language Toolkit) interface to analyze the input data. The input data should be simple sentences which are produced by learners in an exercise and should contain an IP. The steps of the algorithm for the prototype system are listed below.

1) The input will be segmented and the part of speech (POS) information will also be generated by exploiting the segmentor and POS tagger of the Stanford Parser.

2) The dependency parser of the Stanford Parser will provide the structual information of the segmented input and the LP within will be extracted depending on the existense of a "dobj" (direct object) tag. If a "dobj" tag exists, the contents, as well as their POS tags will be extracted, otherwise the output will be "*".

3) Since the extracted LPs will have timestamps, the system will compare the latter LP with the former one to detect whether the learner has changed the translation or not .

C. Output Analysis and Discussion

In order to evaluate the approach, we used the previously collected translations from Class 1 as our testing data. We also chose the V-O phrase "看樱花" (see cherry blossoms) as the target to provide feedback as described in the Section 2. The translations for S1, S2 and S3 are the raw data to input into the system. Because the raw data was compound sentences, we did manual pre-processing to obtain the input sentences which should contain the IP. Examples are shown in Table 3.

TABLE III. EXAMPLES OF PRE-PROCESSED INPUT

Original	如果去看樱花，京都是最好。 (If going to see cherry blossoms, Kyoto is the best.)
	如果我去看樱，京都最好。 (If I go to see cherry, Kyoto is the best.)
Pre-processed	如果去看樱花 (If going to see cherry blossoms)
	如果我去看樱 (If I go to see cherry)

TABLE IV. EXAMPLES OF EXTRACTED PHRASES

No.	verb	vPOS	object	oPOS	V&O
S1	去 (go)	VV	看樱 (see cherry)	NN	去看樱 (go to see cherry)
S1	看 (see)	VV	樱花 (cherry blossoms)	NN	看樱花 (see cherry blossoms)
S2	看 (see)	VV	樱花 (cherry blossoms)	NN	看樱花 (see cherry blossoms)
S2	*	*	*	*	**

StudentNumber	VO in S2	Detection	VO in S8	Detection
Student1	去看樱	changed	看樱花	ok
Student2	看樱花	ok	**	changed
Student3	去赏花	changed	看樱花	ok
Student4	看樱花	ok	来看樱	changed
Student5	赏樱花	changed	来赏花	changed

Figure 1. Examples of change detection

TABLE V. ABOUT EXTRACTION OF THE SYSTEM

	Extraction Rate of All Inputs	Usage of "看樱花"
Week 1	100%	100%
Week 2	100%	14.7%
Week 8	76.5%	38.5%

There are two kinds of outputs provided by the prototype system that are shown in Table 4 and Figure 1. Table 4 shows some examples of the output obtained by the step 1) of the algorithm. If a LP was extracted, then the verb and object, as well as the V-O phrase will be provided to users. It can be observed that not all inputs can be extracted with a V-O phrase. Just like the last example in the table, if the system couldn't find a "dobj" tag, then the output would be "*".

For examining the validity of the feedback in Table 4, we calculated the extraction rate that describes how many V-O phrases there are in the input sentences. The extraction rates are presented in Table 5. Meanwhile, we calculated the percentages of the IP "看樱花" (see cherry blossoms) used by students in the raw data and showed the percentages in the same table. From Table 5 it is clear that in week 1, all students of Class 1 translated "花見" (cherry-blossom viewing) into the IP "看樱花" (see cherry blossoms) because of the hint. Consequently, all inputs were successfully extracted. Apart from "看樱花" (see cherry blossoms), other variations were also extracted in week 2 and week 8, as long as the input contained a V-O phrase. In week 2, although every input contains a V-O phrase, the usage of the IP decreased to 14.7%. Thus, if students have grasped the basic sentence structure, e.g. the V-O structure, all LP would be extracted and Table 4 would provide teachers a visual feedback to confirm what different phrases or wrong phrases are used by students. On the other hand, the extraction rate in week 8 was only 76.5%. In the case, this results from that the two-character words in G2: "看花" (see flowers) and "赏花" (admire flowers) were treated as nouns instead of V-O phrases in the system. It remained a problem when automatically dealing with the 24.5% sentences without a "dobj" tag.

Figure 1 shows examples of some change detection outputs. With the input parsed and extracted, the system then compared the extracted LP of the latter two inputs (S2, S3) with the first one (S1) respectively and generate the outputs showing whether students had changed their translations or not. If a student did not change the translation, then "ok" will be shown in the "Detection" column, otherwise it will be "changed".

According to the results in Figure 1, there are 85.3% of the LPs that have been changed in week 2 and 73.5% that have been changed in week 8 in comparison with the phrases used in week 1. Despite the inputs with no extracted V-O phrases, the percentages are agreements with those manually calculated from the raw data.

Thus, Figure 1 can provide teachers an overview of students' progress in learning process. It can be readily noted that there is only one student who did not changed the translation in all three exercises. There were 7 students who changed their answer in week 2 but then changed back to the most appropriate "看樱花" (see cherry blossoms) in week 8, which demonstrated the effectiveness of the teacher's detailed explanation in week 3. The other 26 students failed to change back to the correct translation they submitted in week 1. This information can help teachers improve instructional strategies, and facilitate individual students to comprehend whether the required grammatical knowledge had been mastered or not as well.

IV. CONCLUSION

In this paper, we first analyzed learning log data from two face-to-face classrooms in Chinese learning. The analysis results revealed that tracking the changes of translation on V-O phrase could help teachers confirm the effects of the provided hint or explanation; and students may benefit from the formative feedback to find out the weak points in the learning process. Thus, we proposed an approach for providing formative feedback and developed a prototype system to test the approach.

It is suggested that the system is effective in providing automated formative feedback for both learners and teachers. Learners can confirm their acquisition throughout the learning process. The feedback on V-O phrases would help teachers grasp the whole picture used by learners and confirm the effects of the current strategies. Because the system focuses on the extraction and comparison of V-O phrases by using the Stanford Parser, thus it is expected to be applied to other languages as long as similar structures can be identified by the parsers.

There still remained some problems in the approach. In the prototype system, the input sentences should be simple sentence so that a pre-processing is needed. Developing an automatically pre-processing function will be our next work soon. The extraction method still needs improvement. As we have explained, it is an important issue to deal with the phrases without a "dobj" tag. In addition, further practical use in classrooms needs to be investigated.

ACKNOWLEDGMENT

This work is supported by JSPS KAKENHI Grant Number JP17K01081.

REFERENCES

[1] H. Kimura, T. Kimura, and O. Shiki, Theory and Practice in Reading and Writing: Nurturing Independent Learning, pp. 124–134, 2010.

[2] P. Duppenthaler, "The effect of three types of feedback on the journal writing of EFL Japanese students," JACET Bulletin, (38), pp. 1-17, 2004.

[3] K. Oi, T. Kamimura, T. Kumamoto, and K. Matsumoto, "A Search for the Feedback That Works for Japanese EFL Students: Content-based or Grammar-based," JACET Bulletin, (32), pp. 91-108, 2000.

[4] A. M. F. Yousef, U. Wahid, M. A. Chatti, U. Schroeder, and M. Wosnitza, "The Impact of Rubric-Based Peer Assessment on Feedback Quality in Blended MOOCs," Communications in Computer and Information Science Computer Supported Education, pp. 462–485, 2016.

[5] I. Goldin, S. Narciss, P. Foltz, and M. Bauer, "New Directions in Formative Feedback in Interactive Learning Environments," International Journal of Artificial Intelligence in Education, vol. 27, no. 3, pp. 385–392, 2017.

[6] P. D. Ware and M. Warschauer, "Electronic feedback and second language writing," Feedback in second language writing: Contexts and issues, pp. 105-122, 2006.

[7] S. W. Yeh and J. J. Lo, "Using online annotations to support error correction and corrective feedback," Computers & Education, 52(4), pp.882-892, 2009.

[8] M. Warschauer and D. Grimes, "Automated writing assessment in the classroom," Pedagogies: An International Journal, 3(1), pp.22-36, 2008.

[9] C. Leacock, M. Chodorow, M. Gamon, and J. Tetreault, "Automated grammatical error detection for language learners," Synthesis lectures on human language technologies, 7(1), pp.109-112, 2014.

[10] S. van Kol and C. Rietz, "Effects of Web-Based Feedback on Students' Learning," International Journal of Teaching and Learning in Higher Education, 28(3), pp.385-394, 2016.

[11] K. Ludvigsen, R. Krumsvik, and B. Furnes, "Creating formative feedback spaces in large lectures," Computers & Education, 88, pp.48-63, 2015.

[12] C. D. Manning, et al, "The stanford corenlp natural language processing toolkit," In ACL (System Demonstrations) pp. 55-60, 2014.

An Approach toward Automatic Error Detection in Learners' English Writing Based on the Source Language

Koichi Kawamura[1], Harumi Kashiwagi[2], Min Kang[1]
[1]Graduate School of Intercultural Studies
[2]Institute for Promotion of Higher Education
Kobe University
Kobe, Japan
email: kawamura51@stu.kobe-u.ac.jp, kasiwagi@kobe-u.ac.jp, kang@kobe-u.ac.jp

***Abstract*— Automatic error detection systems for English writing have been improved since they were first introduced and are being applied to foreign language learning. However, these systems mainly focus on local errors, such as grammatical aspects in the target language and ignore the meaning intended in the source language. As a result, teachers must spend an inordinate amount of time to detect global errors. In this paper, we propose an approach to an automatic error detection system to solve this problem. In order to determine whether the structure of an English sentence is in error or not, criteria for error determination are first needed. Our approach is based on the idea that criteria for error determination are created by the correspondence relation between Japanese and English using sentence patterns. In order to evaluate our approach, by way of illustration, four sentence patterns were selected from the authors' original six sentence patterns. Automatic error detection using these four sentence patterns was carried out on 100 Japanese sentences with subjects and their corresponding English sentences. As a result, we concluded that, using the sentence patterns in the source language, automatic error detection is effective when based on our criteria for error determination.**

Keywords-Error Detection; Sentence Pattern; Global Error; Parser; Source Language; Criteria for Error Determination.

I. INTRODUCTION

For English learners, compared to speaking, reading and listening, writing is the most difficult skill to improve. "Writing abilities are not naturally acquired; they must be culturally (rather than biologically) transmitted in every generation, whether in school or in other assisting environments" [1]. Despite this linguistic feature, writing is not taught enough in schools relative to other skills [2]. It is especially difficult to teach as teachers must detect and correct learners' errors one by one which is very time consuming.

It is accepted that English essays written by learners with low proficiency contain a lot of errors. Of these errors, global errors negatively affect the structure of the whole sentence, and this limits the readers' comprehension. Therefore, it is necessary for teachers not to overlook such errors when proofreading the essay. However, in order to detect global errors teachers must devote an inordinate amount of attention discovering all the potential structural errors. Thus, teachers may have a tendency to overlook some structural errors due to time constraints. For this reason, a support tool for structural error detection is needed in order to reduce the burden on teachers.

On the other hand, a number of automatic error detection systems using natural language processing technology have been tried. They are applied to foreign language learning classes to reduce the burden on teachers and support students to acquire better writing skills. These systems perform excellently with single grammatical errors, such as spelling, article usage, prepositions and aspect. However, few error detection systems look at structural errors. Thus, current automatic error detection systems are limited in that they do not cover all types of learners' errors. In addition, most of these systems are designed to analyze the target language (English) only. This unilateral approach may cause a discrepancy between the system's automatic correction feedback and the learner's intention [3]. In order to overcome these problems, the source language (Japanese) should also be an object of analysis. For these reasons, these systems are of limited general use in classrooms.

In order to support teachers and improve error detection accuracy, an automatic error detection system which can easily identify sentence structure errors, and cope with various types of global errors, and recognize the learners' intention is needed. Therefore, this study proposes just such an automatic error detection system, one which can easily determine whether a sentence is correct or not by comparing the basic sentence elements (subject and predicate) of Japanese and English using parsers based on sentence patterns. This approach is based on the results of our previous study, which showed that "detecting English errors using sentence patterns is more promising than detection that depends on full sentences" [4].

In Section 2, we propose an approach for an automatic error detection system that can determine whether an English sentence structure is in error or not. In Section 3, we detect structural errors according to criteria for error determination. Then we evaluate the accuracy of criteria for error determination created by the correspondence relation between Japanese and English, based on the four sentence patterns selected for illustration. In Section 4, we refer to the efficiency of automatic error detection using the sentence patterns in the source language.

II. APPROACH

To make the detection of global errors easy, we focus on basic sentence elements, by comparing them in the source language and the corresponding target language. To conduct the comparison, we classify the sentence patterns and create criteria for error determination: a rule created based on the correspondence relation between Japanese and English using sentence patterns. We compare the basic sentence elements (primary subject and predicate) of the source language (Japanese) and the corresponding target language (English) using parsers based on sentence patterns and criteria, this approach follows the procedure below.

A. Procedure

1. Prepare Japanese sentences and the corresponding English sentences as analytical data.
2. Set up a Japanese parser, Cabocha and an English parser, the Stanford Parser.
3. Automatically extract sets of sentence elements, a primary subject and a predicate (verb) by a parser based on extraction rules.
4. Automatically classify the sets of a primary subject and a predicate (verb) based on the Japanese sentence patterns.
5. Compare the defined sentence patterns with the extracted sentence patterns based on criteria for determination.
6. Obtain the results of error determination as feedback (ERROR, POSSIBLE, UNKNOWN).

*ERROR stands for "an outright error." POSSIBLE stands for "not an error, but may not be a correct answer." UNKNOWN stands for "indeterminable."

B. Sentence Elements

Although each Japanese and English sentence contains various elements, such as subjects, predicates (verbs), objects, complements, etc., this study examines the set of a primary subject and predicate (verb) only. This is because all major sentence patterns contain a subject and a predicate verb in academic writing [5]-[7]. Additionally, it is efficient for teachers to determine whether the learners' English is grammatically correct by checking sets of a primary subject and a predicate verb only. This will support teachers to detect errors easily since learners' errors are not always clear, and teachers have difficulty determining where the problems lie.

C. Parsers and Extraction Rules

To extract sets of primary subjects and predicates from Japanese sentences, the parser, Japanese Dependency Structure Analyzer, Cabocha [8] was utilized. To extract sets of primary subjects and predicate verbs from the corresponding English sentences, the Stanford Parser [9] was utilized. Table I indicates details of both parsers and extraction rules of subjects and predicates (verb).

TABLE I. EXTRACTION RULES OF CABOCHA AND THE STANFORD PARSER

Parser		**Cabocha 0.69**	**The Stanford Parser 3.6.0**
Target Language		***Japanese***	***English***
Extraction Rule	Subject	A clause including a case particle "が (GA)" or a binding particle "は (WA)" or "も (MO)" which has a dependency structure with the predicate	A nominal subject or a clausal subject
	Predicate (Verb)	The last clause	A verb (transitive or intransitive) or a "be" verb + copula which has a dependency structure with the subject

*が (GA), は (WA), も (MO) are particles in Japanese grammar that immediately follow a noun, a verb, an adjective, and indicate the subject of a sentence.

D. Sentence Patterns and Criteria for Determination

In order to clarify the determinate language behavior, we selected the following six sentence patterns, because they appear frequently in learners' writing. The patterns were classified into two categories (predicate based and subject based). First, the predicate based sentence pattern was sub-classified into four sentence patterns: A) Subject + (ARU / IRU), B) Subject + Noun + (DESU / DEARU / DA), C) Subject + Reporting Verb (OMOU / KANGAERU / KANJIRU / JIKKANSURU), D) Subject + Verb (excluding "be" verb *existence* and reporting verb). Second, the subject based sentence pattern was sub-classified into two sentence patterns: E) ~ (SURU) KOTO + (WA / GA / MO) + predicate (excluding a modal auxiliary verb), F) WATASHI + (WA / GA / MO) + predicate. Table II indicates the Japanese sentence patterns.

The following is a supplementary explanation of each sentence pattern: A) ARU and IRU represent a "be" verb *existence*, B) DESU, DEARU and DA represent an auxiliary verb *state*, C) ~ (TO) OMOU and KANGAERU represent a reporting verb *mental state*, KANJIRU and JIKKANSURU represent a verb *perception*, E) ~ (SURU) KOTO represents an inanimate subject, such as a formal subject, a gerund or an infinitive in English, F) WATASHI represents the personal pronoun "I". Note on Japanese verbs, plain form is used.

TABLE II. JAPANESE SENTENCE PATTERNS

Type		Sentence Patterns with Subject
Predicate Based	A	主語 +(ある / いる) Subject + (ARU / IRU)
	B	主語 + 名詞 +(です / である / だ) Subject + Noun + (DESU / DEARU / DA)
	C	主語 + ～と(思う / 考える / 感じる / 実感する) Subject + Reporting Verb (OMOU / KANGAERU / KANJIRU / JIKKANSURU
	D	主語 + 動詞(存在, 伝達除く) Subject + Verb (excluding "be" verb *existence* and reporting verb)
Subject Based	E	～(する)こと +(は / が / も)+ 述語(法助動詞除く) ~ (SURU) KOTO + (WA / GA / MO) + predicate (excluding a modal auxiliary verb)
	F	私 +(は / が / も)+ 述語 WATASHI + (WA / GA / MO) + predicate

TABLE III. SENTENCE PATTERN AND ITS CRITERIA FOR ERROR DETERMINATION

S.P.	Criteria for Error Determination
A	If predicate verb is not "be" verb, it should be ERROR.
B	If predicate verb is not "be" verb, it should be ERROR.
C	If predicate verb is not "reporting" verb, it should be ERROR.
D	If predicate verb does not meet semantic agreements, it should be ERROR
E	If subject is not "it," "to verb" or "verb-ing," it should be ERROR.
F	If subject is not "I," it should be ERROR.

S.P. is an acronym of "sentence pattern." The above highlighted sentence patterns are dealt with in this study as an illustration.

The predicate based sentence pattern A) "Subject + (ARU / IRU)" and B) "Subject + Noun + (DESU / DEARU / DA)" always correspond with a 'be' verb in English, without the 'be' verb in the English sentences there would be errors. Sentence pattern C) "Subject + reporting Verb (OMOU / KANGAERU / KANJIRU / JIKKANSURU)" always responds with a reporting verb "think" or "feel" in English, without reporting verb "think" or "feel" in the English sentences there would be errors. Sentence pattern D) "Subject + Verb" is the most common, if semantic agreement in terms of predicate (verb) is missing, an error would occur.

The subject based sentence pattern E) "~ (SURU) KOTO + (WA / GA / MO) + predicate" always corresponds with an inanimate subject, such as a formal subject, a gerund or an infinitive in English, without the inanimate subject in the English sentences there would be an error. Sentence pattern F) "WATASHI + (WA / GA / MO) + predicate" is the most basic, without the subject "I" in the English sentences there would be an error.

Table above shows six sentence patterns and their original criteria for determination whether a sentence is correct or not.

III. RESULTS AND DISCUSSION

A. *Results*

In order to evaluate our approach, by way of illustration, automatic error detection using four sentence patterns (A, B, C and F) was carried out on Japanese sentences with subjects and their corresponding English sentences.

This study utilized 1499 sentences for analysis from essay data written by 110 Japanese EFL (English as a foreign language) college students. The proficiency level of all the learners was equivalent to the A1 level of the Common European Framework of Reference (CEFR). All the participants were required to write an essay in Japanese with the following prompts: "It is important for college students to have a part time job" and "Smoking should be completely banned at all the restaurants in the country." They then had to translate the Japanese essay into English. The essay had to be 200 - 300 words, written in under 1 hour, with no use of a dictionary or internet enabled devices.

For parsing, 100 Japanese sentences with subjects and the corresponding English sentences were randomly selected from essay data. As a result of parsing, 75 sentences were analyzed since they had the required one subject only. These 75 sentences were classified into six sentence patterns. In order to obtain feedback, comparisons between Japanese primary subjects and predicates and the corresponding English primary subjects and predicate verbs were conducted based on the extraction by parser and sorted based on sentence patterns.

TABLE IV. SAMPLE RESULTS OF EXTRACTION AND ERROR DETERMINATION

	Results of Extraction				Results of Error Determination			
	JPN		*ENG*		*Type of S.P.*		*S.S.*	
	Sub.	***Pre.***	***Sub.***	***Pre.***	***Sub-based***	***Pre-based***	***Sub-based***	***Pre-based***
1	ことは	大切です	It	is important	E	B	-	POSSIBLE
2	人が	困ります	smoking	is difficult	UNKNOWN	D	UNKNOWN	-
3	可能性も	ある	we	have	UNKNOWN	A	UNKNOWN	ERROR
•	•	•	•	•	•	•	•	•
75	私も	思います	I	think	F	C	POSSIBLE	POSSIBLE

*Sub. is an abbreviation of "subject." Pre. is an abbreviation of "predicate." S.P. is an acronym of "sentence pattern." S.S. is an acronym of "sentence structure." (-) is "unanalyzed" on behalf of N/A in this paper.

Table IV shows sample results of extraction and determination.

TABLE V. EVALUATION RESULTS OF THE PREDICATE BASED SENTENCE PATTERNS AND THE SUBJECT BASED SENTENCE PATTERNS

			Results of Determination by Error Detection System			Results of Manual Determination
Type	*S.P.*		*ER.*	*PO.*	*UN.*	*ER.*
Predicate Based	A	8	4	4	0	5
	B	28	9	19	0	13
	C	9	2	7	0	1
	D	30	-	-	-	-
	Total (A+B+C)	45	23	22	0	17
Subject Based	E	4	-	-	-	-
	F	10	4	0	6	3
	Others	61	-	-	-	-
	Total (F)	10	4	0	6	3

*ER. stands for "ERROR." PO. stands for "POSSIBLE." UN. stands for "UNKNOWN." (-) is "unanalyzed" due to being non applicable.

Table V shows the evaluation results on the accuracy to criteria for error detection of the predicate based sentence patterns (A, B, C) and the subject based sentence pattern (F). Manual determination follows the determination method in our previous works. The numbers in Results of Manual Determination are errors identified by criteria for determination (Table III) based on the meaning.

B. Discussion

Comparing the results of determination by error detection system with the results of manual determination in Table V, we obtained the following information.

Sentence Pattern A: In the results of manual determination, nine errors were the same as in the results of determination by error detection system. The coverage of determination was 80%. To increase the accuracy of error determination, distinction between *existence* "ARU" and *probability* "SURUKOTOMO-ARU" is needed.

Sentence Pattern B: In the results of manual determination, seven errors were the same as in the results of determination by error detection system. The coverage of determination was 69.2%. To increase the accuracy of error determination, the problem arising from conjugation must be solved. Cabocha determines conjugation as a noun, although conjugation is a part of verb. Therefore, adding detailed conditions regarding conjugation to sentence pattern is needed.

Sentence Pattern C: In the results of manual determination, two errors were the same as in the results of determination by error detection system. The coverage of determination was 100%. To maintain the accuracy of error determination, adding more reporting verbs in the list is needed.

Sentence Pattern F: In the results of manual determination, two errors were the same as in the results of determination by error detection system. The coverage of determination was 100%. However, the error detection system over-detects errors. To reduce over-detection it is necessary to create detailed sentence patterns and criteria for error determination to deal with sentences which contain multiple subjects, such as a compound sentence or a complex sentence. This will be the subject of further study.

IV. CONCLUSION

In this study, we proposed an approach toward an automatic error detection system. Developing sentence patterns, which differentiates the system from other language error detection systems, is the key point of our approach. We concluded that using the sentence patterns in the source language, automatic error detection is effective when based on our criteria for error determination. The remaining issue is to expand the number of sentence patterns in order to respond to as wide a range of English essays as possible. Furthermore, developing sentence patterns enables our system to be applied to other languages.

ACKNOWLEDGEMENT

This work was partially supported by JSPS KAKENHI Grant Number JP17K01081.

REFERENCES

[1] W. Grabe and R. B. Kaplan, "Theory and practice of writing: An applied linguistics perspective," Harlow: Pearson Education, p.6, 1996.

[2] Y. Takada, "Saishuuhoukokusho," Eigokyouiku Ni Kansuru Kenkyuu, Monbukagakushou itakukenkyuu, ["Final report," Research on English Education, Contract Research Commissioned by the Ministry of Education, Culture, Sports, Science and Technology], p.12, 2004.

[3] K. Kawamura, H. Kashiwagi, and Min Kang, "On the Potential of Error Analysis Using Source Language in Learner's Written English," Research report of JET conference, JSET, 17(2), pp.225-232, 2017.

[4] K. Kawamura, H. Kashiwagi, and M. Kang, "An Approach of Semi-Automatic Correction Feedback for Learners' English Writing Using the Source Language," Proceedings of Symposium on Language and Sustainability in Asia 2017, SELSA2017, pp.11-16, 2017.

[5] R. Quirk, S. Greenbaum, G. Leech, and J. Svartvik, "A comprehensive grammar of the English language," London, UK: Longman, 1985.

[6] D. Biber, S. Johansson, G. Leech, S. Conrad, and E. Finegan, "Longman grammar of spoken and written English," Essex, UK: Pearson Education Limited, 1999.

[7] S. Ando, "Eigo no ronri, nihongo no ronri [The logic of English, the logic of Japanese]," Tokyo: Taishukan, 1986.

[8] T. Kudo and Y. Matsumoto, "Fast Methods for Kernel-Based Text Analysis," ACL 2003 in Sapporo, Japan, 2003.

[9] D. Klein and C. D. Manning, "Accurate Unlexicalized Parsing," Proceedings of the 41st Meeting of the Association for Computational Linguistics, pp.423-430, 2003.

Best Practices in a Redesigned Online Computer Ethics Course

Cynthia Y. Lester
Department of Computer Science and Engineering
Georgia State University, Perimeter College
Dunwoody, Georgia, USA
e-mail: clester6@gsu.edu

Abstract **– The Babson Survey Research group, in its 13th annual survey of higher education, reported that one in four students is enrolled in online courses. The report also stated that the number of students taking online courses has continued its growth trend of the last 13 years where nearly 5.8 million students take online courses. Furthermore, approximately 28 percent of higher education students are enrolled in at least one online course. While these numbers are not surprising, they do confirm what most educators now know and that is students want to learn on their own terms and in their own environments. However, challenges in the perception of online education still persist, especially in the wake of the most recent scandals surrounding online for profit institutions. Moreover, how to best deliver quality online instruction still plagues many institutions whether they are traditional brick and mortar with an online campus or an online institution where the majority of the programs and students are fully online. Consequently, the objective of this paper is to provide a discourse on best practices in an online learning environment. More specifically, the work uses as its context an online computer ethics course aimed at students in a 2-year degree pathway, at a Research I university that was first piloted in 2014. Since then, the course has been revised and has become a regular offering, part of the required computer science curriculum. Also presented are challenges and lessons learned with hopes that they further the dialogue among educators on how best to design online courses and meet the needs of online students.**

Keywords – computer ethics; community college; learning outcomes; online education; undergraduate computer science.

I. INTRODUCTION

The United States Department of Commerce, Economics and Statistics Administration in its July 2011 report stated that Science, Technology, Engineering, and Mathematics (STEM) occupations are projected to grow by 17.0 percent between 2008 and 2018, compared to 9.8 percent growth for non-STEM occupations [1]. According to the U.S. Bureau of Labor and Statistics in its January 2017 report, there were nearly 8.6 million STEM jobs in 2015, representing 6.2 percent of the U.S. employment [2]. Moreover, STEM degree holders enjoy higher salaries, regardless of whether they are working in STEM or not and they command higher wages, earning 26 percent more than their non-STEM counterparts [1]. In fact, ninety-three out of 100 STEM occupations had wages above the national average [2]. But these higher wages also come at a price. According to the report, over 99 percent of STEM employment included occupations that require some postsecondary education [2]. Additionally, of the ten fastest growing STEM occupations, nearly all required at least a bachelor's degree [2]. So, where does this leave students who are attending 2-year institutions and/or community colleges and choosing STEM disciplines?

In a report entitled, "The Role of Community Colleges in Postsecondary Success," by the National Student Clearinghouse Research Center, it is noted that community colleges play a critical role in increasing the opportunity for many to experience postsecondary education [3]. In particular, these institutions provide a critical pathway for the under-served and disadvantaged students, working adults, and students with family and employment responsibilities [3]. In a report by the Community College Research Center, the leading independent authority on 2-year colleges in the U.S., it was reported that in fall 2015, 38 percent of undergraduate students attending college, were attending a public or private 2-year institution [4]. Moreover, the report stated that of the students who completed a degree at a 4-year institution in 2015-2016, nearly 49 percent had enrolled in a 2-year institution during the previous ten years [4]. Consequently, the need to ensure that students who are attending 2-year institutions receive quality instruction and be exposed to opportunities and various learning experiences is a must. Furthermore, for many of these institutions being able to offer online education for students is also important, because it allows them more flexibility to reach the student population which they traditionally serve.

The Babson Survey Research group, in its 13th annual survey of higher education, reported that one in four students is enrolled in online courses [5]. The report also stated that the number of students taking online courses has continued its growth trend of the last 13 years where nearly 5.8 million students take online courses [5]. Furthermore, approximately 28 percent of higher education students are enrolled in at least one online course [5]. While these numbers are not surprising, they do confirm what most educators already know and that is students want to learn on their own terms and in their own environments. Yet for many students, online education provides the only opportunity for them to achieve their lifelong goal of earning a college degree and provides even more accessibility for those students attending community college.

Online education is especially important for first generation college students, adult learners, students with family obligations, students in remote areas where college/universities are not easily accessible and veterans returning to school. *41 Facts about Online Students* by College Atlas revealed that 37 percent of online students were the first among their family members to attend college and that 60 percent were employed full-time [6]. To this end, 68 percent of those surveyed indicated that the reason they enrolled in online courses was the ability to balance work, family and school responsibilities, while 64 percent stated that they appreciated the ability to study at their convenience [6].

Although online education continues to grow and public institutions continue to seek new and innovative ways to reach today's students, there continue to be challenges. For example, faculty members have reported feeling less confident about online programs [5]. According to the Babson Survey Research report, only 29.1 percent of chief academic officers reported that their faculty accept "the value and legitimacy of online education [5]." Additionally, academic leaders who regard online learning as critical to their long-term strategic efforts dropped 7.5 percentage points from 70.8 percent in 2015 to 63.3 percent in 2016 [5].

When it comes to community colleges and online education, researchers have found differing opinions. In an Inside Higher Ed survey, published April 17, 2015, it was reported that "50 percent of two-year-college presidents agreed that more courses could be moved online without adversely affecting students at their institutions [6]." This stands in contrast to reports that community college students are also less likely to do well in online courses [7]. For example, in a report by the U.S. News and World Report, researchers at the University of California-Davis, found that community college students throughout California were 11 percent less likely to finish and pass a course if they opted to take the online version instead of the traditional face-to-face version of the same class. The work was presented on April 18, 2015, at the American Educational Research Association's annual conference in Chicago in April 2015 [8]. Furthermore, one of the authors of the paper went on to note that in their study they found that in every subject, face-to-face students were doing better than their counterparts taking the online version [8].

Consequently, the objective of this paper is to provide a discourse on best practices in an online learning environment. More specifically, the paper presents an update on an online course intended to teach computer ethics aimed at STEM pathway students who are enrolled in an Associate's degree granting pathway within a Research I university. The author first presented the development of the course in the proceedings of the Seventh International Conference on Mobile, Hybrid, and On-line Learning in the work entitled, "Developing a Computer Ethics Course for Online Learners [9]." The current work focuses on course improvements and results, challenges faced and lessons learned.

The paper is organized into the following sections. Section II introduces the course and provides the rationale for course revisions. Sections III and IV present a course overview and the redesigned modules. Section V includes the results, while sections VI and VII present the discussion and concluding thoughts.

II. FRAMEWORK

A. *Background – Pre-consolidation*

As previously stated, course development was described in the work entitled in "Developing a Computer Ethics Course for Online Learners [9]." The course description, topics covered and learning outcomes remained the same. However, there was one significant change in the course design which included the prerequisites of the course. When the course was developed and implemented in 2014, it only had one prerequisite which was the successful completion of *CSCI 1301 - Principles of Computer Science I* with a "C" or better, or permission of the Instructor and Department Chair [10]. At that time, it was decided that CSCI 1301 would be the course prerequisite because it emphasized structured, top-down development and testing of computer programs. At the conclusion of the course, students would be able to utilize critical thinking and analytical skills to successfully analyze, develop and implement programs in a modern programming language.

In 2014, when the course was developed it was done so as a part of Georgia Perimeter College. At that time, Georgia Perimeter College was the largest 2-year institution in the state of Georgia with the largest freshman and sophomore enrollments in the state, making it the top producer of transfer students to 4-year institutions within the state [11]. It had five campus locations throughout the Atlanta-metro area and serviced approximately 22,000 students either face-to-face or through its online campus. Roughly 10 percent of the student body took all their classes online [11]. The number of students choosing one of the STEM disciplines was roughly 10 percent [12].

B. *Background – Post-consolidation*

In 2016, Georgia Perimeter College consolidated with Georgia State University. As a result, the new Georgia State University has six campuses throughout metro Atlanta, an online campus, and is a national leader in serving students from diverse backgrounds with a student population of over 51,000. Perimeter College became the 2-year arm of the university and provides instruction to approximately 21,000 students, still at its five campus locations throughout the Atlanta metro area and online. It is through Georgia State University's Perimeter College, that students can still earn an associate's degree. However, as a result of the consolidation, many associate degree pathways made significant changes to their curricula and one of those was the computer science pathway.

In consultation with the Director for Undergraduate Studies for the computer science department at the Atlanta campus and with the author (who serves as the computer science and engineering department chair at Perimeter College), it was decided to change the prerequisites for the computer ethics course such that it mirrored prerequisites for 2000-level courses at the main campus. To this end, the new prerequisites for the course became *CSC 1301 and CSC 1302, each with a grade of C or higher or permission of the department* [13]. The addition of CSC 1302 further strengthened the skill set of students had coming and hoped to ensure that students were ready for the rigor of 2000-level computer science courses. The next sections provide an overview of the course followed by the redesigned course modules.

III. Course Overview

A. Course Description

CSC 2920- Ethical and Social Issues in Computing, is a three hour course dedicated to the study of social, ethical, and legal effects of computing on society and its users. Ethical concepts, professional codes of ethics, and the influence of computing on individuals, organizations, and the global economy will be addressed. Students will utilize critical thinking and problem solving skills to analyze and debate case studies on topics some of which include privacy; intellectual property; computer crimes; system failures and implications; and, the impact of technology on society [13].

The course continued to utilize the College's Desire 2 Learn (D2L) learning management system as its online portal. Although redesigned after the consolidation with enhanced features, this allowed the author to disseminate information, engage students in discussions and perform student assessments.

B. Topics Covered

The topics covered in the CSC 2920 remained the same which included [13]:

- Basic concepts and historical overview of computer ethics
- Introduction to issues and themes in ethical computing
  - Privacy
  - Freedom of Speech
  - Intellectual Property
  - Computer and Network Crime
  - Evaluating and Controlling Technology
  - Error, Failures and Risks
- Professional ethics and responsibilities

C. Learning Outcomes

By the end of the course, students were still expected to [13]:

- Explain and evaluate the ramifications of technological advances brought by the advent of the computer on individuals, organizations and society
- Identify ethical and legal issues related to computer use
- Develop solutions based on the computer professional code of ethics
- Effectively and succinctly communicate through speech, writing, and presentation the themes of the course

D. Student Assessments

One change that was made was in the area of student assessments. In the pilot study of the course, students were required to write and submit a term paper (8 percent of the course grade). Although in the pilot study survey, students noted that at first they were somewhat apprehensive about writing a "term paper" for a computer science class, they enjoyed the assignment and that overall the class average was a B [9]. However, the author removed the paper in order to give more weight to class participation and incentivize students' online interaction in the course. Consequently, the new areas (with grade weight) in which students were assessed included:

- Class Participation = 10%
- Case Study = 10%
- Programming Assignment = 5%
- Exams = 50%
- Final exam = 25%

The next section discusses three areas of changes in course content. The first is the addition of a new module entitled the Class Passport and the other two areas of change are to the student assessment areas of class participation and case studies.

IV. Redesigned Course Modules

A. Class Passport

To engage students from the very beginning, a class passport module was developed. Much like the definition of the word, "passport," the passport module symbolized a travel document for the rest of the course and once students completed viewing it, they were granted access to the rest of the course material. This high-level of interaction ensured that students reviewed the following: 1) online honor code policy; 2) the attendance and participation policy; 3) the dropping and withdrawal policy; 4) instructor's expectations which were presented in video format; and, 5) the course syllabus and semester schedule. Also, as part of the passport module, the first discussion post was presented which asked students to address the following:

- Where you are from?
- Why you are taking this class?
- What area of computer science interests you the most?
- What are your career plans?
- Is this your first online computer science or online college class?

In particular, it was the answer to the last question that helped the author gauge how best to interact with students.

B. Class Participation

Previously, class participation accounted for only 2 percent of the overall course grade [10]. However, based on recommendations from students and from colleagues who reviewed the course, the instructor changed the weight of class participation to 10 percent of the course grade.

Participation now carried as much weight as student case study presentations, which emphasized to students that participating in discussion posts was just as important as the case study that they were to present to their peers. It should be noted that an increase from 2 percent to 10 percent for participation in an online class seems negligible, especially when students report feelings of loneliness in online classes. However, because exams and the final exam must be weighted 75 percent of the course as required by the college's curriculum committee, only the additional 8 percent was available for use in the class participation category. Hence, the author redistributed the weight and increased the class participation category.

There were total of five discussion posts based on central themes. Discussion questions were posted in concert with student case study presentations and students were given approximately one week to respond. To guide their response, they were asked to:

- Provide an overview of the theme based on textbook concepts
- State their opinion
- State the student presentation that best supported their opinion
- To encourage responses and replies, the instructor would often comment on student posts.

C. *Case Study Presentations*

The author re-worked this module completely. When the course was first developed, this module was named class debates. The intent was for students to be assigned opposing sides to discuss course topics. However, many students did not understand how to "debate" a topic but instead just recounted the topic background that was initially presented by the author in the directions.

Therefore, to encourage more critical thinking where arguments and solutions could be presented, the author asked a question at the end of the case study background and challenged students to:

- Use the case study background as a framework only for the presentation
- Provide an introduction to the topic utilizing theoretical concepts covered in the textbook.
- Discuss how the use of technology impacts your given role
- Use similar cases/scenarios to further explain your position (news articles, cases in the textbook, etc.)
- Present your opinion of the situation (even if it differs from your given role).

An example of a case study based on the themes, "Privacy, Technology, and Security" is as follows:

In March, the House of Representatives approved the Congressional Review Act (CRA), undoing privacy restrictions imposed on ISPs during the Obama administration. The Senate also passed the CRA]. Advocates who support privacy noted that the move means Verizon, Comcast or AT&T can continue tracking and sharing people's browsing and app activity without permission. While supporters of broadband providers said the privacy rules were onerous and unfairly strapped regulations on telecom carriers, but not on web companies such as Facebook and Google that also provide access to online content. As asked in the textbook, "Technological and social changes make people feel uncomfortable, but does that mean the changes are unethical?"

Directions once again included that the presentation of the material should be no less than ten (10) minutes and no more than fifteen (15) minutes. The presentation should include at least three (3) scholarly references from which the information was gathered. Additionally, students were encouraged to be creative with technology beyond the use of PowerPoint in order to promote interaction and advanced technology use. Students were also informed that use of PowerPoint only, would garner very few points. Lastly, students were informed that they would be assessed on their use of technology, style and delivery of the content.

D. *Programming Assignment*

The programming assignment which counted for five percent of the total course grade was designed to engage students' critical thinking and problem solving skills while also focusing on the course content of ethics. As a result of the new prerequisites, the programming assignment was also redesigned to include not only the concepts from CSC 1301 but also some higher level concepts taught in CSC 1302. Since Java was taught as the programming language in both courses, the program description was specific to a Java implementation. Yet, keeping in mind that this was not a "programming course," students were informed that they would be assessed on their design, efficiency, and implementation of the program as a whole.

E. *Exams*

Since exams counted for 75 percent of the course assessment as required by the curriculum committee, the author added another module which included lectures and videos on how to adequately prepare for the exams and the final exam (which was comprehensive). Students were told how many questions would be on each exam and the types of questions (i.e., multiple choice, matching, essay, etc.). Students were also informed that the exam would be available for 24 hours, but that once started, it would end 120 minutes later. By providing this level of detail, it was the anticipation of the author to level the playing field between those who had not taken an online course previously and those who had (approximately 36 percent had not taken an online course). Also, the announcement feature with e-mail in D2L was heavily used as a reminder about upcoming exams and logistics.

Once the exams had been graded and reviewed by the author, exam review notes were posted. The author utilized the question statistics and question details features in D2L to determine questions themes on which students had difficulty. If 25 percent or more of the students answered a question incorrectly, the instructor reviewed that question and its corresponding theme and also engaged students in feedback.

The next section presents the results of student assessments in two areas, class participation and the exams. Results were not available from the case study presentations for reasons explained later in the discussion section.

V. RESULTS

A. *Class Participation*

As noted, class participation was worth 10 percent of the overall grade and was implemented through discussion posts. There were a total of five discussion posts. Figure 1 shows the overall number of students participating in the discussion posts. Figure 2 shows students participating by discussion post.

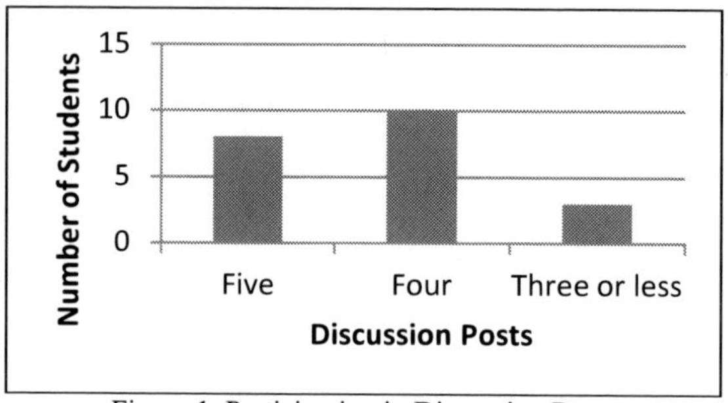

Figure 1. Participation in Discussion Posts

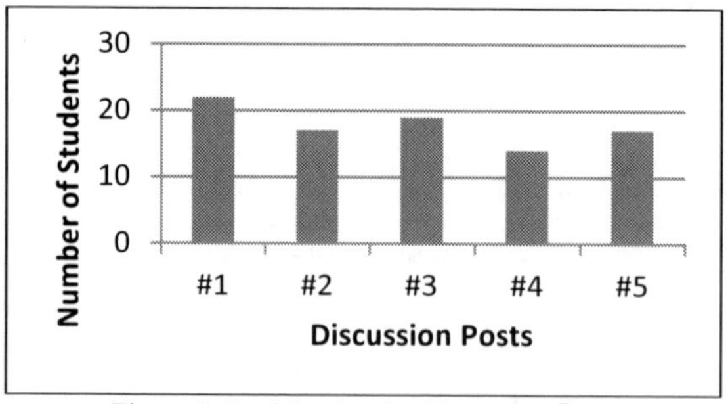

Figure 2. Participation by Discussion Post

B. *Exams*

There were total of three exams and one final exam. The instructor used the statistics in the D2L to gather information not only about the class performance as a whole on each exam, but also how students performed on individual questions. By utilizing question statistics and question details, the instructor was able to develop exam review notes which focused on the themes covered in the question. Figure 3 shows the number of questions on which 25 percent or more the students answered incorrectly. Figure 4 shows the types of question by exam on which 25 percent or more of the students answered incorrectly.

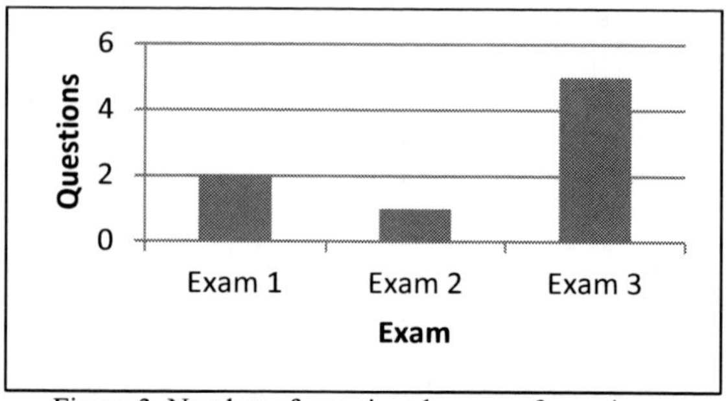

Figure 3. Number of questions by exam for review

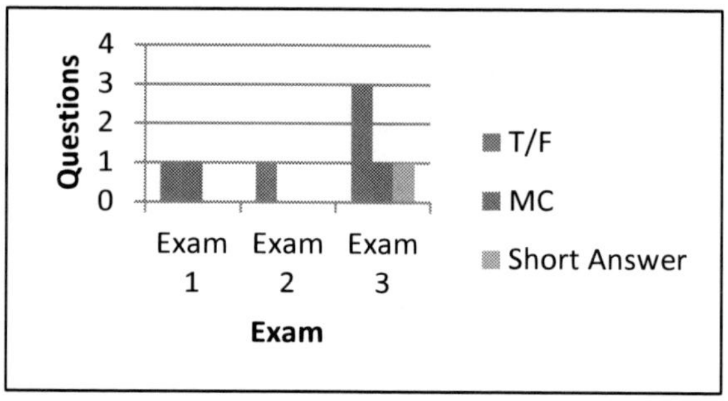

Figure 4. Questions for review by question type

The next section provides an overview of the results presented, followed by concluding thoughts.

VI. DISCUSSION

Overall, the instructor was pleased with the changes in course content and the heightened level of interaction. Results show that on average, the majority of the students participated in the discussion posts (approximately 18 each time). The results also show that participation varied according to topic, but remained strong throughout the semester.

As it relates to the exams, while it was not presented in the results section, the author can attest that with the heightened level of communication and constant reminders about the exam and exam logistics, no students missed taking any of the exams, a first since the author began teaching the course in 2014. However, what is presented in the results section that needs more attention is on the concepts and wording of the questions for exam #3. It may be that the wording of the T/F questions need to be revised and/or that the short answer question was too challenging to complete in the time provided. Only little over half of the students attempted to answer the question.

While the author was pleased with the overall modifications to course, one point of concern and an obvious challenge is the case study module and student assessment. The author spent significant time redesigning the module with updated content and directions. The author had hoped that students would submit case study presentations that encouraged a higher level of critical inquiry which promoted discussion and challenged ways of thinking. Although students were challenged in their way of thinking and conveying the ethical implications of the material, many presentations lacked the critical analysis of the literature needed to support their claims. This is a work in progress, one that the author will again revisit.

VII. Conclusion

In closing, the purpose of this work is to further a discussion on how best to teach computer ethics in an online environment and to identify best practices. The author presents revisions to a course that was initially offered as a pilot study. Since the first offering in 2014, the course has been offered each year and has grown in popularity. However, certain challenges still remain which include how to truly assess if by the end of the course students are able to meet the learning outcome of being able to, "Explain and evaluate the ramifications of technological advances brought by the advent of the computer on individuals, organizations and society." The author thought that by redesigning the case studies and providing students with a framework that presentations would engage critical thinking. However, results from this module were inconclusive.

Another challenge that the author did not anticipate was that the redesign of several modules and the addition of a new module would significantly increase course development time. In an article title, "Does it take more or less time to facilitate and develop and online course? Finally some answer", twenty-nine percent of survey participants stated that they spent over 100 hours developing their first online course [14]. The article went on to explain that number of hours was probably due to the fact that 59 percent of respondents developed over 90 percent of the course without any assistance, which included developing content, assessments, assignments, and time associated with course design [14]. Although the author used lectures from the first implementation of the course, the assessments, assignments, and other materials associated with the course redesign were new. Additionally, because the intent was to increase the level of interaction and engagement in the redesigned course, additional hours were spent on this aspect. Therefore, the author spent approximately 70+ hours in the redesign.

However, through these efforts some best practices did emerge, which were in the redesign of the course and that the author will carry forward into the next course offering:

- Use of the introductory discussion post to gather insightful information on students' background
- Restricting access to course content until the Class Passport module has been completed
- Expanded use of the announcement feature with email
- Utilization of the question statistics with details

In closing, as more and more students choose to take classes online and institutions increase their offerings to meet the demands of those students, so does the debate on how best to offer quality instruction. This is especially important to educators who are interested in increasing opportunities for those who desire to experience postsecondary education and in expanding the STEM pipeline. By carefully examining course content, delivery, and also understanding who our students are, we further our goal as educators in helping students who cross our "virtual pathways" to succeed.

References

[1] D. Langdon, G. McKittrick, D. Beede, B. Khan, and M.Doms. "STEM: Good jobs and for the Future," U.S. Department of Commerce, Economics and Statistics Administration. http://www.esa.doc.gov/sites/default/files/reports/documents/stemfinalyjuly14_1.pdf. *[Retrieved: February 2018].*

[2] U.S. Bureau of Labor and Statistics, Spotlight on Statistics. https://www.bls.gov/spotlight/2017/science-technology-engineering-and-mathematics-stem-occupations-past-present-and-future/pdf/science-technology-engineering-and-mathematics-stem-occupations-past-present-and-future.pdf *[Retrieved: February 2018].*

[3] National Clearinghouse Research Center. The Role of Community Colleges in Postsecondary Success. https://studentclearinghouse.info/onestop/wpcontent/uploads/Comm-Colleges-Outcomes-Report.pdf. *[Retrieved: February 2018].*

[4] *Community Colleges for International Development.* https://www.ccidinc.org/single-post/2017/05/04/Community-College-Enrollment-and-Completion *[Retrieved: February 2018].*

[5] 2015 Online Report Card - Tracking Online Education in the United States https://onlinelearningconsortium.org/read/online-report-card-tracking-online-education-united-states-2015/ *[Retrieved: February 2018].*

[6] 41 Facts About Online. Students https://www.collegeatlas.org/41-surprising-facts-about-online-students.html *[Retrieved: February 2018].*

[7] Free Community College, Structure Pathways: Survey of 2-Year College Leaders. https://www.insidehighered.com/news/survey/free-community-college-structured-pathways-survey-2-year-college-leaders. *[Retrieved: February 2018].*

[8] Studies: Online Courses Unsuccessful at Community Colleges. https://www.usnews.com/news/articles/2015/04/27/studies-online-courses-unsuccessful-at-community-colleges *[Retrieved: February 2018].*

[9] C. Lester, "Developing a Computer Ethics Course for Online Learners" Proceedings of the Seventh International Conference on Mobile, Hybrid, and On-line Learning. Pp. 27-32. ISBN: 978-1-61208-385-8.

[10] C. Lester, 2014. CSCI 2900-099- Ethical and Social Issues in Computing. Course Syllabus, summer 2014. Unpublished syllabus, Department of Computer Science and Engineering, Georgia State University, Perimeter College, Decatur, GA.

[11] The University System of Georgia, 2012. http://www .usg.edu/. *[Retrieved: February 2018].*

[12] C. Lester, Georgia Perimeter College STEM Annual Report Form 2011-2012. Report submitted to the USG STEM Initiatives II Office. Unpublished report, University System of Georgia, STEM Initiatives, Atlanta, GA.

[13] C. Lester, CSCI 2920-Ethical and Social Issues in Computing. Course Syllabus, spring 2017. Unpublished syllabus, Department of Computer Science and Engineering, Georgia State University, Perimeter College, Decatur, GA.

[14] D. Morrison, "Does it Take More or Less Time to Facilitate and Develop an Online Course? Finally, Some Answers," https://onlinelearninginsights.wordpress.com/2015/05/08/does-it-take-more-or-less-time-to-facilitate-and-develop-an-online-course-finally-some-answers/ *[Retrieved: February 2018].*

Educator-Oriented Tools for Managing the Attention-Aware Intelligent Classroom

Evropi Stefanidi, Maria Korozi, Asterios Leonidis, Maria Doulgeraki, and Margherita Antona
Institute of Computer Science
Foundation for Research and Technology – Hellas (FORTH)
Heraklion, Crete, Greece
email: {evropi, korozi, leonidis, mdoulger, antona}@ics.forth.gr

Abstract—**The emergence of Intelligent Classrooms and in particular classrooms that are equipped with appropriate infrastructure for identifying the students' attention levels, has raised the need for appropriate educator-friendly tools that facilitate monitoring and management of these educational environments. This paper presents two such systems: LECTORviewer and NotifEye. LECTORviewer is deployed on the educator's personal workstation and offers an overview of the students' attention levels. Additionally, through its intuitive user interface, educators can provide their input regarding ambiguous behaviors or scheduled interventions that aim to reengage distracted, tired or unmotivated students to the educational process. NotifEye is a smart watch application for educators that aims to communicate, in a mobile fashion, important events occurring during a lesson (e.g., 60% of students are tired). This work presents the functionality of these tools and the usability findings of a heuristic evaluation experiment conducted with UX experts for LECTORviewer.**

Keywords-Classroom management; intelligent classroom; monitoring student attention.

I. INTRODUCTION

The introduction of technology in the school environment has been associated with enhancing the students' performance and has encouraged several technology-driven curriculum renewal projects [1]. The rate of technological development is ever increasing, a fact that influenced the emergence of innovative approaches towards incorporation of Information and Communication Technologies (ICTs) in the classroom environment. Whereas once the overhead projector was considered a cutting-edge tool in the classroom [2], today the concept of the smart classroom is a reality [3].

According to researchers, technology can be used effectively as a cognitive tool as well as instructional media, and can be helpful in classroom settings by promoting inquiry, helping communication, constructing teaching products, and assisting students' self-expression [4]. Research in [2] shows that by combining Ambient Intelligence (AmI) technologies [5] with social and behavioral analysis inside a smart classroom, an active analysis of the effectiveness of the lecture can be conducted. Moreover, ICT can monitor learners' behavior during learning activities to improve the educational process, such as identifying whether a learner is paying attention to the lecture or not [6]. Student attention monitoring has been proven to lead to better student achievements [7] and a more pleasant and effective learning process.

Research has shown that live monitoring of a class is possible and beneficial, not only in the more obvious case of distant learning [6][8], where monitoring is deemed necessary, as the educator cannot rely on physical observation to perceive the status of the participants, but also in a physical classroom [8], as the large number of students hinders the educator's ability to quickly draw conclusions. The kind and extent of monitoring in each case naturally varies, but students' management is necessary in both cases, since the educator has to adjust and adapt the lesson according to the students' needs at any given moment. Nevertheless, this is a cumbersome task for the educator to perform while pursuing specific educational goals in the short time frame of a lesson period. Technology can automate trivial monitoring and managing tasks, and present appropriate information to the educator either during classroom downtime (e.g., quiz, problem-solving, essay writing), or after class as a reflection on the overall process. Moreover, it has the ability to collect information from multiple visible and invisible sources, that can not only reveal problematic behaviors that the educator missed to detect (e.g., mind wandering), but most importantly provide indications about the reasons of inattention; the latter is especially important in classrooms with a large number of students, where the educator cannot focus on every student.

In such settings, educator-friendly tools, which aim to help educators in managing and monitoring the attention-aware smart classrooms effectively, are necessary. This paper presents LECTORviewer and NotifEye, which equip educators with intuitive interfaces for performing the necessary managing tasks. Their functionalities include monitoring student attention levels and applying targeted interventions to distracted, tired or unmotivated students in order to reengage them in the educational process.

Regarding the structure of this paper, in Section 2, related work is discussed, while Section 3 presents the requirements that guided the design and development process. Section 4 describes the features of the in-vitro Intelligent Classroom that currently hosts these systems, while Sections 4 and 5 focus on LECTORviewer and NotifEye respectively. Finally, the findings of a preliminary heuristic evaluation are analyzed in Section 6, while conclusions and plans for further improvements are described in Section 7.

II. RELATED WORK

The ability to handle disruptive student behaviors in a classroom is a critical factor in any educational setting and greatly affects the overall learning process [9]. Effective and efficient classroom management and active monitoring of student progress and attention have been long since identified as key instructional factors, with significant relationships to positive student achievement outcomes [7]. Equipping educators with context-aware visualization tools [8] allows to quickly detect problems stemming from inattentive behaviors and identify their causes.

Towards addressing inattention, class monitoring is augmented with attention-aware artifacts embedded in the physical environment that observe relevant parameters and report their findings [10]. Upon inattention detection, targeted interventions are delivered to the inattentive students [11]. Such instructional interventions have been proven to both re-engage students in the learning process and promote self-monitoring and self-regulation [12]. Specifically, in educational contexts, interventions positively influence the students' performance, independent of their educational background or their learning abilities [13].

Various Graphical User Interface (GUI) applications have been developed which simplify classroom management activities, such as teacher-student communication [14], management of learning assets [15][16], distant learning [17], real-time activity monitoring [18], and on-the-fly creation of educational software [19]. These applications utilize the data resulting from monitoring and management of the classroom in order to produce appropriate visualizations that the educator can explore so as to reflect and improve lecturing.

Classroom monitoring has been the focus of multiple research attempts. Intelligent Tutoring Systems (ITS) [20] monitor and assess learners' affective and cognitive state. Their potential to influence learning is greatly enhanced by the tutor's ability to accurately assess the student's state in real-time and then use this state as a basis to provide timely feedback or alter the instructional content. Thus, tailored and personalized educational experiences can be provided through monitoring student interactions in real-time and adapting learning events to the individual. In [21], the emotional state of the user is monitored via sensors that measure physiological signals (i.e., Electrocardiogram (ECG) and Galvanic skin response (GSR)) and appropriate interventions are provided when necessary.

In [22], a monitoring instrument to assess students' perceptions of their learning environments was developed and validated. The purpose was to assist teachers, teacher educators and researchers to monitor and guide changes towards outcome-based classroom learning environments. Biofeedback methodology is used in [23], to investigate interactions among learners' affective states, metacognitive processes, and learning outcomes during multimedia learning. The developed model emphasizes cognitive processes and metacognitive monitoring and control.

It is therefore obvious that the advancement of technology has allowed various monitoring techniques to be developed. Although quite a lot of research has been conducted on monitoring the classroom with respect to student interactions, physiological variables, and physiological signals in real-time [24], there is a lack of research and development of tools for educators that can monitor attention and take appropriate actions in the classroom setting.

III. REQUIREMENTS

This Section presents the requirements for both LECTORviewer and NotifEye, which have been collected through an extensive literature review and an iterative elicitation process based on multiple collection methods, including brainstorming, focus groups, observation and scenario building.

R1. Real-time Classroom Monitoring: The system should permit real-time behavior monitoring of individual students and the entire classroom.
R2. Intervention Management: When interventions are about to start, educators should be able to cancel, postpone or easily configure them.
R3. Educator's Control over the System: The educator should always have full control of the system and be able to turn on or off the monitoring and intervention mechanisms (either for the entire classroom of for specific individuals).
R4. Educator's Input: The educator should be able to (i) disapprove system decisions regarding identified behaviors, (ii) disambiguate behaviors (e.g., thinking vs. mind wandering), and (iii) override system suggestions in case they do not serve the students' needs.
R5. System Analytics regarding Intervention- and Attention- related Data: Statistics and data about the overall operation should be visible, such as attention and inattention percentage, total times that an intervention was initiated, and success rates of interventions.
R6. Full Overview of System's Decisions: The educator should have access to the detailed log of events that occurred during the lesson time.
R7. Reduce Educator's cognitive Load: The UI should be educator-friendly so that the teaching activities are not burdened by cumbersome interfaces. Furthermore, there should be alternative representations of the same information to serve different situations.
R8. Do not hinder the lecture: The acquired information should be presented in a subtle, yet effective, manner.

All these requirements are realized by LECTORviewer and NotifEye, which aim to support educators in their daily activities within the attention aware intelligent classroom.

IV. THE INTELLIGENT CLASSROOM

The systems presented in this paper are employed in-vitro inside a technologically augmented classroom, where educational activities are enhanced with the use of pervasive and mobile computing, sensor networks, artificial intelligence, multimedia computing, middleware and agent-based software [25]-[27]. In more detail, the hardware infrastructure includes both commercial and custom-made artifacts, which are embedded in traditional classroom equipment and furniture. In particular, the classroom contains: (i) a commercial touch sensitive interactive whiteboard, (ii) technologically augmented student desks [27] that integrate various sensors (e.g., Kinect, eye-tracker, camera, microphone.), (iii) a personal workstation and a smart watch for the educator, as well as (iv) various ambient facilities appropriate for monitoring the overall environment and the learners' actions (e.g., microphones, user-tracking devices).

The Intelligent Classroom relies on the AmI-Solertis middleware infrastructure [28] that facilitates: (i) the deployment, execution and monitoring of the various artifacts in the classroom, (ii) their encapsulation in an interoperable ubiquitous ecosystem and (iii) the collection, analysis and storage of environment-related data.

A sophisticated framework, named LECTOR [29], is responsible for identifying inattentive behaviors and intervening to re-engage distracted, tired or unmotivated students to the educational process. Specifically, LECTOR observes the students' actions (SENSE), identifies the individuals who show signs of inattention (THINK) and consequently undertakes the necessary actions to restore their engagement by applying appropriate interventions (ACT). Actually, interventions are applications running on private (e.g., student's desk, teacher's watch) or public (e.g., classroom board) hosts, instantiated at a key point in time with appropriate content. Currently, LECTOR features two types of interventions, namely quizzes and multimedia presentations that aim to ensure active student participation in the main course. Furthermore, taking into consideration the fact that most students thrive in encouraging environments, their private artifacts are equipped with a messaging mechanism able to provide encouraging messages when deemed necessary. The same mechanism is employed on the teacher's smart watch in order to display subtle messages suggesting changes in the lecture format (e.g. recapitulation of the lecture topics, initiation of a discussion relevant to the current course, repetition of specific material, etc.).

However, LECTOR would be ineffective without exploiting the expertise of educators. To this end, two interconnected tools are introduced, namely LECTORviewer [6] and NotifEye; the former provides an overview of the students' attention levels and asks the educator's opinion regarding ambiguous behaviors or scheduled interventions, while the latter provides notifications regarding important events occurring during the lesson time and can serve as an input to the former. The architecture of the intelligent classroom is depicted in Figure 1.

V. LECTORVIEWER

LECTORviewer is a web-based tool for managing the attention-aware intelligent classroom. It is deployed on the educator's personal workstation and allows the observation and customization of LECTOR's decisions regarding either individual students or the classroom as a whole. In more detail, LECTORviewer offers the following:

- One-click enabling or disabling of the LECTOR's monitoring facility.
- One-click enabling or disabling of the LECTOR's intervention mechanism.
- An overview of the attention level of the entire classroom that also facilitates focusing on particular students.
- A mechanism that asks the educator's opinion regarding ambiguous student behaviors.
- A mechanism that gives educators control over approving or dismissing an intervention.

These functionalities are provided through an intuitive user interface which mainly consists of (i) a main dashboard that displays information regarding all the classes an educator teaches, and (ii) the representations of each class (i.e., class view) containing details about its students, displayed either in a seating chart layout or a list view.

All the classes that an educator teaches can be found in a sortable list on the main dashboard, where valuable information is available to the educator: (i) the schedule of the class (e.g., the assignments that are close to a deadline), (ii) reminders of important events (e.g., scheduled exam), (iii) details about the fluctuation of the attention levels during the last lesson, and (iv) number of successful interventions. This type of information not only helps educators to have an overview of the class and better organize future lessons, but also to judge the efficiency and quality of past lessons based on the students' attention levels. Moreover, by viewing the statistics about the effectiveness of past interventions, educators can acquire an understanding of the kind of interventions that are appropriate for a specific class or student, and therefore more effectively choose and manage interventions in the future.

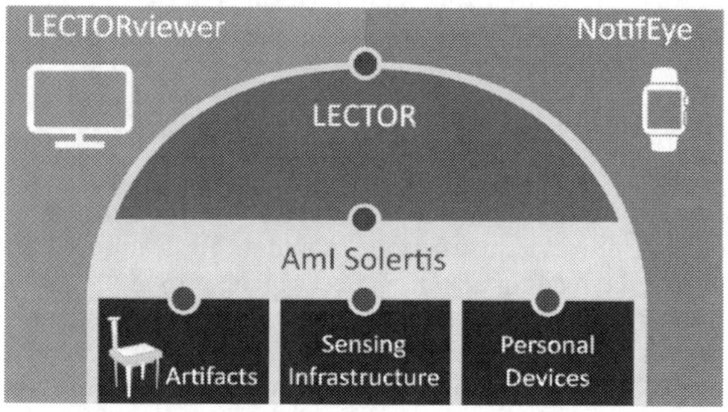

Figure 1. The architecture of the intelligent classroom.

During a lesson, through LECTORviewer's class view, the educator can get insights regarding students that are not paying attention due to factors like fatigue, mind wandering, or lack of motivation. However, in some cases, the ability to disambiguate student activities depends on information that only a human can provide. For instance, students laughing at a teacher's joke is not an indicator of inattention. To that end, when the system identifies a behavior that can be misinterpreted, it asks for the educator's opinion. These three states (i.e., attentive, not attentive and needs revision) are coded with appropriate colors (i.e., green, red and orange) which are used throughout the user interface so as to help educators easily distinguish the current status of the students.

At the top of the "class view" (see Figure 2a), the educator can see at a glance the attention percentage of the classroom as a whole. A pie chart, located at the top left of the page, uses the aforementioned colors to display the percentage of attentive or inattentive behaviors, and situations that require revision. At the center of the chart, the percentage of attentive students is displayed using bold and large fonts so as to ensure that the educator will be able to see it even from a distance. Furthermore, the legends of the chart can be used as filters that modify its contents, thus enabling educators to customize it according to their needs. The representation as a pie chart was

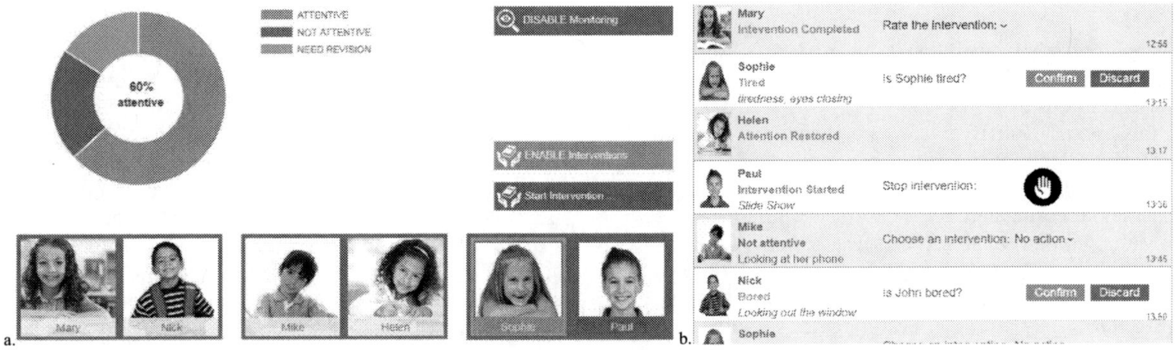

Figure 2. Snapshots of LECTORviewer's (a) class-view and (b) detailed log.

considered as the most appropriate alternative to communicate this type of information to educators by displaying all the data simultaneously; that is because a person's visual system needs less time to understand graphs (rather than tables), which give numbers shape and form [30].

In addition, in order to ensure that educators can freely activate or deactivate the monitoring and intervention mechanisms according to the class's needs, the top of the page contains the appropriate controls so as to be easily accessible. This functionality is important for an environment full of students where unforeseen situations can emerge; for example, the educator could observe that interventions are not effective or disrupt the course's flow at a given moment, and may wish to stop the system from making suggestions. Apart from merely (de)activating interventions, educators can select to start a specific intervention when deemed necessary. The latter ensures that educators do not rely on the system's decisions alone; on the contrary, they can initiate custom interventions in case the system (i) fails to identify that the students require remedial actions, or (ii) suggests an inappropriate one.

Apart from managing the classroom as a whole, the educators can focus on individual students as well. In more detail, there are two alternative layouts available for browsing through the classroom students and observing their status. By default, a "seating chart" layout is displayed, where students are represented in a form that resembles their actual seating arrangements, while the educator can easily switch to a "list view" layout, with a rich sorting functionality (e.g., alphabetical order, attention level order). For each student, LECTORviewer displays useful information regarding their status, as well as the likely reason a student is inattentive.

When the list view of the class is enabled, more functionality regarding each individual student is displayed. For each student, additional information is available, such as details regarding their learning style, attention level, and the reason that led the system to identify that they have lost focus, if that is the case. Furthermore, in order to provide enough context to the educator, in case of inattention or behaviors that need revision, relevant tags that reveal the reason are available. An indicative tag is "Mobile", which is used to annotate the behavior of students who are not paying attention because they are looking at their smartphones. Finally, next to each student the educator can find the appropriate controls for enabling or disabling LECTOR's monitoring and intervention mechanisms for that individual. This is required in a class that is constituted of different students with varying backgrounds, personalities, behaviors, needs and learning patterns [31].

Additionally, a detailed log (see Figure 2b) is available for each classroom that allows educators to revisit –even at a later time– LECTOR's decisions and mark them as accurate or not. A mini view of the log is always available at the sidebar of the "class view", enabling educators to observe in real time LECTOR's decisions without navigating to a new page. However, if needed, the educator can select to view the entire attention log, through which they can (i) confirm or invalidate an identified student behavior, (ii) stop an active intervention and optionally replace it with another one, and (iii) rate elapsed interventions. Providing such information is really important for "calibrating" LECTOR to a specific classroom environment and its students, since this process makes the decision-making mechanisms more accurate and less prone to false positives. This is a cumbersome task, which requires recalling various incidents that occurred during a significant amount of time. In order to minimize the amount of information someone has to remember, LECTORviewer's log is equipped with a sophisticated filtering mechanism, while each log entry is accompanied with abundant contextual information (e.g., timestamp, teacher's activity at the time).

Finally, on the top right of the screen, important upcoming activities concerning the current lesson are visible. This enables the educator to have a quick overview of tasks that are time-critical, thus giving the opportunity to better organize activities, while also serving as a reminder. Icons visible next to each upcoming activity aid the fast recognition of the activity with just a quick glance.

VI. NOTIFEYE

NotifEye (see Figure 3) is a smart watch application able to provide subtle interventions to educators. Employing such wearable devices to act as intervention hosts seemed natural, since in addition to indicating time they: (i) are increasingly available in the market, (ii) support notifications and reminders, and (iii) are appropriate for private interventions.

To this end, NotifEye can be used to provide informative interventions regarding important incidents that occur during a lesson. In more detail, the application is able to display messages dictated by LECTOR, while at the same time the watch vibrates to alert the user. For example, when the entire classroom displays signs of inattention, NotifEye is instructed to deliver the short yet meaningful message "CLASSROOM TIRED", accompanied with an exclamation mark icon. The use of self-explanatory icons that require little effort to see and understand was imperative for an application running on a wearable small-screen device whose target audience must not be distracted from its main task (i.e., teaching tasks).

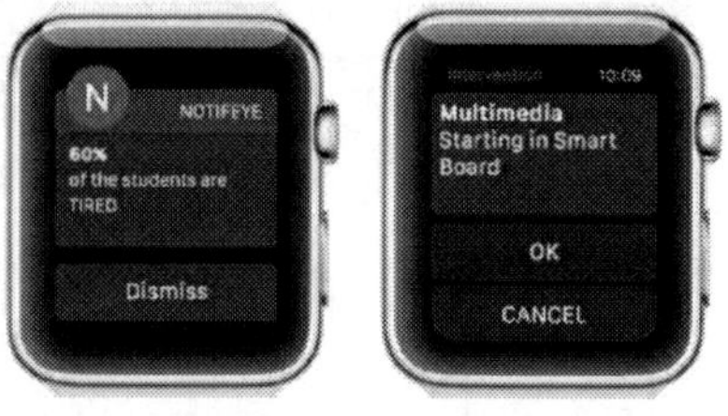

Figure 3. Snapshot of NotifEye.

Furthermore, apart from delivering notifications, the educator's smart watch is used as an input device through which useful information to LECTOR can be communicated. Specifically, when a class-wide intervention is about to start, NotifEye displays a message asking for approval; in case the educator rejects it, LECTOR is notified so as to increase the cancelation percentage of the selected intervention accordingly.

VII. Preliminary Evaluation

An iterative design process was followed throughout the development lifecycle of LECTORviewer and NotifEye. The first phase involved the creation of low fidelity paper prototypes exhibiting the entire functionality of the system. These were initially assessed by three (3) Human Computer Interaction experts during a cognitive walkthrough evaluation experiment in order to uncover any usability errors [6].

In the case of NotifEye, no important problems were identified. On the contrary, the evaluation of LECTORviewer revealed some issues related to the complexity of the most frequently used screens, and secondly to the metaphors used in the design, suggesting their refinement in order to simplify the interaction paradigm used to execute time-critical or common functions expected to occur on a daily basis. Subsequently, an improved vertical high fidelity interactive prototype [32] was created integrating the feedback received and was re-assessed by five (5) UX experts via heuristic evaluation [33] in order to test the overall usability and address any problems before conducting a full-scale user-based evaluation with the target audience (i.e., educators).

The problems identified through that experiment where ranked according to their severity by the evaluators. The severity ratings range from zero ("not a usability problem") to four ("Usability catastrophe") [33][32][31][30][29][33] and are used to indicate how serious each problem is and how important is to fix it. Next, the development team ranked each problem with an ease-of-fix ranking ranging from zero ("would be extremely easy to fix") to three ("would be difficult to fix") to designate the amount of effort needed to address it. This process revealed 16 usability issues out of which 2 were ranked as cosmetic problems only, 7 were identified as minor usability problems, and the remaining 7 were ranked as major issues, hence the most important to fix. Major and minor issues have been prioritized in the list below, with the most severe and hardest to fix problems listed first.

Priority 3

- The extra information that is provided in the list view should also be available in the seating chart view (ease-of-fix 1)
- There should be a summary log for each class, containing diagrams that display how many interventions have been done during a lesson, and the success rate of interventions (ease-of-fix 1)
- It was not clear that the pie chart of attention had filters (ease-of-fix 0)
- The percentages of the pie chart should be immediately visible without having to hover over them (ease-of-fix 0)
- The focus of the main screen should be the students, everything else is of secondary importance. The pie chart and buttons in the upper part of the screen is of secondary importance and should be located elsewhere (ease-of-fix 0)
- There should be a way to see in which mode I am viewing the class: while the lesson is taking place, or not? (ease-of-fix 0)

Priority 2

- There should not be paging in the log for the same day, for each day there should be infinite scrolling (ease-of-fix 1)
- Instead of the label "need revision" the label "uncertain" should be used (ease-of-fix 0)
- In the seating chart layout, there should also be an indication of where the educator's desk is located, for orientation purposes (ease-of-fix 0)
- Current time should be visible somewhere on the interface (ease-of-fix 0)
- The messages displaying the status of a student should be clearer (ease-of-fix 0)
- It is not clear that the orange color represents the state that the educator must revise the system's decision (ease-of-fix 0)
- It is not clear that the STOP hand icon stops an active intervention (ease-of-fix 0)

According to the above list, fixing the identified issues requires minimum effort on behalf of the developers.

VIII. Conclusions and Future Work

This paper has presented the educator-friendly tools LECTORviewer and NotifEye, which aim to assist educators in monitoring and managing the attention-aware intelligent classroom. In particular, LECTORviewer provides an overview of the students' attention levels and asks the educator's opinion on ambiguous behaviors or automatically initiated interventions, while NotifEye aims to bring to her knowledge important events occurring during the lesson time. The heuristic evaluation of LECTORviewer, conducted with UX experts, revealed various usability issues, which will be incorporated in the next version, to be used to conduct a full-scale user-based evaluation of the tool with the targeted end-users (i.e., educators) to fine-tune it before its final release. Similar evaluation experiments are being planned for NotifEye.

Acknowledgment

This work is supported by the FORTH-ICS internal RTD Programme 'Ambient Intelligence and Smart Environments'.

References

[1] C. Moersch, "Levels of technology implementation (LoTi): A framework for measuring classroom technology use," Learn. Lead. Technol., vol. 23, pp. 40–40, 1995.

[2] M. M. Groves and P. C. Zemel, "Instructional technology adoption in higher education: An action research case study," Int. J. Instr. Media, vol. 27, no. 1, p. 57, 2000.

[3] D. C. Niemeyer, Hard facts on smart classroom design: Ideas, guidelines, and layouts. Rowman & Littlefield, 2003.

[4] Y. Baek, J. Jung, and B. Kim, "What makes teachers use technology in the classroom? Exploring the factors affecting facilitation of technology with a Korean sample," Comput. Educ., vol. 50, no. 1, pp. 224–234, 2008.

[5] D. J. Cook, J. C. Augusto, and V. R. Jakkula, "Ambient intelligence: Technologies, applications, and opportunities," Pervasive Mob. Comput., vol. 5, no. 4, pp. 277–298, 2009.

[6] E. Stefanidi, M. Doulgeraki, M. Korozi, A. Leonidis, and M. Antona, "Designing a Teacher-Friendly Editor for Configuring the Attention-Aware Smart Classroom," in International Conference on Human-Computer Interaction, 2016, pp. 266–270.

[7] R. Spicuzza, J. Ysseldyke, A. Lemkuil, S. Kosciolek, C. Boys, and E. Teelucksingh, "Effects of curriculum-based monitoring on classroom instruction and math achievement," J. Sch. Psychol., vol. 39, no. 6, pp. 521–542, 2001.

[8] L. France, J.-M. Heraud, J.-C. Marty, T. Carron, and J. Heili, "Monitoring virtual classroom: Visualization techniques to observe student activities in an e-learning system," in Advanced Learning Technologies, 2006. Sixth International Conference on, 2006, pp. 716–720.

[9] A. Brouwers and W. Tomic, "A longitudinal study of teacher burnout and perceived self-efficacy in classroom management," Teach. Teach. Educ., vol. 16, no. 2, pp. 239–253, 2000.

[10] D. Börner, M. Kalz, and M. Specht, "Lead me gently: Facilitating knowledge gain through attention-aware ambient learning displays," Comput. Educ., vol. 78, pp. 10–19, 2014.

[11] J. Cain, E. P. Black, and J. Rohr, "An audience response system strategy to improve student motivation, attention, and feedback," Am. J. Pharm. Educ., vol. 73, no. 2, p. 21, 2009.

[12] A. B. de Bruin and T. van Gog, Improving self-monitoring and self-regulation: From cognitive psychology to the classroom. Elsevier, 2012.

[13] R. J. Waller, "A review of single-case studies utilizing self-monitoring interventions to reduce problem classroom behaviors," Freeman, vol. 1999, no. 2005, 2008.

[14] I. D. Beatty, "Transforming student learning with classroom communication systems," ArXiv Prepr. Physics0508129, 2005.

[15] J. Cole and H. Foster, Using Moodle: Teaching with the popular open source course management system. O'Reilly Media, Inc., 2007.

[16] M. Loving and M. Ochoa, "Facebook as a classroom management solution," New Libr. World, vol. 112, no. 3/4, pp. 121–130, 2011.

[17] M. Turoff and S. R. Hiltz, "Software design and the future of the virtual classroom®," J. Inf. Technol. Teach. Educ., vol. 4, no. 2, pp. 197–215, 1995.

[18] G. Mathioudakis et al., "Ami-ria: real-time teacher assistance tool for an ambient intelligence classroom," in Proceedings of the Fifth International Conference on Mobile, Hybrid, and On-Line Lerning (eLmL 2013), 2013, pp. 37–42.

[19] Y.-J. Lee, "Empowering teachers to create educational software: A constructivist approach utilizing Etoys, pair programming and cognitive apprenticeship," Comput. Educ., vol. 56, no. 2, pp. 527–538, 2011.

[20] M. Chaouachi and C. Frasson, "Mental workload, engagement and emotions: an exploratory study for intelligent tutoring systems," in Intelligent Tutoring Systems, 2012, pp. 65–71.

[21] K. Brawner and B. Goldberg, "Real-time monitoring of ecg and gsr signals during computer-based training," in Intelligent Tutoring Systems, 2012, pp. 72–77.

[22] J. M. Aldridge, R. C. Laugksch, M. A. Seopa, and B. J. Fraser, " Development and Validation of an Instrument to Monitor the Implementation of Outcomes - based Learning Environments in Science Classrooms in South Africa," Int. J. Sci. Educ., vol. 28, no. 1, pp. 45–70, 2006.

[23] A. C. Strain, R. Azevedo, and S. D'Mello, "Exploring relationships between learners' affective states, metacognitive processes, and learning outcomes," in International Conference on Intelligent Tutoring Systems, 2012, pp. 59–64.

[24] P. Chalfoun and C. Frasson, "Cognitive priming: assessing the use of non-conscious perception to enhance learner's reasoning ability," in International Conference on Intelligent Tutoring Systems, 2012, pp. 84–89.

[25] A. Leonidis et al., "A glimpse into the ambient classroom," Bull. IEEE Tech. Comm. Learn. Technol., vol. 14, no. 4, pp. 3–6, 2012.

[26] [26] C. Stephanidis, A. A. Argyros, D. Grammenos, and X. Zabulis, "Pervasive Computing@ ICS-FORTH," in Workshop Pervasive Computing@ Home, 2008.

[27] C. Savvaki, A. Leonidis, G. Paparoulis, M. Antona, and C. Stephanidis, "Designing a technology–augmented school desk for the future classroom," in International Conference on Human-Computer Interaction, 2013, pp. 681–685.

[28] A. Leonidis, D. Arampatzis, N. Louloudakis, and C. Stephanidis, "The AmI-Solertis System: Creating User Experiences in Smart Environments," in Proceedings of the 13th IEEE International Conference on Wireless and Mobile Computing, Networking and Communications, 2017.

[29] M. Korozi, A. Leonidis, M. Antona, and C. Stephanidis, "LECTOR: Towards Reengaging Students in the Educational Process Inside Smart Classrooms," in International Conference on Intelligent Human Computer Interaction, 2017, pp. 137–149.

[30] U. M. Fayyad, A. Wierse, and G. G. Grinstein, Information visualization in data mining and knowledge discovery. Morgan Kaufmann, 2002.

[31] R. M. Felder and R. Brent, "Understanding student differences," J. Eng. Educ., vol. 94, no. 1, pp. 57–72, 2005.

[32] J. Nielsen, Usability engineering. Elsevier, 1994.

[33] J. Nielsen, Severity Ratings for Usability Problems: Article by Jakob Nielsen. nnGroup, 1995.

Integrating Office 365 Into Your Curriculum:

A Backward Design Professional Learning Course

Katharine McClelland
Instructional Technology and Leadership
Duquesne University
Pittsburgh, PA USA
mcclellandk@duq.edu

***Abstract*—To meet the learning needs of teachers and students, a professional learning course was developed on newly introduced instructional technology, Microsoft Office 365 Suite. This poster presentation shares the development, implementation, and impact of the professional learning course.**

Keywords-professional learning; backward design.

I. Introduction

New for 2015-2016 school year, the West Allegheny School District introduced the Microsoft Office 365 Suite of online tools to both staff and students. Over the summer months, the school's technology specialists dedicated countless hours to switching over each staff member and creating student accounts within the new Office 365 platform. After making the switch, administration recognized a need to provide training on how to best use this instructional technology within the classroom.

II. Design of Course

To meet this need, a professional learning course called *Integrating Office 365 Into Your Curriculum* was developed using the backward design model (see Appendix B for course layout). The course was designed to introduce the learner to each of the tools available through the Office 365 Suite including: Email, Tasks, People, Calendar, OneNote, Class Notebook, OneDrive, Online Word, Excel, & PowerPoint, Video, Sway, and Yammer. All learning objectives and instructional methodologies included as part of the course were aligned to the International Society for Technology Education (ISTE) Standards for Teachers and Danielson's Framework for Teaching. Throughout the course, teachers were required to align their work to the PA or national standards for their content area.

Each session was designed to include not only learning how to use the focus feature, but also best practices for integrating the technology into the curriculum which were discussed in detail during the sessions. Throughout the course the learners were expected to collaborate with colleagues, to increase their exposure and the quality of their lesson designs. As the course progressed, the learning activities were designed to challenge the learner to achieve higher by developing increasingly productive lessons that showed growth in student learning.

The learning was designed to be assessed through formal and informal observations by both administration and peers as well as self-reflection and student feedback. It was the ultimate goal of the course that the learner developed a firm understanding of each of the tools available and how integrating the instructional technologies within their curriculum impacted student learning.

III. Conclusion

This poster presentation will describe the development and implementation of the course, the learning outcomes and activities for each session, and share the testimonials of the teachers as a result of the implementation of the instructional technologies. Additionally, the presenter will provide evidence to support the design of the course linked to research-based best practices including Gagne's Nine Levels of Learning, the backward design model, and the SAMR model. The appendices included at the end of this paper provide a detailed layout of the backward design process followed for the entire course (Appendix A) and each session (Appendix B).

References

[1] C. Danielson, "The framework for teaching evaluation instrument," 2013.

[2] E. R. Hamilton, J. M. Rosenberg, and M. Akcaoglu, "The substitution augmentation modification redefinition (SAMR) model: A critical review and suggestions for its use," TechTrends, 2016, vol. 60, issue 5, pp. 433-441.

[3] International Society for Technology Education, "ISTE standards for teachers," 2008.

[4] C. Pappas, "How to apply Gagné's 9 events of instruction in e-learning," eLearning Industry, 2015.

[5] G. Wiggins, and J. McTighe, "The understanding by design guide to creating high-quality units," 2011, Alexandria, VA: ASCD.

APPENDIX A: PROFESSIONAL LEARNING COURSE PLAN

Stage 1
If the desired result is for the learner to…
Understand… How to use office 365 tools within his/her content area to improve the learning of his/her students. *And thoughtfully consider the question…* How can integrating technology into the curriculum enhance student learning and positively impact achievement? *While considering distinguished practice in the Framework for Teaching (Act 82), particularly the listed areas:* 1a. Demonstrating Knowledge of Content and Pedagogy 1d. Demonstrating Knowledge of Resources 1e. Designing Coherent Instruction 2c. Managing Classroom Procedure 2e. Organizing Physical Space 3c. Engaging Students in Learning 3d. Using Assessment in Instruction 4a. Reflecting on Teaching 4b. Maintaining Accurate Records 4e. Growing and Developing Professionally *And showing mastery in the following ISTE Standards for Teachers:* 1. Facilitate and inspire student learning and creativity 2. Design and develop digital age learning experiences and assessments 3. Model digital age work and learning 4. Promote and model digital citizenship and responsibility 5. Engage in professional growth and leadership *As well as the PA Core Standards and/or national standards that correspond with his/her content area.*

Stage 2
Then evidence is needed of the learner's ability to…
Use each of the office 365 tools in his/her teaching practice within his/her content area. Reflect on his/her teaching practice and identify areas of strength as well as areas for growth. *Then, the tasks to be assessed need to include…* Implementation of office 365 tools within instructional practices. Impact of instructional technology on student learning. Reflection of teaching practice and student learning.
Stage 3
Then, the learning activities need to help the learner…
Understand how to use and integrate each of the office 365 tools in his/her instructional practice. Design quality lessons using one or more of the office tools. Work collaboratively with colleagues to develop lessons that integrate instructional technology. Implement designed lessons then gather student feedback and students' reflection of learning as a result of the lesson. Reflect on implemented lessons and student learning to improve teaching practice.

APPENDIX B: PROFESSIONAL LEARNING LESSON PLANS

Session 1—Introduction of Office 365 Suite with a Focus on Email, Tasks, People, & Calendar	
Stage 1—Desired Results	
Established Goals: The learner will be able to use the email, tasks, people, and calendar features of office 365 for professional responsibilities. The learner will be able to design a lesson focusing on students use of email, tasks, people, and calendar stressing the importance of digital citizenship. The learner will be able to teach the lesson he/she designed focusing on students use of email, tasks, people, and calendar and appropriately assess the learning of his/her students.	
Understandings: The importance of digital citizenship How to use email, tasks, people, and calendar features of Office 365 with students	Essential Questions: How can integrating technology into the curriculum enhance student learning and positively impact achievement?
The learner will know… How to use email, tasks, people, and calendar features.	The learner will be able to… Design a lesson integrating student email, tasks, people, and calendar features of Office 365 focusing on digital citizenship. Teach the lesson he/she developed to his/her students.
Stage 2—Assessment Evidence	
Performance Tasks: Complete the tutorial on how to use email, tasks, people, and calendar features of Office 365. In content area teams, collaboratively design a lesson introducing student email, tasks, people, and calendar features to the students, stressing the importance of digital citizenship. In content area teams, design a lesson aligned to the course curriculum that integrates the use one or more of the newly taught features of Office 365. In content area teams, collaboratively design an assessment on digital citizenship and recently taught features of Office 365.	Other Evidence: Observation (by administration and/or peer) Teacher reflection Student's reflection of learning Student's feedback of lesson Evaluation of student work
Methods of Assessment: Observation throughout professional learning session	

Discussion during professional learning session
Completion of session feedback form
Observation of lesson implementation
Review of teacher reflection, student's reflection of learning, and student's feedback of lesson
Evaluation of student work

Stage 3—Learning Plan

Learning Activities:
The learners will be divided into content area teams for the entire session.
For each feature—email, tasks, people, and calendar—the following will occur:

- The learner will complete the individual interactive tutorial.
- The learner will engage in a small group discussion around the feature, recording highlights of the group's discussion and ideas for integration on chart paper.
- Each small group will share with the large group their thoughts and ideas for integration.

The groups will collaboratively design a lesson introducing students to digital citizenship and the office tools—email, tasks, people, and calendar.
The groups will collaborative design a lesson aligned to the course curriculum that integrates the use one or more of the newly taught technology.
The groups will collaborative design an assessment on digital citizenship and recently taught technology.

Activities to be Completed Outside of Scheduled Sessions:
Reflect on lesson implementation and student learning.
Gather feedback from students on their interpretation of their learning.

Session 2—Using OneNote and Class Notebook

Stage 1—Desired Results

Established Goals:
The learner will be able to use OneNote.
The learner will be able to design a Class Notebook for each course he/she teaches.
The learner will be able to design a lesson that introduces and integrates the Class Notebook into his/her course curriculum.

Understandings:	Essential Questions:
The importance of digital citizenship How to use OneNote How to create a Class Notebook The features of the Class Notebook and how to integrate them into the curriculum	How can integrating technology into the curriculum enhance student learning and positively impact achievement?
The learner will know…	The learner will be able to…
How to use OneNote How to create a Class Notebook for each course he/she teaches. How to effectively use Class Notebook to benefit the learning of his/her students.	Create a Class Notebook for each course he/she teaches. Design a lesson that introduces and integrates Class Notebook into his/her course curriculum. Teach the lesson he/she developed to his/her students.

Stage 2—Assessment Evidence

Performance Tasks:	Other Evidence:
Complete the tutorial on how to use OneNote and Class Notebook. Create a Class Notebook for each course taught. In content area teams, collaboratively design a lesson introducing and integrating Class Notebook into the course curriculum. In content area teams, collaboratively design a student project that requires the use of the collaboration feature of Class Notebook. In content area teams, collaboratively design a rubric for evaluation of the student project.	Observation (by administration and/or peer) Teacher reflection Student's reflection of learning Student's feedback of lesson Evaluation of student work

Methods of Assessment:
Observation throughout professional learning session
Discussion during professional learning session
Completion of session feedback form
Observation of lesson implementation
Review of teacher reflection, student's reflection of learning, and student's feedback of lesson
Evaluation of student work

Stage 3—Learning Plan

Learning Activities:
With a thought partner, the learner will

- complete the individual interactive tutorial on One Note.
- complete the individual interactive tutorial on Class Notebook.
- create a Class Notebook for each course he/she teaches.

In content area groups, the learners will

- collaboratively design a lesson introducing and integrating Class Notebook into the course curriculum.
- collaboratively design a student project that requires the use of the collaboration feature of Class Notebook.
- collaboratively design a rubric for evaluation of the student project.

Activities to be Completed Outside of Scheduled Sessions:
Schedule a time to observe a colleague teaching the collaboratively designed lesson (each learner must observe a minimum of one colleague).
Once all content area team members have completed their observations, meet as a team to discuss the lesson and modify for future use.
Reflect on lesson implementation and student learning.
Gather feedback from students on their interpretation of their learning.

Session 3—Using OneDrive and Online Word, Excel, & PowerPoint

Stage 1—Desired Results

Established Goals:
The learner will be able to use OneDrive and Online Word, Excel, and PowerPoint.
The learner will be able to create a shared folder for each of his/her classes.
The learner will be able to design a lesson that introduces OneDrive and Online Word, Excel, and PowerPoint to his/her students.
The learner will be able to create a lesson that requires students to use either Online Word, Excel, or PowerPoint and submit to the teacher via OneDrive.

Understandings:	Essential Questions:
The importance of digital citizenship	How can integrating technology into the curriculum enhance

How to use OneDrive, Online Word, Excel, and PowerPoint How to create a shared OneDrive folder for each of his/her classes How to integrate OneDrive, Online Word, Excel, and PowerPoint into the course curriculum	student learning and positively impact achievement?
The learner will know… How to use OneDrive. How to create a shared OneDrive folder for each of his/her classes. How to effectively use Online Word, Excel, and PowerPoint within the course curriculum.	The learner will be able to… Create a shared OneDrive folder for each class period he/she teaches. Design a lesson that introduces OneDrive and Online Word, Excel, and PowerPoint to his/her students. Design a lesson requires the students to use Online Word, Excel, or PowerPoint and submit through OneDrive. Teach the lesson he/she developed to his/her students.
Stage 2—Assessment Evidence	
Performance Tasks: Complete the tutorials on how to use OneDrive, Online Word, Online Excel, and Online PowerPoint. Create a OneDrive shared folder for each class. In content area teams, collaboratively design a lesson introducing and integrating OneDrive and Online Word, Excel, and PowerPoint to the students. In content area teams, collaboratively design a student project that requires the use of either Online Word, Excel, or PowerPoint and submission through OneDrive. In content area teams, collaboratively design a rubric for evaluation of the student project.	Other Evidence: Observation (by administration and/or peer) Teacher reflection Student's reflection of learning Student's feedback of lesson Evaluation of student work
Methods of Assessment: Observation throughout professional learning session Discussion during professional learning session Completion of session feedback form Observation of lesson implementation Review of teacher reflection, student's reflection of learning, and student's feedback of lesson Evaluation of student work	
Stage 3—Learning Plan	
Learning Activities: The learners will be divided into content area teams for the entire session. For each feature—OneDrive, Online Word, Online Excel, Online PowerPoint—the following will occur: • The learner will complete the individual interactive tutorial. • The learner will engage in a small group discussion around the feature, recording highlights of the group's discussion and ideas for integration on chart paper. • Each small group will share with the large group their thoughts and ideas for integration. The groups will collaboratively design a lesson introducing students OneDrive and Online Word, Excel, and PowerPoint. The groups will collaboratively design a lesson that requires the students to use either Online Word, Excel, or PowerPoint and submit through OneDrive. The groups will collaboratively design a rubric to evaluate the students project.	
Activities to be Completed Outside of Scheduled Sessions: Schedule a time to observe a colleague teaching the collaboratively designed lesson (each learner must observe a minimum of one colleague). Once all content area team members have completed their observations, meet as a team to discuss the lesson and modify for future use. Reflect on lesson implementation and student learning. Gather feedback from students on their interpretation of their learning.	
Session 4—Using Video	
Stage 1—Desired Results	
Established Goals: The learner will be able to upload, share, and download a video from the Video feature of Office 365. The learner will be able to design a lesson that requires students to view, upload, and/or share a video using the Video feature of Office 365.	
Understandings: The importance of digital citizenship How to use the Video feature of Office 365	Essential Questions: How can integrating technology into the curriculum enhance student learning and positively impact achievement?
The learner will know… How to use the Video feature of Office 365.	The learner will be able to… Upload, share, and download a video from the Video feature of Office 365. Design a lesson that requires students to view, upload, and/or share a video using the Video feature of Office 365.
Stage 2—Assessment Evidence	
Performance Tasks: Complete the tutorial on how to use Video. With a thought partner, design a lesson introducing the Video feature to your students. With a thought partner, design a lesson that requires students to view, upload, and/or share a video using the Video feature of Office 365. With a thought partner, collaboratively design a rubric for evaluation of the lesson.	Other Evidence: Observation (by administration and/or peer) Teacher reflection Student's reflection of learning Student's feedback of lesson Evaluation of student work
Methods of Assessment: Observation throughout professional learning session Discussion during professional learning session Completion of session feedback form Observation of lesson implementation	

Review of teacher reflection, student's reflection of learning, and student's feedback of lesson
Evaluation of student work

Stage 3—Learning Plan

Learning Activities:
With a thought partner, the learner will
- complete the individual interactive tutorial on Video.
- design a lesson introducing the Video feature to your students.
- design a lesson that requires students to view, upload, and/or share a video using the Video feature of Office 365.
- design a rubric for evaluation of the lesson.

Activities to be Completed Outside of Scheduled Sessions:
Reflect on lesson implementation and student learning.
Gather feedback from students on their interpretation of their learning.

Session 5—Using Sway

Stage 1—Desired Results

Established Goals:
The learner will be able to create a presentation using Sway.
The learner will be able to design a lesson introducing and integrating Sway to his/her students.

Understandings: The importance of digital citizenship How to use Sway	Essential Questions: How can integrating technology into the curriculum enhance student learning and positively impact achievement?
The learner will know… How to use Sway	The learner will be able to… Create a presentation using Sway. Design a lesson that introduces and integrates Sway into the curriculum.

Stage 2—Assessment Evidence

Performance Tasks: Complete the tutorial on how to use Sway. With a thought partner, design a lesson using Sway introducing the Sway to the students. With a thought partner, design a lesson that requires students to use Sway to complete a project. With a thought partner, design a rubric to evaluate the student project.	Other Evidence: Observation (by administration and/or peer) Teacher reflection Student's reflection of learning Student's feedback of lesson Evaluation of student work

Methods of Assessment:
Observation throughout professional learning session
Discussion during professional learning session
Completion of session feedback form
Observation of lesson implementation
Review of teacher reflection, student's reflection of learning, and student's feedback of lesson
Evaluation of student work

Stage 3—Learning Plan

Learning Activities:
With a thought partner, the learner will
- complete the individual interactive tutorial on Sway.
- design a lesson using Sway introducing the Sway to the students.
- design a lesson that requires students to use Sway to complete a project.
- design a rubric to evaluate the student project.

Activities to be Completed Outside of Scheduled Sessions:
Schedule a time to observe a colleague teaching the collaboratively designed lesson (each learner must observe a minimum of one colleague).
Once all content area team members have completed their observations, meet as a team to discuss the lesson and modify for future use.
Reflect on lesson implementation and student learning.
Gather feedback from students on their interpretation of their learning.

Session 6—Using Yammer

Stage 1—Desired Results

Established Goals:
The learner will understand the features of Yammer and how they can benefit his/her students learning.
The learner will be able to design a lesson introducing and integrating Yammer into his/her curriculum.

Understandings: The importance of digital citizenship How to use Yammer with students	Essential Questions: How can integrating technology into the curriculum enhance student learning and positively impact achievement?
The learner will know… How to use Yammer	The learner will be able to… Create a Yammer group for each course he/she teaches and any extra curricular activity he/she supervises. Design a lesson that introduces and integrates Yammer into the curriculum.

Stage 2—Assessment Evidence

Performance Tasks: Complete the tutorial on how to use Yammer. Create a Yammer group for each course and extra curriculum activity you are responsible for. Design a lesson that introduces and integrates Yammer into the curriculum.	Other Evidence: Observation (by administration and/or peer) Teacher reflection Student's reflection of learning Student's feedback of lesson Evaluation of student work

Methods of Assessment:
Observation throughout professional learning session
Discussion during professional learning session
Completion of session feedback form
Observation of lesson implementation
Review of teacher reflection, student's reflection of learning, and student's feedback of lesson
Evaluation of student work

Stage 3—Learning Plan

Learning Activities:
Complete the tutorial on how to use Yammer.
Create a private Yammer group for each course and extra curricular activity you are responsible for and invite your students.

As a content area team, create a private Yammer and assure all team members are members of the Yammer group.
Join at least one other group on Yammer (private or public).
Design a lesson that introduces and integrates Yammer into the curriculum.
Design a lesson that requires students to use Yammer as a collaboration tool for a project.
Design a rubric for evaluation of the project.
Complete the evaluation of this session via the Yammer poll found under the *Best Teaching Practices Using Office 365* group.

Activities to be Completed Outside of Scheduled Sessions:
Schedule a time to observe a colleague teaching the collaboratively designed lesson (each learner must observe a minimum of one colleague).
Once all content area team members have completed their observations, meet as a team to discuss the lesson and modify for future use.
Reflect on lesson implementation and student learning.
Gather feedback from students on their interpretation of their learning.

Session 7—Integrating Multiple Office 365 tools

Stage 1—Desired Results

Established Goals:
The learner will be able to design and implement a lesson or unit that incorporates multiple office 365 technologies.

ISTE Standards
1. Facilitate and inspire student learning and creativity
2. Design and develop digital age learning experiences and assessments
3. Model digital age work and learning
4. Promote and model digital citizenship and responsibility
5. Engage in professional growth and leadership

Framework for Teaching Components
1a. Demonstrating Knowledge of Content and Pedagogy
1d. Demonstrating Knowledge of Resources
1e. Designing Coherent Instruction
2c. Managing Classroom Procedure
2e. Organizing Physical Space
3c. Engaging Students in Learning
3d. Using Assessment in Instruction
4a. Reflecting on Teaching
4b. Maintaining Accurate Records
4e. Growing and Developing Professionally

Understandings:	Essential Questions:
The importance of digital citizenship How to use Email, Tasks, People, Calendar, OneNote, Class Notebook, OneDrive, Online Word, Excel, & PowerPoint, Video, Sway, Yammer, Delve, and Newsfeed	How can integrating technology into the curriculum enhance student learning and positively impact achievement?
The learner will know…	**The learner will be able to…**
How to effectively use more than one office tool to enhance the learning of his/her students.	Design a lesson that integrates multiple features of Office 365. Design a rubric to evaluate the lesson.

Stage 2—Assessment Evidence

Performance Tasks:	Other Evidence:
In content area teams, collaboratively design a lesson that integrates multiple office 365 tools. In content area teams, collaboratively design a rubric to evaluate the lesson.	Observation (by administration and/or peer) Teacher reflection Student's reflection of learning Student's feedback of lesson Evaluation of student work

Methods of Assessment:
Observation throughout professional learning session
Discussion during professional learning session
Completion of session feedback form
Observation of lesson implementation
Review of teacher reflection, student's reflection of learning, and student's feedback of lesson
Evaluation of student work

Stage 3—Learning Plan

Learning Activities:
In content area groups, the learners will
- collaboratively design a lesson that integrates multiple office 365 tools.
- collaboratively design a rubric for evaluation of the lesson.

Each content area group will share their lesson design with the entire group. The rest of the group will provide feedback and suggestions.
All members of the groups will individually complete the feedback form for the course.

Activities to be Completed Outside of Scheduled Sessions:
Schedule a time to observe a colleague teaching the collaboratively designed lesson (each learner must observe a minimum of one colleague).
Once all content area team members have completed their observations, meet as a team to discuss the lesson and modify for future use.
Reflect on lesson implementation and student learning.
Gather feedback from students on their interpretation of their learning.

Applying Mixed Reality Techniques for the Visualization of Programs and Algorithms in a Programming Learning Environment

Santiago Sánchez, María Ángeles García, María del Carmen Lacave, Ana Isabel Molina,
Carlos González, David Vallejo, Miguel Ángel Redondo
Universidad de Castilla-La Mancha
Paseo de la Universidad, 4, 13071 Ciudad Real (Spain)
Email: {Santiago.Sanchez, MariaAngeles.GMarin, Carmen.Lacave, AnaIsabel.Molina,
Carlos.Gonzalez, David.Vallejo, Miguel.Redondo}@uclm.es

***Abstract*—Program and algorithm visualization has been a research topic for more than 25 years. Correct graphical representations have a demonstrated impact on how students understand programming concepts. Previous works on visualization tools based on trees and graphs representations tend to be too difficult for teachers to use them in their classrooms and for students to understand how they work. Moreover, new mixed reality learning environments can improve this learning experience thanks to the latest technology on the market. This paper discusses a whole new set of graphical representations used to visualize programs and algorithms through augmented reality devices. It also presents these visualizations integrated into the architecture of a newly mixed reality programming learning feature for the COLLECE 2.0 Eclipse plugin, a collaborative and distributed environment for programming learning. This new approach is expected to improve students' learning experience in introductory programming courses.**

Keywords-Program visualization; algorithm visualization; augmented reality; programming learning; eclipse.

I. INTRODUCTION

Programming learning through graphical representations is a field in which researchers have been working for more than 25 years. The main purpose of these works is to reduce the level of abstraction that programming requires to facilitate its understanding [1], fulfilling the objectives of level 2 of Bloom's taxonomy [2]. Researchers have proven that the cognitive capacities of the human being are optimized to process information in a multimodal way (i.e., visual, tactile, and aural). Nevertheless, computer programs are usually presented in a textual way (one dimension), wasting all the power of our brain [3].

On the other hand, teachers' difficulties to create these graphic representations prevent the results of these works from becoming popular in classrooms [4].

However, in recent years, this work has been intensified and redirected, due to the rise of hardware devices and technological advances that allow much more expressive representations. In this sense, the integration of immersive technologies into programming learning tools can contribute to improve learning results.

The use of these emerging technologies enables a multimodal interaction-based process, which facilitate active learning. Among the different devices that offer this kind of interaction, it is worth highlighting those that integrate mixed reality capabilities. These provide a natural learning environment where the student's actions in the physical world influence the virtual one. Mixed reality glasses Microsoft HoloLens hold a dominant position on the market as a device capable of mixing the physical and virtual worlds, covering most of the continuum of virtuality defined by Milgram and Kishino from augmented reality to augmented virtuality [5], but especially focused on the first one. Thus, it is possible to expand the capabilities of traditional programming learning systems. To do that, new graphic representation techniques and new architectures that enable their manipulation need to be defined.

In this context, the work discussed in this article emerges, encompassed within a more ambitious scenario whose final objective consists in building a new generation of programming learning tools based on interactive technologies [6].

The contribution described in this article represents an approximation for the graphical representation of programs and algorithms through mixed reality, as well as a potential architecture to support it. As a practical application, this approach is integrated into COLLECE 2.0, a collaborative and distributed environment for programming learning through problem solving, which is based on the Eclipse platform [7], currently available for download at http://blog.uclm.es/grupochico/proyecto-iapro/collece-2-0/.

This article shows the proposed architecture as a complete environment oriented to programming learning, highlighting the new visualization capabilities of programs and algorithms. The rest of the paper is organized as follows. In Section 2, some similar solutions are presented, as well as previous works on which this work is based. Then, Section 3 focuses on the proposal of this work and the system architecture. Section 4 discusses the different tests performed to obtain the set of final visualizations. Finally, Section 5 draws some final conclusions and suggests possible lines of future work.

II. RELATED WORK

Works on visualization of programs and algorithms are very varied and provide results both for and against the effectiveness of their use in the educational context. Within the first group, in [8], it was made an evaluation of the extrinsic and intrinsic motivation of the students, resulting that these motivations increase when using visualizations of programs and algorithms in the classroom. In [9], it was proposed the resolution of the problem of the knapsack through a textual animation, in which the students had to identify the problem that was finally implemented, obtaining very satisfactory results. In another work [10], the Alice tool was used to teach how to solve recursive problems through 3D visualizations that represent lines of code. Although the students did not successfully solve the problems, they demonstrated certain facilities to deal with them. Similar results were obtained in [11], where the use of the Jeliot tool improved the students' understanding of control structures and loops. In [12], some experiences were made trying to discover why it is so difficult for students to understand recursive programming; they concluded that using visualization tools to display the trace of the program helps them understand how the programs work and how to solve the exercises better.

Among the works that reflect their skepticism about the effectiveness of visualizations in programming learning, the following are noticeable. In [1], it was shown that the algorithm visualization technology is educationally effective depending on how it is used, rather than on the quality of the visualizations. In [13], it was studied the effectiveness of teaching from the teacher's point of view and learning from the student's point of view. In the first case, it was concluded that the teacher must put too much effort in contrast to what these visualizations actually provide, while in the second case no substantial benefits were achieved. In this work it is concluded that for the visualizations to be pedagogically useful, they must support students' interaction and promote active learning, as stated in [4] and [14]. In this sense, the works of [15] and [16] come together through the idea that the teaching community is quite reluctant to incorporate visualization tools, due to the costs of installation, learning, creation, and maintenance that they imply, as well as the fear of losing control of the classes while the applications are used.

However, there are several tools that try to alleviate these disadvantages, which have been analyzed considering the taxonomy defined by Myers [3], which classifies the visualization of programs according to the information to be rendered (i.e., code, data, or algorithm) and to its nature: dynamic or static. SRec [17] is able to dynamically visualize the trace of recursive algorithms; those studied in [15], for functional programming (Kiel and WinHIPE) and object-oriented programming (BlueJ and Jeliot); JAVENGA [18], used in the visualization of network and graph algorithms; Visual LinProg [19], to visualize algorithms of linear problems; VISBACK [20], for dynamic visualization of recursive backtracking algorithms using trees; ALGOLIPSE [21], to visually represent the execution of algorithms on data structures and recursive algorithms; among others.

All the analyzed applications are framed in traditional interaction systems. Regarding the use of mixed reality techniques for teaching in the classroom, several experiments have been conducted, and, although they are not directly related to the visualization of programs and algorithms, it demonstrates the advantages they offer. Thus, in [22], a mixed reality environment, SMALLab, was created, aimed at primary and secondary school students, which allowed students to express themselves using their own bodies and improving the learning process. In [23], objects of the physical world replicated in a virtual world (i.e., cross-reality objects [24]) were used so that students could remotely work in a digital laboratory; the evaluation performed with the students positively demonstrated the use of this technology [25]. On the other hand, in [26], a system of cameras, projectors, and Cuisenaire rods (wooden sticks with different measures) was used to satisfactorily teach mathematical concepts to children. Some more related experiments with programming were conducted in [27], where a set of augmented reality physical markers were used to answer different programming questions, visualizing different 3D models related to the questions. The students enjoyed the activities and the work concluded that there was an increase in their motivation to learn programming concepts, but not so much to understand them, since more tests had to be done. Finally, a systematic literature review on the topic is conducted in [28], where the authors draw some conclusions related to the advantages of using augmented reality in education, such as learning gains, motivation, interaction and collaboration, and its main purpose, related to explain a topic of interest as well as providing additional information.

As a final remark in this section, it is important to highlight that the work described in this article is based on COLLECE [29], a groupware tool where multiple users can work collaboratively, thanks to a turn-based approach, in a shared source file written in Java. A series of improvements were made on this tool that resulted in COLLECE 2.0 [7], a complete programming learning environment, based on Eclipse, with collaboration capabilities oriented to real-time project editing, version control, communication, and other awareness-related elements. This environment has been extended with techniques of mixed reality, although without including techniques of improved visualization of programs and algorithms.

III. ARCHITECTURE

The architecture of the proposal presented in this paper is based on the Eclipse development environment. This platform is used by most of the students who learn programming, mainly because of the facilities it offers. It features native support for the Java programming language, syntax autocompletion, project management, program compilation and execution tools, and extensibility capabilities through plugins. This system of plugins enables us to build complete applications that directly benefit from the possibilities offered by Eclipse. Thanks to this feature, and taking advantage of the familiarity of the students with Eclipse, the COLLECE 2.0 programming learning environment was built as a modular Eclipse plugin [30].

COLLECE 2.0 is proposed as a development environment that serves first-year undergraduate students in Computer Science to learn the basics of programming by solving problems, such as those studied in introductory programming courses (e.g., CS101). For this, the environment offers different mechanisms that facilitate learning and collaborative work among students, highlighting project-oriented work sessions, multi-user editing of source code in real time, tele-pointers, blocking of code regions, communication through chat, and statement of the problem to be solved, among others. Regarding the implementation, as stated before, it is based on Eclipse plugin, whose architecture relies on a set of modules that are responsible for different tasks, such as synchronization between users, which follows a client-server network model where a central server takes control and maintains session synchronization among the rest of the clients that connect to it. A server can manage different work sessions at the same time. These work sessions maintain the global context between the connected clients and the server, that is, the data of the users, the status of the associated projects, and the information related to the server itself. All this information and the related interactions are presented to the user through different views developed using the set of Eclipse SWT widgets.

One of the features implemented in COLLECE 2.0 is the capability to visualize programs and algorithms through an external augmented reality device that facilitates the interaction with the system. The device, introduced in Section 1, facilitates the reconstruction of the physical space, identifying typical elements of the environment, such as the floor, walls, tables, and chairs. Thanks to this, we can precisely indicate the position of the physical world where the program or algorithm is required to be visualized, in addition to sharing the visualization with another user who also uses the device simultaneously, or interacting with the visualization through gestures and voice recognition. This interaction allows the user to perform tasks, such as examining the value of the variables, advancing backward or forward in the execution of the algorithm, as if it were a debugger, or discovering certain characteristics of the program when the user physically approaches the visualization, among others.

The integration of the augmented reality device with the environment is done through a new Eclipse plugin that works together with COLLECE 2.0. This new plugin is responsible for performing an analysis of the program to be viewed to extract the relevant information, in addition to establishing and maintaining a network connection between the device and the system to exchange information related to the user's own visualization and physical context.

IV. Definition of Visual Representations

The methodology used to provide COLLECE 2.0 with the representations used during the visualization of algorithms and programs has gone through an exhaustive process of refinement, thanks to the collaboration of several experts, teachers, and students, who have contributed different ideas by conducting surveys. The participants answered several questions, which are now listed:

- How would you graphically represent a condition statement: IF … THEN … ELSE …?
- How would you graphically represent a selection statement: SWITCH … CASE …?
- How would you graphically represent the execution of a loop?
- How would you graphically represent the definition of a function?
- How would you graphically represent the return value of a function?
- How would you graphically represent the evaluation of an expression?

The results obtained were very varied, although most of the participants agreed on the use of flow diagrams to make the representations. Those that did not, contributed certain designs related to boxes (expressions), spirals (loops), telephones (function definitions), and branches (control sentences). From the study of these designs, a representation based on roads was extracted (see Figure 1), sufficiently abstract and scalable to represent any type of program.

This set of roads and traffic signs enables the visualization of the program execution flow in a natural way for the user, since he/she is familiar with them in his/her daily life. The fact that students are familiar with roads and signs facilitates the use of these metaphors to help them understand programs and algorithms through their static representation.

Using this metaphor, a modular set of blocks have been designed to construct the visual representations. These representations are explained below by referencing them numerically according to Figure 1.

The representation associated with the condition statements, IF ... THEN ... ELSE (1), shows a fork with two branches in which the left branch supposes the execution when the condition to be evaluated is fulfilled (THEN), while the right branch involves the execution when this condition is not (ELSE).

As in the previous representation, the selection sentences, SWITCH ... CASE ... (2), use a fork, but this time with three branches. However, in this case, the central branch which represents the selected case during the evaluation of the expression is exclusively used, leaving the other two as merely symbolic branches. This has been decided in order to

Figure 1. Set of visual representations: (1) condition statement IF … THEN … ELSE …, (2) selection statement SWITCH … CASE …, (3) loop execution, (4) function definition, (5) function return value, (6) expression evaluation.

improve the scalability of the visualization process if the number of cases of the sentence increases disproportionately.

The proposed representations for the loops (3) are based on the metaphor of roundabouts, where a vehicle can travel indefinitely and cyclically. However, the concept has undergone certain modifications to improve scalability (e.g., to support nested sentences), making exhaustive use of the different lanes of the road. Conceptually, the visualization is interpreted through a vehicle (which would represent the step-by-step execution of the program) that would reach the roundabout in the north where the condition of the loop would be evaluated. If this condition is fulfilled, the vehicle would execute the iteration of the loop taking the second exit of the roundabout. Once the iteration has been completed, the vehicle would reach the roundabout in the south, where the condition would be evaluated again. In case this time the condition was not fulfilled, the vehicle would leave the loop taking the third exit of the roundabout.

Regarding function definitions (4), their representation is conceptually based on the traffic signal of exit to city from highway, indicating the beginning of a function, which will be followed by another set of representations indicating the body of the function and, finally, its return sentence. This representation shows information about the type of data that the function returns, the input arguments, and the name of the function itself.

Function returns (5) are represented as a traffic signal that mimics the one existing in real life and that denotes end of city. This representation shows the name of the function from which it is returning and the variable whose value is returned.

Finally, the evaluation of expressions (6), such as, for example, the assignments to variables or the invocations to functions, are represented as a box that contains the expression that will be executed. These boxes are located on the roads, representing the position where they would be in the program.

The representations discussed here are used to display the program statically in order to provide an overview of its structure. The system makes a direct association between certain sentences of the language and their corresponding representation. The set of sentences to be visualized is rich enough to represent any program with them. However, no distinction is made between the types of loops, such as the classics "for", "while" and "do ... while", and their different variants, but all of them are encompassed in a single representation, thus abstracting the user from the language implementation details.

These representations have been evaluated through a pilot test with a small sample of student. Two questions have been presented for the students after they have worked with the representations:

- Q1: I think the proposed notation can be motivating for those who are learning to program.
- Q2: I like the proposed representation to model algorithms.

These preliminary obtained results showed a positive feedback from the students, who found the representations useful and easy to understand. However, in depth evaluations have to be conducted in order to better analysis of the results.

V. Example of Applying Representations

To test the set of representations, a visualization of a function was made. The code for that function is showed in Figure 2, which checks whether the numbers in a list are even, and in that case, increases them by one unit; otherwise, it decrements them. This function is visualized through a graphical representation in Figure 3.

```
public static int [] changeNums(int [] nums) {
   for (int i = 0; i < nums.length; i++) {
      if (nums[i] % 2 == 0) {
         nums[i]++;
      }
      else {
         nums[i]--;
      }
   }
   return nums;
}
```

Figure 2. Sample code listing for further program visualization.

Thanks to the rendered visualization, a user can quickly identify the elements of the program. In this case, the visualization includes the definition of a function ("changeNums") that includes a loop with a condition statement and its two possible branches. Finally, it shows

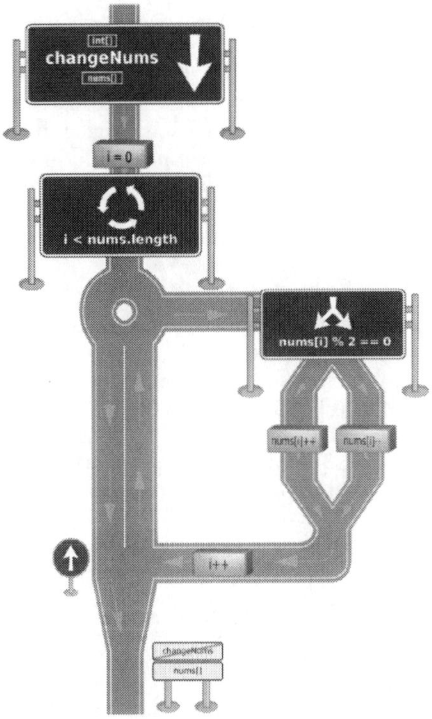

Figure 3. Visual representation of a function definition.

Figure 4. 3D visual representation of the Bubblesort algorithm seen through an augmented reality device.

how the definition of the function ends and the variable that returns ("nums").

Thanks to the representations generated in the physical space and visualized through the augmented reality device, Figure 4 graphically shows the Bubblesort algorithm displayed on a table, as seen by a user of the system. This visualization includes 3D elements associated to each of the 2D representations that have been introduced in the previous section. We can identify the definition of a function with two loops, one of them nested within the other, which also contains a one-branch condition statement.

VI. Conclusion and Future Work

The visualizations discussed in this paper are static representations that need to be rigorously evaluated before obtaining any conclusion regarding their effectiveness. However, its flexibility and scalability to represent programs and algorithms is highlighted as shown in the representation of the algorithms proposed in this paper, involving an advance over other algorithm representation tools, such as those mentioned in Section 2.

The next step will be composing a selection of relevant algorithms with these representations to evaluate their effectiveness with undergraduate students in the first courses of introduction to programming.

In these experiments, the effectiveness of the representations to visualize programs and algorithms will be evaluated, both subjectively and objectively (through eye-tracking techniques).

Acknowledgment

This research has been funded by the Ministry of Economy, Industry and Competitiveness, and the European Regional Development Fund through the project TIN2015-66731-C2-2-R.

References

[1] C. D. Hundhausen, S. A. Douglas, and J. T. Stasko, "A meta-study of algorithm visualization effectiveness," *Journal of Visual Languages & Computing*, vol. 13, pp. 259-290, 2002.

[2] B. S. Bloom, "Taxonomy of educational objectives. Vol. 1: Cognitive domain," *New York: McKay*, pp. 20-24, 1956.

[3] B. A. Myers, "Taxonomies of visual programming and program visualization," *Journal of Visual Languages & Computing*, vol. 1, pp. 97-123, 1990.

[4] G. Törley, *Algorithm visualization in programming education* vol. 4, pp. 68-80, 2009.

[5] P. Milgram and F. Kishino, "A taxonomy of mixed reality visual displays," *IEICE TRANSACTIONS on Information and Systems*, vol. 77, pp. 1321-1329, 1994.

[6] M. Ortega *et al.*, "iProg: development of immersive systems for the learning of programming," *Proceedings of the XVIII International Conference on Human Computer Interaction*, Cancun, Mexico, 2017, pp. 1-6.

[7] S. Sánchez, M. A. Redondo, D. Vallejo, C. González, and C. Bravo, "COLLECE 2.0: A distributed real-time collaborative programming environment for the Eclipse platform," *Proceedings of the International Conference Interfaces and Human Computer Interaction 2017*, Lisbon, Portugal, 2017, pp. 136-142.

[8] J. Á. Velázquez-Iturbide, I. Hernán-Losada, and M. Paredes-Velasco, "Evaluating the Effect of Program Visualization on

Student Motivation," *IEEE Transactions on Education*, vol. 60, pp. 238-245, 2017.

[9] C. Kann, R. W. Lindeman, and R. Heller, "Integrating algorithm animation into a learning environment," *Computers & Education*, vol. 28, pp. 223-228, 1997.

[10] W. Dann, S. Cooper, and R. Pausch, "Using visualization to teach novices recursion," *ACM SIGCSE Bulletin*, vol. 33, pp. 109-112, 2001.

[11] R. B.-B. Levy, M. Ben-Ari, and P. A. Uronen, "The Jeliot 2000 program animation system," *Computers & Education*, vol. 40, pp. 1-15, 2003.

[12] C. Lacave, A. I. Molina, and J. Giralt, "Identificando algunas causas del fracaso en el aprendizaje de la recursividad: Análisis experimental en las asignaturas de programación," *Jornadas de Enseñanza Universitaria de la Informática (19es: 2013: Castelló de la Plana)*, Castellón de la Plana, Spain, 2013, pp. 225-232.

[13] T. L. Naps, G. Rößling, V. Almstrum, W. Dann, R. Fleischer, C. Hundhausen, et al., "Exploring the role of visualization and engagement in computer science education," *ACM SIGCSE Bulletin*, pp. 131-152, 2002.

[14] L. Fernández and J. Á. Velázquez, "Estudio sobre la visualización de las técnicas de diseño de algoritmos," *Proceedings of the VII Congreso Internacional de Interacción Persona-Ordenador*, pp. 315-324, 2007.

[15] A. Pérez Carrasco, "Sistema Generador de Animaciones Interactivas para la Docencia de Algoritmos Recursivos," Ph.D. Dissertation, Universidad Rey Juan Carlos, Spain, 2011.

[16] J. Urquiza Fuentes, "Generación semiautomática de animaciones de programas funcionales con fines educativos," Ph.D. dissertation, Universidad Rey Juan Carlos, Spain, 2008.

[17] L. Fernández-Muñoz, A. Pérez-Carrasco, J. Á. Velázquez-Iturbide, and J. Urquiza-Fuentes, "A framework for the automatic generation of algorithm animations based on design techniques," *Proceedings of the European Conference on Technology Enhanced Learning*, pp. 475-480, 2007.

[18] T. Baloukas, "JAVENGA: JAva-based Visualization Environment for Network and Graph Algorithms," *Computer Applications in Engineering Education*, vol. 20, pp. 255-268, 2012.

[19] V. Lazaridis, N. Samaras, and A. Sifaleras, "An empirical study on factors influencing the effectiveness of algorithm visualization," *Computer Applications in Engineering Education*, vol. 21, pp. 410-420, 2013.

[20] J. F. Pérez Mena, "VisBack Herramienta para la visualización de algoritmos de backtracking," B.S. Thesis, Universidad de Castilla-La Mancha, Spain, 2015.

[21] L. A. Fava, M. A. Schiavoni, J. Rosso, A. C. Falcone, and L. Ronconi, "ALGOLIPSE: una herramienta educativa para mejorar la comprensión de algoritmos y estructuras de datos," *Proceedings of the XXII Congreso Argentino de Ciencias de la Computación (CACIC 2016)*, 2016, pp. 1280-1290.

[22] S. Hatton, D. Birchfield, and M. Colleen, "Learning metaphor through mixed-reality game design and game play," *Proceedings of Sandbox 2008: An ACM SIGGRAPH Videogame Symposium, Sandbox'08*, pp. 67-74, 2008.

[23] A. Peña-Ríos, V. Callaghan, M. Gardner, and M. J. Alhaddad, "Remote mixed reality collaborative laboratory activities: Learning activities within the InterReality portal," *Proceedings of the 2012 IEEE/WIC/ACM International Conference on Web Intelligence and Intelligent Agent Technology Workshops, WI-IAT 2012*, pp. 362-366, 2012.

[24] J. A. Paradiso and J. A. Landay, "Cross-reality environments," *IEEE Pervasive Computing*, vol. 8, pp. 14-15, 2009.

[25] P. Rios, C. Anasol, V. Callaghan, M. Gardner, and M. J. Alhaddad, "Experiments with collaborative blended-reality laboratory technology for distance learners," *Proceedings of The Immersive Learning Research Network Conference*, 2015.

[26] S. Marichal, A. Rosales, F. G. Perilli, A. C. Pires, E. Bakala, G. Sansone, *et al.*, "CETA: Designing mixed-reality tangible interaction to enhance mathematical learning," *Proceedings of the 19th International Conference on Human-Computer Interaction with Mobile Devices and Services, MobileHCI 2017*, 2017, pp. 1-13.

[27] N. Salazar Mesía, G. Gorga, and C. V. Sanz, "EPRA: Herramienta para la Enseñanza de conceptos básicos de programación utilizando realidad aumentada," *X Congreso sobre Tecnología en Educación & Educación en Tecnología (TE & ET)*, Corrientes, Argentina, 2015, pp. 426-435.

[28] J. Bacca, S. Baldiris, R. Fabregat, S. Graf, and Kinshuk, "Augmented reality trends in education: A systematic review of research and applications," *Educational Technology and Society*, vol. 17, pp. 133-149, 2014.

[29] C. Bravo, R. Duque, and J. Gallardo, "A groupware system to support collaborative programming: Design and experiences," *Journal of Systems and Software*, vol. 86, pp. 1759-1771, 2013.

[30] S. Sánchez, M. Á. García, C. Bravo, and M. Á. Redondo, "Sistema COLLECE mejorado para soportar aprendizaje colaborativo de la programación en tiempo real sobre Eclipse," *IE Comunicaciones*, vol. 26, pp. 73-82, 2017.

Developing, Understanding and Evaluating Augmented Reality Framework for Universities in Saudi Arabia

Muteeb Saad Alahmari
Curtin Business School
School of Information Systems
Perth, Australia
M.alahmari4@postgrad.curtin.edu.au

Abstract— Technology has introduced new tools such as Augmented Reality (AR), the application of which may improve learning outcomes. AR is the integration of digital information with the user environment in real time. Despite the fact that technologies have been implemented in Saudi Arabia's education sector, several issues exist that are associated with the traditional methods of teaching and learning i.e. students' lack of motivation concerning independent learning, collaborative learning, and skills-acquisition, which are a part of the current pedagogy. To resolve the problems associated with traditional teaching and learning methods, the Augmented Reality approach will be examined and assessed in Saudi Arabia's higher education sector, through the development of a new AR model. This research aims to develop, understand and evaluate the AR framework in order to determine the factors (e.g., willingness, perception, motivation, and acceptance) that will have the most influence on AR adoption especially regarding students' learning outcomes in Saudi Arabia. A set of recommendations will be suggested for the adoption of AR in Saudi Arabia's higher education sector. This study will employ a mixed-methods research design (Explanatory Sequential Design), whereby the data will be collected using both quantitative (online survey) and qualitative methods (semi-structured interviews).

Keywords-Augmented Reality; Higher Education; Saudi University; Integration.

I. INTRODUCTION

Schuemie [4] described Human-Computer Interaction (HCI) as a discipline that is concerned with designing, evaluating and implementing interactive computing systems for the use of individuals. User experiences such as satisfaction, motivation, attention, and emotion are essential in HCI to improve the efficiency of these technologies. The effectiveness of new technologies, such as Augmented Reality, has inspired the higher education sector to utilize them for teaching and learning [5]. In the area of learning, the increased learning demands and enhanced learning outcomes have given rise to many issues in university curricula. Consequently, it has now become more challenging to adhere to traditional methods of teaching and learning. Hence, with the increased role of computers in day-to-day activities, it is expected that several computer systems will be integrated into the learning environment. Technological innovations such as AR and Virtual Reality (VR) have a potential use in education. Integrating AR technology into the classroom needs to be evaluated in order to determine its effectiveness for learners. AR technology has become a well-known research topic, and has been widely explored and used in many settings including training and education. Thus, in this study, AR will be examined and assessed in the context of Saudi Arabia's higher education sector, through the development of a new model of AR.

This paper has been organized according to the following sections. In Section II, AR and VR are discussed and compared. Section III explains AR technology. Section IV reviews the extant literature on the use and effectiveness of AR in education. This is followed in Section V by a detailed description of the Saudi education system. The research methods and research question are presented in Section VI. In Section VII, an initial AR framework and the research outcomes are identified based on the literature review. Section VIII discusses future work and concludes the paper.

II. VR AND AR

VR is defined by McLellan [6] as "a class of computer-controlled multisensory communication technologies that allow more intuitive interactions with data and involve human senses in new ways." (p.461). McGlashan and Axling [7] elucidated that VR is a graphical two- or three-dimensional interface that enables the communication between the user and computer, while AR is the next step after VR. Azuma et al. [8] defined AR as a system that enhances the real world with artificial objects by means of computer-generated sensory input such as graphics, video sound, or a Global Positioning System (GPS) data. Azuma [9] identified three advantages of an AR system: it mixes real and virtual; it is interactive in the real world; and it registers in 3-D.

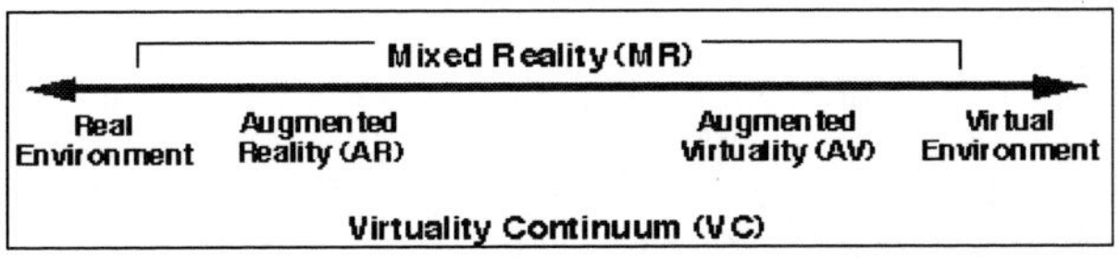

Figure 1. Simplified representation of a "virtuality continuum" [3]

Total immersion is provided in the VR environment while AR integrates the information in the user's existing view. Figure 1 depicts Milgram and Kishino's [3] representation of the real world and virtual world objects combined in a simple display.

In order to process the scene, the VR system presents an entirely artificial environment; whereas, AR processes the information from different resources and superimposes it onto the users' environment [5]. Nevertheless, Di Serio et al. [10] reported that involvement, navigation, and interaction are features that AR and VR have in common.

III. AR TECHNOLOGY

There are two main AR software application types, both of which have recently become available to educators: (a) a marker-based or vision-based AR and (b) a markerless or location-based AR. The marker-based AR presents the virtual object and digital media (i.e., text, 3D models, graphics, video, and audio) to the users when they point a camera at a visual marker (e.g., 2D target, Quick Response code (QR)). The markerless AR uses the user's location, like GPS, and then the application integrates the virtual content with an exact location on or within the users' real environment. The marker-based AR type will be addressed in this research.

A. Marker-based AR System process

This process uses a software application to recognize images, such as a QR or a physical object, then generates the augmented virtual content, and enhances this information onto the recognized object (see Figures 2 and 3).

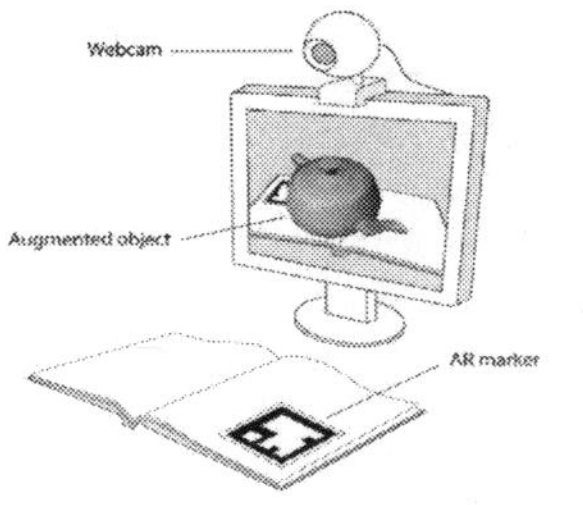

Figure 2. The concept of AR- based [2]

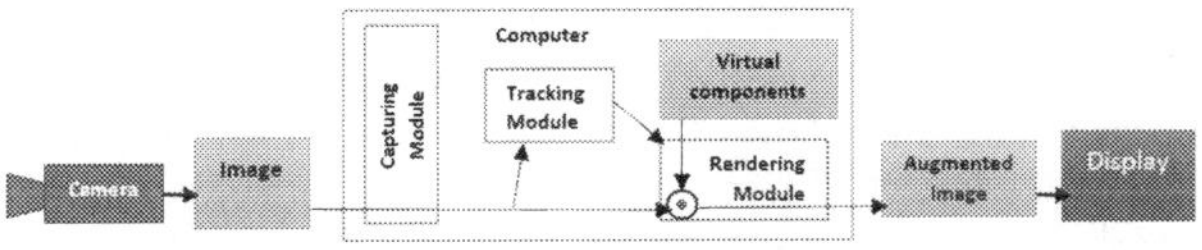

Figure 3. AR Marker-based AR architecture [1]

Mainly, an AR system captures the real world or images, analyzes them and compares them with features identified by the designer and displays the results to the end user.

B. AR displays

AR displays can be categorized into three types based on their position between the viewer and the real environment: Head-Worn Displays (HWD), handheld displays, and Projection displays. HWD is worn on the head, allowing images to be displayed in front of users' eyes. Projection displays are used to direct chosen virtual information to the real objects to be augmented. Handheld is a flat-panel Liquid Crystal Display (LCD) that some AR systems use by connecting a camera to run a video see-through-based augmentation. The handheld display is used as a magnifying glass or a window that shows the real objects with an AR overlay. Zhou et al. [11] suggested "Handheld displays are a good alternative to Head Mounted Display (HMD) and Head-Mounted Projective Display (HMPD) systems for AR applications, particularly because they are minimally intrusive, socially acceptable, readily available and highly mobile"(p.198).

IV. AR IN EDUCATION

In the literature, AR has been acknowledged as an effective technological tool that assists students to understand a range of science-based domains, such as environmental science [12]. The study has shown that AR has a strong positive emotional impact on the student. Moreover, a study on the use of AR has produced significant results and encouraged researchers to investigate its use in the field of education [13]. The result indicated that no studies have investigated the "educational" field (teacher training). A study by Bujak et al. [14] which compared AR with traditional computer devices inside and outside a mathematics classroom suggested that AR as a collaborative learning tool will better motivate students to learn. AR allows learners to interact with virtual objects in the real world. Combining the educational content with AR technology builds new automated applications to enhance the effectiveness of learning and teaching. Bujak et al. [14] discussed how AR allows students to interact naturally, which can improve learning by attaching data to objects and locations in the students' surroundings. Another study by Kamarainen et al. [15] assessed the use of AR technology as a means of facilitating students' understanding and interpretation when measuring water quality. Results indicated that AR allows students to interact in real time and that leads to improvement in interpretation flexibility. However, the use of AR in education has limitations. According to Bacca et al. [13], common limitations of applying AR in education are the students' attitudes and the difficulty of using AR applications. Hsiao et al. [12] reported that students need to pay much more attention when using AR for the first time. Environment constraints, such as inadequate infrastructure and lack of AR equipment, are common obstacles that educators need to be aware of when integrating AR and VR into education. Therefore, accessibility and usability factors are important issues that need to be considered in future work [10]. Additionally, Dunleavy and Dede [16] found that cognitive overload, culture, and type of institute are important issues that play significant roles in the adoption of AR in education.

A. Effectiveness of AR regarding students' learning outcomes

Many studies have reported the different effects that these technologies have on students' learning outcomes. A study by Wojciechowski and Cellary [17] showed that AR technology improves students' motivation to learn. Bacca et al. [13] hypothesized that AR is an effective learning tool owing to its combination of actual world and virtual world objects. Its superimposition of information and its enabling of the visualization, exploration, manipulation and interaction with objects within computer-generated surroundings allow learning to take place at the learner's own pace. Findings have confirmed that AR produces positive learning outcomes for students in the faculties of medicine and science [8] [18]. In addition, AR provides enjoyment that significantly influences students' intention to use this technology in the future. Furthermore, Jou and Wang [19] found that teaching approaches, such as AR, have the most effect on students' motivation to learn. From the psychological perspective, Bujak et al. [14] identified the psychological factors that enhance a learning environment that uses AR: students are able to interact naturally, and this can lead to an increase in the transparency of the interface between students and educational content. Additionally, Bujak et al. concluded that the AR environment could enhance learning by attaching data to objects and locations in the students' surroundings. Akçayır and Akçayır [20] demonstrated that most of the advantages of AR in educational settings relate to students' learning outcomes associated with motivation, attitude, and learning achievement.

B. Influence of students 'characteristics with AR technology.

According to Cheng and Tsai [2], few studies have taken into account the students' characteristics when students are engaged with AR in science education [21][23]. In the Squire and Jan [22] study, students were divided into three groups according to their age. Older students were found to be more interactive during AR game tasks, whereas younger students rejected the researchers' hypothesis regarding the AR game task. Albrecht et al. [24] investigated the emotional and cognitive impact that AR technology could have on students' learning process compared with the impact of traditional methods. The results showed that there was a significant decrease in student fatigue and a slight increase in student drive. However, despite the scant support from various researchers for the effectiveness of AR, other researchers have stressed its significance in the learning field classroom environment or as an evaluation tool [14][25][26] the classroom environment, or as an evaluation tool. Researchers Ausburn and Ausburn [27] highlighted that there are a few studies that explore and explain the effect of AR regarding theoretical perspectives and models. Several studies [28] [30] also argued that more research on AR is needed to investigate the emotional, social and cognitive dimensions of human experience in the virtual world rather than just technical issues. Cheng and Tsai [2] suggested, "more research is required to explore learning experience (e.g., motivation or cognitive load) and learner characteristics (e.g., spatial ability or perceived presence) involved in AR" (p.449). Various factors such as emotional, social, and personal beliefs, prior knowledge, and cognition have been mentioned in the literature as important issues that need to be examined to determine their influence on student learning outcomes when teaching methods have included technology compared with traditional methods.

V. SAUDI EDUCATION SYSTEM

The process of teaching and learning in the Saudi education system is still lacking vital elements such as enhancing students' personal skills and motivation by encouraging critical thinking, self-learning, and engagement [31]. The current approaches to learning and teaching in Saudi Arabia's higher education sector were reviewed by Alnassar and Dow [32]. They noted the following major challenges: a lack of motivation to develop and improve the teaching methods; the current curriculum does not sufficiently encourage students' critical thinking, self-learning, and problem-solving skills; the lack of adequate teacher training for faculty members. Furthermore, [33] stated that the higher education system in Saudi Arabia encounters difficulties in meeting outcome quality in relation to work needs. Saudi universities are trying to confront these challenges by developing a contemporary curriculum and advanced technological teaching facilities [34]. Despite the learning and teaching issues in the Saudi education system, there are some reasons for optimism. Studies are continuously being conducted by the Ministry of High Education in Saudi Arabia in order to develop an adequate e-learning infrastructure. Alrasheed et al. [35] reported that in developing countries, such as Saudi Arabia, many universities and schools depend on traditional teaching methods and ignore alternative and more effective methods, such as the use of technology in the classroom. Consequently, Saudi Arabia allocated a large budget to support the growth of the education sector and introduce new education programs [36]. One of the largest projects for the redevelopment of the education sector in SA is the King Abdullah University of Science and Technology (KAUST). The aim of this project is to redevelop and improve the learning environments by integrating a digital environment and technologies into the classroom. The Ministry of Education has established twenty-seven technical centers to develop teaching methods and improve teachers' performance in class [37]. The Saudi Arabian government is working hard to reform the education sector in line with sophisticated market needs.

A. Integration of technologies in education in Saudi Arabia

The integration of technologies in universities is rapidly increasing to simplify the delivery of education. Therefore, to enhance student learning, a large number of studies have focused on finding better technological solutions that are compatible with pedagogy [39][40]. Collaborative e-learning is one of the popular pedagogical technologies that were integrated into Saudi Universities to improve education. Al Saif [41] indicated that collaborative e-learning plays a significant role in increasing the number of students enrolling at universities. Smart Tablet technology was introduced in Saudi Arabia's education sector to investigate its potential benefits and enhance student learning outcomes by increasing the level of engagement in the learning process [42]. Also, several studies [43][44] examined the acceptance by students in Saudi Arabia of mobile learning in higher education. The results revealed that more than 65 percent of students are using online learning services and more than 62 percent are learning via electronic resources daily. Also, smartphones, iPads, and Tablets were the preferred learning devices of the majority of students. However, some studies [37] [42] [45] [46] identified several limitations: delay of the integration or rather the implementation of these technologies in SA education institutions; the lack of an adequate infrastructure; and the culture and personal beliefs, which have a significant impact on the utilization of technology in classrooms. Nowadays, new innovative technologies such as AR and VR introduce individuals to a new way of interacting with the world in three dimensions and two dimensions. Universities need to adjust and develop new methods of teaching and learning. In this study, these innovative technologies are introduced into the education system in Saudi Arabia's universities with consideration given to the aforementioned limitations.

B. Learning Technologies in SA

A study by Abou-Elhamd et al. [47] examined the adoption of VR in medical education in Saudi Arabia. Students used the Voxel-Man TempoSurg simulator to learn about the anatomy of the temporal bone in three dimensions. They found that teachers and students consider the virtual environment to be a powerful learning tool. Another learning technology used in SA higher education is virtual Avatar to represent a female tutor in online learning [48]. The Avatar technology was used to resolve the issue of a gender-segregated society in online learning. Based on that study, virtual Avatar is considered as a good learning technology for both male and female students. Nevertheless, certain limitations can prevent the adoption of these technologies in SA education; these include technical problems and the acceptance by students of a virtual teacher. However, all the previously mentioned studies have noted that the use of VR has several serious limitations associated with training, time, resources, technical problems, and personal beliefs. These studies would have been more useful if they had focused on suggesting a framework for adopting these kinds of technologies in SA education, and determining the effects of student characteristics on student learning outcomes when using VR technology.

VI. RESEARCH METHODS AND RESEARCH QUESTION

The rapid development of technologies has created difficulties in understanding Information Technology (IT) practices, impacts, usage, and capabilities. IT has become an integral part of individuals' lives and has evolved rapidly. Therefore, Information Systems (IS) researchers often face challenges in identifying sufficient findings and theories that provide essential insights into a phenomenon of interest. Consequently, a mixed-methods design can be employed as a powerful mechanism to help IS researchers to deal with such situations [49]. Given the research purpose and problem statement, this study will adopt a case study approach using mixed-methods research design (Explanatory Sequential Design) wherebythe data will be collected by both quantitative (online survey) and qualitative methods (SS interviews), analyzed separately, and then merged in one study [50] [51].

This research approach has been selected because a general understanding of the research problem can be provided by the quantitative data and their subsequent analysis. The statistical results will then be further refined and explained by eliciting participants' views through interviews (qualitative phase) [52] [54]. Since 2011, most AR studies have used the mixed-methods approach [55] which involves the collection of both quantitative and qualitative data [56][58] to achieve the research objective(s).

The purpose of using a sequential mixed-methods approach is to provide a comprehensive picture of a phenomenon by using qualitative data results to deliver a rich explanation of quantitative data and analysis [49][59]. In this study, the mixed-methods approach is used to provide an in-depth understanding of the potential use of AR technology in education, and to unearth more factors. The research philosophy in this study is pragmatism, taking an abductive approach to explore the use of AR in education and then generate a conceptual framework [60]. Pragmatism has been suggested for IS researchers and recommended by mixed methodologists as one of the preferred paradigms for modifying the use of mixed-methods research [49]. Therefore, this study will take a mixed-methods (abduction) approach that is both qualitative (based on deduction) and quantitative (based on induction) in order to examine the use of, and users' attitudes toward, new technology learning methods in Saudi Arabia's universities. This research aims to identify the new factors that must be considered when developing AR for Saudi Arabia.

Firstly, quantitative data will be gathered in order to understand students', teachers', and learning department staff's reactions to the AR teaching method, and to develop a set of new factors from the survey[49]. In other words, survey data will be used to determine the factors influencing the effectiveness of AR as a learning tool. In the the next phase, the qualitative method will be used to explore the quantitative results from the survey in more depth to gain more insights, reasons, deeper understanding, and explanation of these constructed factors.

A. The participants

The study population will comprise students, teachers (academics) and e-learning department staff from three publicly-funded universities in Saudi Arabia. These universities are an appropriate choice as this study will focus on the introduction of AR technology in the tertiary education sphere.

B. Quantitative online survey

In this study, quantitative data will be used to measure attitude, AR pedagogical contribution, willingness, acceptance, ICT infrastructure, sociocultural factor, etc. and to identify the factors for the proposed framework. Accordingly, an online survey via Qualtrics will be conducted by sending a hyperlink to the all participants (students, teachers (academics), and learning department staff).

This study will use the Statistical Package of Social Sciences IBM SPSS Statistics (version 24) for data analysis and conduct exploratory factor analysis (EFA) for statistical testing of the data collected from the questionnaire in order to identify factors. EFA is commonly used in the domains of psychology and education [61].

C. Qualitative Interviewing

The quantitative data collected via an online survey will be supported/supplemented by qualitative data gathered during face-to-face interviews. The researcher will use semi-structured, face-to face-interviews with a selected number of subjects to collect the data necessary to achieve the research objective and to support the data obtained from the online survey results. The selection of potential interviewees will be based on their knowledge of AR. People who are highly familiar with AR will be able to provide the researcher with rich information and various perspectives on the use of AR in education. The aim of the interviews is to answer the 'why' questions and to better explain the findings derived from quantitative data and analysis, and unearth additional factors.

The qualitative data gathered from the interviews will be analyzed using general qualitative analysis techniques, such as Nvivo software (version 11).

VII. RESEARCH OUTCOMES

Several studies [2] [14] [62] [66] have attempted to show that AR will improve student learning outcomes; however, no study to date has appropriately identified the effect on learning outcomes of the individual's characteristics, such as emotional, personal, social, and cognitive influences in combination with the technology. After comparing these studies, some of the factors were found to be missing in some models, and none would be appropriate for higher education in SA. According to limitations and suggestions offered by related studies [37] [42,] [45] [46] [48] personal and social factors have a significant influence on the utilization of technology in the context of higher education in Saudi Arabia. Compared with other developing regions, this country has solid roots in religious and tribal histories dating back to the eighteenth century. Moreover, Saudi Arabia is one of the most traditional of the Muslim countries, especially regarding the status of women [67]. The religious and cultural restrictions in Saudi Arabian society cannot countenance gender-desegregation [68]. Alturise and Alojaiman [69] indicated that "the strict application of Islamic law has led to its education system being segregated according to gender, which has far-reaching implications for the educational environment which puts it at odds with the open-access culture practiced in many other countries" (p.46). Therefore, the adoption of technology by Saudi Arabia presents a significant cultural challenge to the development of its learning system.

Moreover, cognitive and emotional considerations were identified as important factors that must be dealt with when integrating AR [2] [14] [24] [55] [70] [71].

To the best of this researcher's knowledge, none of the studies reviewed thus far has addressed all of these dimensions comprehensively. Hence, this study will attempt to address the gap in the literature of theoretical frameworks for using AR in learning by including these dimensions: emotional factors (EF), personal factors (PS), social factors (SF), and cognitive factors (CF).

A. AR initial Framework

Figure 4 demonstrates the conceptual framework that includes all these factors. The conceptual framework classifies the relevant factors in AR learning system development and acceptance in SA. Based on Gregor [72] theory taxonomy, this theoretical framework is related to theory for an explanation of the phenomena and provides a deeper understanding of why and what a relation between constructs.

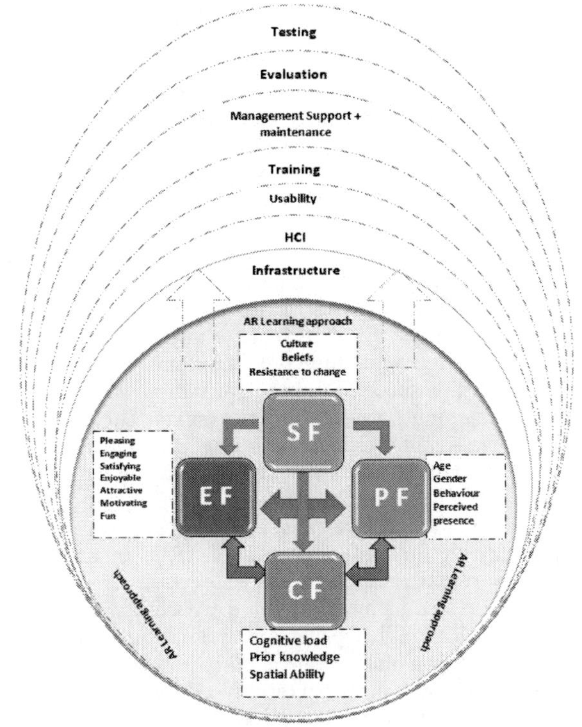

Figure 4. Augmented Reality Framework for Universities in Saudi Arabia

The gray arrows indicate the factors' relationships that were derived from the literature review (INTERACT model) [73], while the blue arrows (the influence of SF on other factors) will be tested in this research via the mixed-methods approach. Until recently, no study has been conducted on the use of AR in Saudi Arabian universities. The initial model will be examined and assessed by several stakeholders in Saudi universities.

B. *Social factor (SC)*

Culture can influence what is learned and how it is learned [74]. From a social perspective, culture is what a society or community share in terms of attitudes, values, and beliefs. Learning and teaching styles differ across cultures and need to be understood. Furthermore, the context of the institutions plays a role in the use of technology. Windschitl and Sahl [75] stated that "The ways in which those teachers eventually integrated computers into classroom instruction were powerfully mediated by their interrelated belief systems about learners in their school, about what constituted 'good teaching' in the context of the institutional culture, and about the role of technology in students' lives" (p.165). Therefore, a different learning approach, such as a new technology can also be influenced by cultures and beliefs.

C. *Personal Factor (PF)*

Personal characteristics such as gender, age, and level of education can influence the attitude toward using technology for educational purposes [76]. Hence, the successful adoption and integration of technology into teaching will be influenced by the personal characteristics of potential users [77]. Consequently, these factors will be considered in the AR learning environment, particularly in this research. Furthermore, case studies conducted by Hayes et al. [78] who investigated students' experience of presence in a mixed reality environment, found that perceived presence may impact on learning outcomes.

D. *Emotion Factor (EF)*

The learning process in higher education can be affected by emotion. Motivated students can confidently demonstrate their level of knowledge. Emotion plays a significant role in both teacher and learner behaviours and in learner motivation and self-esteem [79]. Several studies [80][81] have concluded that the positive impact of a virtual learning environment on emotions would improve students' cognitive processes and performance. According to the findings of previous studies [82] [84], in order to integrate cognitive and affective processes, emotional design research is needed.

E. *Cognitive factor (CF)*

The thinking processes of students can be supported, guided, and extended when computer technology is involved in the learning process [85]. However, technology may pose additional processing demands and increase students' cognitive load which prevents them from learning [2] [86]. Kalyuga and Liu [87] suggested that the cognitive characteristics of learners should be considered in order to guarantee the instructional effectiveness of any technological innovation; otherwise, students will become frustrated. Moreover, the level of students' prior knowledge can influence student learning outcomes in virtual learning and this should be considered in AR learning. Cai et al. [88] indicated that "With sufficient prior knowledge, whether we use abstract objects in teaching causes no impact on learning; this suggests that the influence of a technological innovation must be closely correlated with the students' prior knowledge".

F. *Technological Infrastructure*

In order to develop, deliver, monitor, test, control or support information technology services in universities, certain hardware, software, networks, facilities, etc. are required to operate and manage an information technology environment. Technology infrastructure is a complex issue and universities' decision-makers need to realize the importance of technology infrastructure as a means of improving teaching and enhancing learning outcomes. Altameem [89] stated that some of the universities in SA still have a weak infrastructure, which makes people reluctant to use the available services and systems.

G. *Human-Computer Interaction (HCI)*

HCI is the study of interactions between computers and people and is an interdisciplinary field comprising computer science, engineering, and ergonomics; its human side includes psychology, physiology, sociology and cognitive sciences [90]. According to [91], the purpose of HCI is to design a system that is aligned with users' needs and requirements.

H. Usability

Usability is about assuring users that the system is effective, efficient, safe to use, easy to use and evaluate, enjoyable, and satisfying [91]. To ensure usability, the user should participate in the development process to prevent future user frustration and error and meet the users' requirements. According to Cheng and Tsai [2], usability issues must be considered in AR technology because, without well-designed interfaces, students might encounter difficulties when using AR.

I. Maintenance and Support

After careful planning and hard work, the integrated technologies in organisations need to be updated to ensure that they are running flawlessly. Maintenance and support are required after implementing new technologies to keep the system running efficiently and effectively. The National Center for Education [92] stated that "support services, training, and certification must be ongoing to ensure successful post-implementation use of technology". Thus, the implementation of new technologies such as AR in universities should be supported and maintained by them or outsourced to contractors to achieve the desired goals.

J. Training

Training in the use of technologies should be introduced when universities intend to integrate technology in an educational environment. The main goal of training is to introduce teachers and students to various appropriate technologies that shift the traditional learning method to an efficient learning approach that will enhance learning outcomes. In order to achieve this goal, adequate training is needed to encourage both teachers and students to use the technology. Follow-up training has been acknowledged as a significant factor in integrating technology in the classroom [93]. Finally, in order for new technologies to be used appropriately in education, good in-service training is essential.

K. Testing

The testing stage will allow users to test the new system via a list of web browsers to ensure that the programme code is accurate and meets the intended functional requirement. [63]defined the user test as "a systematic approach to evaluating user performance in order to inform and improve usability design" (p.430). The AR system must be tested to determine whether it meets the expectations of the authorized entity.

L. Evaluation

System evaluation is an important phase when developing or updating a system. When a system is introduced or released, an evaluation should be conducted. Regular evaluation is an important means of identifying the outcomes of using AR in education and improving its efficiency.

VIII. Conclusion

In conclusion, the aim of this study was to develop and evaluate the AR framework in Saudi Arabia's higher education sector. This is a pioneering study in its field in that it attempted to extend the literature by classifying the factors that will have the most influence on AR adoption, especially on students' learning outcomes in Saudi Arabia. The results of this study will create awareness of the potential advantages and the weaknesses of adopting AR technology for teaching and learning purposes in SA universities. It is anticipated that this study will contribute to the theoretical and academic knowledge regarding the important factors that are needed for the successful implementation of AR for teaching and learning purposes in universities. The context of Saudi Arabia's higher education sector presents a set of ambiguities and uncertainties that require careful examination prior to the widespread introduction of AR in university pedagogy. By combining various approaches drawn from extant literature on the implementation of AR in universities globally, this research suggests a framework of factors which could support an integrated and well-considered incorporation of AR in higher education in Saudi Arabia.

In future work, we plan to extend current research by implementing an AR system in Saudi universities and evaluating its impact on student learning outcomes.

REFERENCES

[1] S. Siltanen and V. t. tutkimuskeskus, *Theory and Applications of Marker-based Augmented Reality*. VTT, 2012.

[2] K.-H. Cheng and C.-C. Tsai, "Affordances of augmented reality in science learning: Suggestions for future research," *Journal of Science Education and Technology*, vol. 22, no. 4, pp. 449-462, 2013.

[3] P. Milgram and F. Kishino, "A taxonomy of mixed reality visual displays," *IEICE TRANSACTIONS on Information and Systems*, vol. 77, no. 12, pp. 1321-1329, 1994.

[4] M. J. Schuemie, *Human-computer Interaction and Presence in Virtual Reality Exposure Therapy*. TU Delft, Delft University of Technology, 2003.

[5] L. Johnson, R. Smith, A. Levine, and K. Haywood, "The 2010 Horizon Report: Australia-New Zealand Edition. Austin, Texas: The New Media Consortium," ed, 2010.

[6] H. McLellan, "Virtual realities," *Handbook of Research for Educational Communications and technology*, pp. 457-487, 1996.

[7] S. McGlashan and T. Axling, "Talking to agents in virtual worlds," in *UK VR-SIG Conf*, 1996.

[8] Azuma, Y. Baillot, R. Behringer, S. Feiner, S. Julier, and B. MacIntyre, "Recent advances in augmented reality," *IEEE Computer Graphics and Applications*, vol. 21, no. 6, pp. 34-47, 2001.

[9] Azuma, "A survey of augmented reality," *Presence: Teleoperators and virtual environments*, vol. 6, no. 4, pp. 355-385, 1997.

[10] Á. Di Serio, M. B. Ibáñez, and C. D. Kloos, "Impact of an augmented reality system on students' motivation for a visual art course," *Computers & Education*, vol. 68, pp. 586-596, 2013.

[11] F. Zhou, H. B.-L. Duh, and M. Billinghurst, "Trends in augmented reality tracking, interaction and display: A review of ten years of ISMAR," presented at the Proceedings of the 7th IEEE/ACM International Symposium on Mixed and Augmented Reality, 2008.

[12] K.-F. Hsiao, N.-S. Chen, and S.-Y. Huang, "Learning while exercising for science education in augmented reality among

adolescents," *Interactive Learning Environments,* vol. 20, no. 4, pp. 331-349, 2012/08/01 2012.

[13] J. Bacca, S. Baldiris, R. Fabregat, S. Graf, and Kinshuk, "Augmented Reality Trends in Education: A Systematic Review of Research and Applications," in *Educ. Technol. Soc.* vol. 17, ed, 2014, pp. 133-149.

[14] K. R. Bujak, I. Radu, R. Catrambone, B. MacIntyre, R. Zheng, and G. Golubski, "A psychological perspective on augmented reality in the mathematics classroom," *Computers & Education,* vol. 68, pp. 536-544, 2013.

[15] A. M. Kamarainen *et al.*, "EcoMOBILE: Integrating augmented reality and probeware with environmental education field trips," *Computers & Education,* vol. 68, pp. 545-556, 2013.

[16] M. Dunleavy and C. Dede, "Augmented reality teaching and learning," in *Handbook of Research on Educational Communications and Technology*: Springer, 2014, pp. 735-745.

[17] R. Wojciechowski and W. Cellary, "Evaluation of learners' attitude toward learning in ARIES augmented reality environments," *Computers & Education,* vol. 68, pp. 570-585, 2013.

[18] T. Huk, "Who benefits from learning with 3D models? The case of spatial ability," *Journal of Computer Assisted Learning,* vol. 22, no. 6, pp. 392-404, 2006.

[19] M. Jou and J. Wang, "Investigation of effects of virtual reality environments on learning performance of technical skills," *Computers in Human Behavior,* vol. 29, no. 2, pp. 433-438, 2013.

[20] M. Akçayır and G. Akçayır, "Advantages and challenges associated with augmented reality for education: A systematic review of the literature," *Educational Research Review,* vol. 20, pp. 1-11, 2// 2017.

[21] P. M. O'Shea, C. Dede, and M. Cherian, "Research Note: The Results of Formatively Evaluating an Augmented Reality Curriculum Based on Modified Design Principles," *International Journal of Gaming and Computer-Mediated Simulations (IJGCMS),* vol. 3, no. 2, pp. 57-66, 2011.

[22] K. D. Squire and M. Jan, "Mad City Mystery: Developing Scientific Argumentation Skills with a Place-based Augmented Reality Game on Handheld Computers," *Journal of Science Education and Technology,* journal article vol. 16, no. 1, pp. 5-29, 2007.

[23] K. Squire and E. Klopfer, "Augmented reality simulations on handheld computers," *The Journal of the Learning Sciences,* vol. 16, no. 3, pp. 371-413, 2007.

[24] U.-V. Albrecht, K. Folta-Schoofs, M. Behrends, and U. Von Jan, "Effects of Mobile Augmented Reality Learning Compared to Textbook Learning on Medical Students: Randomized Controlled Pilot Study," *Journal of Medical Internet Research,* vol. 15, no. 8, 2013.

[25] K.-E. Chang, C.-T. Chang, H.-T. Hou, Y.-T. Sung, H.-L. Chao, and C.-M. Lee, "Development and behavioral pattern analysis of a mobile guide system with augmented reality for painting appreciation instruction in an art museum," *Computers & Education,* vol. 71, pp. 185-197, 2014.

[26] H.-K. Wu, S. W.-Y. Lee, H.-Y. Chang, and J.-C. Liang, "Current status, opportunities and challenges of augmented reality in education," *Computers & Education,* vol. 62, pp. 41-49, 2013.

[27] L. J. Ausburn and F. B. Ausburn, "Spheres of reality: A conceptualization of desktop virtual environments in career and technical education and an implementation training model," in *Proceedings of the National Career and Technical Education Research and Professional Development Conference, Las Vegas, NV. Retrieved from http: www. public. iastate. edu/~ lannan/ACTER/2010/wednesday. shtml*, 2010: Citeseer.

[28] S. A. Barab, T. D. Sadler, C. Heiselt, D. Hickey, and S. Zuiker, "Erratum to: Relating narrative, inquiry, and inscriptions: Supporting consequential play," *Journal of Science Education and Technology,* vol. 19, no. 4, pp. 387-407, 2010.

[29] G. Hokanson *et al.*, "Studying Native American culture in an immersive virtual environment," in *2008 Eighth IEEE International Conference on Advanced Learning Technologies*, 2008, pp. 788-792: IEEE.

[30] M. Patera, S. Draper, and M. Naef, "Exploring magic cottage: A virtual reality environment for stimulating children's imaginative writing," *Interactive Learning Environments,* vol. 16, no. 3, pp. 245-263, 2008.

[31] A. K. Hamdan, "The Reciprocal and Correlative Relationship between Learning Culture and Online Education: A Case from Saudi Arabia," *International Review of Research in Open and Distance Learning,* vol. 15, no. 1, pp. 309-336, 2014.

[32] S. A. Alnassar and K. L. Dow, "Delivering High-Quality Teaching and Learning for University Students in Saudi Arabia," in *Higher Education in Saudi Arabia: Achievements, Challenges and Opportunities*, L. Smith and A. Abouammoh, Eds. Dordrecht: Springer Netherlands, 2013, pp. 49-60.

[33] M. A. Alkhazim, "Higher education in Saudi Arabia: Challenges, solutions, and opportunities missed," *Higher Education Policy,* vol. 16, no. 4, pp. 479-486, 2003.

[34] L. Smith, *Higher Education in Saudi Arabia : Achievements, Challenges and Opportunities / edited by Larry Smith, Abdulrahman Abouammoh.* Dordrecht: Dordrecht : Springer Netherlands : Imprint: Springer, 2013.

[35] A. Alrasheed, A. Basahi, A. Alrowais, M. Alrwaished, M. Alrwaily, and H. Alsuaik, "Study of teaching science in both elementary and middle schools stages in boys and girls schools in Saudi Arabia," *Riyadh: King Abdul-Aziz City for Science and Technology,* 2003.

[36] U.-S. A. B. Council, "The Education Sector in the Kingdom of Saudi Arabia," *Retrieved on December,* vol. 15, p. 2015, 2009.

[37] K. K. Amoudi and O. Sulaymani, "The Integration Of Educational Technology In Girls'classrooms In Saudi Arabia," *European Journal of Training and Development Studies,* vol. 1, no. 2, pp. 14-19, 2014.

[38] EON, "EON Reality and Midwam Open New Interactive Digital Center (IDC) in the Kingdom of Saudi Arabia," 2016.

[39] M. Goos, "Using Technology to support effective mathematics teaching and learning: what counts?," 2010.

[40] V. G. Zakirova and E. E. Purik, "Creative Environment Formation in Design Professional Training," *International Journal of Environmental and Science Education,* vol. 11, no. 9, pp. 2323-2332, 2016.

[41] A. Al Saif, "The motivating and inhibiting factors affecting the use of web-based instruction at the University of Qassim in Saudi Arabia," *ETD Collection for Wayne State University,* pp. 1-17, 2005.

[42] G. Almalki, G. Finger, and J. Zagami, "Introducing SMART Table technology in Saudi Arabia education system," *Editorial Preface,* vol. 4, no. 2, 2013.

[43] A. B. Nassuora, "Students acceptance of mobile learning for higher education in Saudi Arabia," *American Academic & Scholarly Research Journal,* vol. 4, no. 2, p. 1, 2012.

[44] A. Badwelan, S. Drew, and A. A. Bahaddad, "Towards Acceptance M-Learning Approach in Higher Education in Saudi Arabia," *International Journal of Business and Management,* vol. 11, no. 8, p. 12, 2016.

[45] A. Al-Alwani, "Barriers to integrating information technology in Saudi Arabia science education," R. Aust, Ed., ed: ProQuest Dissertations Publishing, 2005.

[46] R. S. Al-Jarf, "Connecting Students across Universities in Saudi Arabia," *Online Submission,* 2005.

[47] K. A. Abou-Elhamd, A. Al-Sultan, and U. Rashad, "Simulation in ENT medical education," *The Journal of Laryngology & Otology,* vol. 124, no. 03, pp. 237-241, 2010.

[48] R. Adham, K. Lundqvist, and P. Parslow, "The Use of Avatars in Gender Segregated Online Learning within MOOCs in Saudi Arabia," presented at the Global Learn 2016, Limerick, Ireland, 2016. Available: https://www.learntechlib.org/p/172713

[49] V. Venkatesh, S. A. Brown, and H. Bala, "Bridging the qualitative-quantitative divide: Guidelines for conducting mixed methods research in information systems," *MIS Quarterly,* vol. 37, no. 1, pp. 21-54, 2013.

[50] N. V. Ivankova, J. W. Creswell, and S. L. Stick, "Using Mixed-Methods Sequential Explanatory Design: From Theory to Practice," *Field Methods,* vol. 18, no. 1, pp. 3-20, 2006.

[51] R. B. Johnson, A. J. Onwuegbuzie, and L. A. Turner, "Toward a Definition of Mixed Methods Research," *Journal of Mixed Methods Research,* vol. 1, no. 2, pp. 112-133, 2007.

[52] G. B. Rossman and B. L. Wilson, "Numbers and Words: Combining Quantitative and Qualitative Methods in a Single Large-Scale Evaluation Study," *Evaluation Review,* vol. 9, no. 5, pp. 627-43, 1985.

[53] A. Tashakkori, *Mixed methodology : combining qualitative and quantitative approaches / Abbas Tashakkori, Charles Teddlie.* Thousand Oaks, Calif.: Thousand Oaks, Calif. : Sage Publications, 1998.

[54] J. W. Creswell, *Research design: Qualitative, quantitative, and mixed methods approaches*. Sage publications, 2013.

[55] P. Chen, X. Liu, W. Cheng, and R. Huang, "A review of using Augmented Reality in Education from 2011 to 2016," in *Innovations in Smart Learning*, E. Popescu *et al.*, Eds. Singapore: Springer Singapore, 2017, pp. 13-18.

[56] C. Teddlie and A. Tashakkori, "Major issues and controveries inthe use of mixed methods in the social and behvioral sciences," *Handbook of mixed methods in social & behavioral research,* pp. 3-50, 2003.

[57] J. W. Creswell, *Educational research : planning, conducting, and evaluating quantitative and qualitative research / John Creswell.* Upper Saddle River, N.J.: Upper Saddle River, N.J. : Merrill, 2002.

[58] C. Teddlie and A. Tashakkori, *Foundations of mixed methods research: Integrating quantitative and qualitative approaches in the social and behavioral sciences*. Sage, 2009.

[59] A. Bryman, "Integrating quantitative and qualitative research: how is it done?," *Qualitative Research,* vol. 6, no. 1, pp. 97-113, 2006.

[60] M. a. Saunders, *Research methods for business students / Mark Saunders, Philip Lewis, Adrian Thornhill,* Seventh edition.. ed. Harlow Pearson Education, 2016.

[61] T. Brown and A. Onsman, "Exploratory Factor Analysis: A Five-step guide for novices," *Australasian Journal of Paramedicine,* vol. 8, no. 3, pp. 1-14, 2013.

[62] H. K. Wu and Y. L. Huang, "Ninth - grade student engagement in teacher - centered and student - centered technology - enhanced learning environments," *Science Education,* vol. 91, no. 5, pp. 727-749, 2007.

[63] J. Preece and L. Keller, "Human Computer Interaction," *ISBN: 0-201-62769-8. Addison Wesley,* 1989.

[64] O. S. Patrick, M. Rebecca, J. Catherine, and D. Chris, "Lessons Learned about Designing Augmented Realities," *International Journal of Gaming and Computer-Mediated Simulations (IJGCMS),* vol. 1, no. 1, pp. 1-15, 2009.

[65] N.-S. Chen, D. C.-E. Teng, C.-H. Lee, and Kinshuk, "Augmenting paper-based reading activity with direct access to digital materials and scaffolded questioning," *Computers & Education,* vol. 57, no. 2, pp. 1705-1715, 9// 2011.

[66] K. J. Carlson and D. J. Gagnon, "Augmented Reality Integrated Simulation Education in Health Care," *Clinical Simulation in Nursing,* vol. 12, no. 4, pp. 123-127, 4// 2016.

[67] R. Baki, "Gender-Segregated Education in Saudi Arabia: Its Impact on Social Norms and the Saudi Labor Market," *Education Policy Analysis Archives,* vol. 12, no. 28, p. n28, 2004.

[68] A. Onsman, "It is better to light a candle than to ban the darkness: government led academic development in Saudi Arabian universities," *Higher Education,* journal article vol. 62, no. 4, pp. 519-532, 2011.

[69] F. Alturise and B. Alojaiman, "Benefits and challenges of using ICT in Saudi Arabia universities: A literature review," in *International conference on advanced in computing, Engineering and Learning Technologies*, 2013, vol. 2, pp. 2-46.

[70] E. S. Billings and C. Mathison, "I Get to Use an iPod in School? Using Technology-Based Advance Organizers to Support the Academic Success of English Learners," *Journal of Science Education and Technology,* journal article vol. 21, no. 4, pp. 494-503, 2012.

[71] M. Bower, C. Howe, N. McCredie, A. Robinson, and D. Grover, "Augmented Reality in education – cases, places and potentials," *Educational Media International,* vol. 51, no. 1, pp. 1-15, 2014.

[72] S. Gregor, "The nature of theory in information systems," *MIS quarterly,* pp. 611-642, 2006.

[73] S. Domagk, R. N. Schwartz, and J. L. Plass, "Interactivity in multimedia learning: An integrated model," *Computers in Human Behavior,* vol. 26, no. 5, pp. 1024-1033, 9// 2010.

[74] J. Munro, "Social-cultural influences on learning," ed: University of Melbourne. Retrieved, 2012.

[75] M. Windschitl and K. Sahl, "Tracing Teachers' Use of Technology in a Laptop Computer School: The Interplay of Teacher Beliefs, Social Dynamics, and Institutional Culture," *American Educational Research Journal,* vol. 39, no. 1, pp. 165-205, 2002.

[76] J. Schiller, "Working with ICT: Perceptions of Australian principals," *Journal of Educational Administration,* vol. 41, no. 2, pp. 171-185, 2003.

[77] C. Buabeng-Andoh, "Factors influencing teachers' adoption and integration of information and communication technology into teaching: A review of the literature," *International Journal of Education and Development using Information and Communication Technology,* vol. 8, no. 1, p. 136, 2012.

[78] A. T. Hayes, S. E. Hardin, and C. E. Hughes, "Perceived Presence's Role on Learning Outcomes in a Mixed Reality Classroom of Simulated Students," in *Virtual, Augmented and Mixed Reality. Systems and Applications: 5th International Conference, VAMR 2013, Held as Part of HCI International 2013, Las Vegas, NV, USA, July 21-26, 2013, Proceedings, Part II,* R. Shumaker, Ed. Berlin, Heidelberg: Springer Berlin Heidelberg, 2013, pp. 142-151.

[79] J. M. Dirkx, "The meaning and role of emotions in adult learning," *New directions for adult and continuing education,* vol. 2008, no. 120, pp. 7-18, 2008.

[80] B.-K. Kye and Y. Kim, "Investigation on the relationships among media characteristics, presence, flow, and learning effects in augmented reality based learning," *Journal of Educational Technology,* vol. 24, no. 4, pp. 193-223, 2008.

[81] B. Dalgarno and M. J. W. Lee, "What are the learning affordances of 3 - D virtual environments?," *British Journal of Educational Technology,* vol. 41, no. 1, pp. 10-32, 2010.

[82] B. Park, L. Knörzer, J. L. Plass, and R. Brünken, "Emotional design and positive emotions in multimedia learning: An eyetracking study on the use of anthropomorphisms," *Computers & Education,* vol. 86, pp. 30-42, 2015/08/01/ 2015.

[83] T.-C. Huang, C.-C. Chen, and Y.-W. Chou, "Animating eco-education: To see, feel, and discover in an augmented reality-based experiential learning environment," *Computers & Education,* vol. 96, pp. 72-82, 2016/05/01/ 2016.

[84] J. L. Plass, S. Heidig, E. O. Hayward, B. D. Homer, and E. Um, "Emotional design in multimedia learning: Effects of shape and color on affect and learning," *Learning and Instruction,* vol. 29, pp. 128-140, 2014/02/01/ 2014.

[85] S. J. Derry and S. P. Lajoie, *Computers as cognitive tools*. Lawrence Erlbaum Associates Pub., 1993.

[86] M. Dunleavy, C. Dede, and R. Mitchell, "Affordances and Limitations of Immersive Participatory Augmented Reality Simulations for Teaching and Learning," *Journal of Science Education and Technology,* vol. 18, no. 1, pp. 7-22, 2008.

[87] S. Kalyuga and T.-C. Liu, "Guest editorial: managing cognitive load in technology-based learning environments," *Educational Technology & Society,* vol. 18, no. 4, pp. 1-8, 2015.

[88] S. Cai, F.-K. Chiang, Y. Sun, C. Lin, and J. J. Lee, "Applications of augmented reality-based natural interactive learning in magnetic field instruction," *Interactive Learning Environments,* pp. 1-14, 2016.

[89] A. Altameem, "What drives successful E-learning? An empirical investigation of the key technical issues in Saudi Arabian Universities," *Journal of Theoretical and Applied Information Technology,* vol. 53, no. 1, pp. 63-70, 2013.

[90] İ. A. Erdem, "Vision-based human-computer interaction using laser pointer," Middle East Technical University, 2003.

[91] T. Issa and P. Isaias, "Usability and Human Computer Interaction (HCI)," in *Sustainable Design*: Springer, 2015, pp. 19-36.

[92] S. National Center for Education, *Technology @ your fingertips: a guide to implementing technology solutions for education agencies and institutions* (Technology at your fingertips, no. vii, 102 p.). Washington, DC: National Center for Education Statistics : National Cooperative Education Statistics System : National Forum on Education Statistics, 1997, pp. vii, 102 p.

[93] S. Martin and M. Vallance, "The impact of synchronous inter-networked teacher training in Information and Communication Technology integration," *Computers & Education,* vol. 51, no. 1, pp. 34-53, 2008/08/01/ 2008.

A User-centric Design and Pedagogical-based Approach for Mobile Learning

Mohammed Bahja
IRAC Group, School of Computer Science and Technology
University of Bedfordshire
Luton, United Kingdom
E-mail: Mohammed.Bahja@beds.ac.uk

Rawad Hammad
Research and Learning Solutions
King's College London
London, United Kingdom
E-mail: Rawad.Hammad@kcl.ac.uk

***Abstract*—The adoption of various learning technologies in education has gained momentum in the last couple of decades due to: (i) their ability to meet stakeholders' requirements and (ii) offering a wide variety of services that are accessible from different platforms, such as mobile learning and online learning. Despite the success of mobile learning, certain limitations and shortcomings have been reported in literature, such as the insufficient design and limited support provided to stakeholders. This paper focuses on reviewing the studies relating to m-learning application for identifying the issues and challenges limiting its adoption, and proposes a pedagogy-informed and user-centric design framework for mobile learning artifacts which would address the issues identified. The findings from the review revealed that user-centric issues, such as privacy, security, usability, learnability, and socio-cultural aspects (including adaptability of the application, sustainability, integration with pedagogical approaches) are the main factors affecting users in adopting an m-learning approach. Considering these issues, a user-centric framework integrated with socio-cultural aspects, design and technology attributes is proposed.**

Keywords- m-learning; pedagogy; user-centric design; user-centric methodology; software engineering; software development methodology.

I. INTRODUCTION

The rapid developments across the Internet and telecommunication technologies have paved the way for developing and adopting innovative and efficient methods of learning in many fields. Various innovative technologies such as mobile technologies, Internet and communication technologies have been applied in educational sector. This has enriched teaching and learning processes, and consequently has reflected on learning flexibility, effectiveness and efficiency. It is estimated that 47% of the worldwide organizations are using mobile devices in their training programs, as it enhances the user engagement in learning and helps in knowledge retention [1]. The global market for mobile learning, henceforth m-learning, is expected to cross $12.2 billion in 2018 as it is advancing at a fast rate [2]. Accordingly, a rapid increase in the mobile workforce was observed in the recent years, which is expected to double or triple its size in 2018 [3]. Since stakeholders expect answers at their fingertips, the real-time access to information on mobile devices boosts the adoption of m-learning [4]. In addition, the number of mobile devices would increase to three on average by the end of 2018 [5]. Furthermore, the amount of time spent on using mobile devices is significantly increasing in the recent years as mobile devices become more reliable in accessing various types of information [6].

Though there is a rapid increase in the m-learning approaches, there have been various challenges identified with it. *First*, the traditional teaching can have one to one access, where the learner's abilities are assessed and accordingly the teaching process is modified to suit the learner's abilities [7], where it is not clear how this could happen via m-learning. *Second*, the insufficient support provided via m-learning platforms across various contexts [7]. *Third*, the impact of design on effective learning, where design in this context refers to system design rather than learning content design. *Fourth*, the difference in mobile usage habits and attitudes across the regions [8]. Other challenges identified include security, accessibility, contents accuracy, adaptability, etc. [9]. As stated above, most of these issues are associated with theory and practice of teaching, and user-centered factors.

Therefore, this paper is an attempt to understand how a pedagogy-informed and user-centric design methodology could be useful for m-learning. The rest of this paper is organized as follows. Section II reviews the related work in m-learning and pedagogy. Section III introduces the user-centric design framework methodology for developing m-learning systems. Section IV addresses the user-centric design methodology. Section VI concludes the paper and suggests future research directions.

II. M-LEARNING AND PEDAGOGY

M-Learning is the process of learning across multiple contexts using various social interactive features on the mobile devices [10]. Learning in educational field varies from one region to another depending on the socio-cultural aspects. Integrating socio-cultural and methods underpinning them (i.e., pedagogy) into mobile technological environments is one of the major challenges in m-learning. This aspect has been the focus of research in many studies. In this context pedagogy refers to theory, methods and practices of teaching and learning, which can include various approaches. Therefore, the concept of 'one-size-fits-all' would be an impractical approach in developing m-learning platforms [11]. Consequently, integrating pedagogical theories and models with technology is inevitable to design effective and efficient m-learning platforms [12].

In addition to these concerns, it is also very important to consider the user-centric aspects such as attitudes, behavior, usability, learnability etc. in developing m-learning platforms. Literature studies [13] investigate the attitudes of students and educators in the Arab region towards m-learning identified significant difference in students' attitudes towards m-learning, while positive attitudes were observed among the educators. Another recent study by Chung et al. [14] identified that the students' behavioral intentions had high positive correlations with mobile devices' compatibility, self-efficacy, perceived ease of use; the majority of the students showed positive approach towards adopting m-learning.

However, Khan et al. [15] reveals the need to increase awareness, training, and motivation for adopting m-learning approach among students and educators. Moreover, students in secondary school have positive perceptions about m-learning but their m-learning adequacy levels are identified as not sufficient enough to put it in to practice. The above-mentioned studies reveal that m-learning platform features and usability aspects could influence the attitude towards their adoption. Likewise, the adoption of m-learning would be dependent on various user-centric attributes, such as level of education, age, awareness etc. Abachi and Muhammad [16] investigate the impact of m-learning on educators and learners, and found that great enthusiasm was shown by the users regarding augmented reality-based m-learning platforms. Though, the users favored the adoption of m-learning, they have expressed concerns in relation to security and coverage (completeness, accuracy).

Another important perspective of evaluation is to assess how the mobile platform adaptation could influence the learning process. M-learning has a dynamic scope as the users would be constantly moving and the context from which they learn can be changing. Therefore, adaptation according to these changes by the mobile platforms is essential for providing effective and dynamic learning process. Nevertheless, Garcia-Cabot et al. [17] finds that mobile adaptation had limited impact on the learning process, since students learn in similar contexts despite the fact that they use different ways to access learning contents.

On one hand, technological aspects of m-learning platforms design need further investigation in order to embed the best teaching practices into innovative m-learning. Such technological aspects could influence various features and characteristics such as usability, learnability, ease of use, understandability, quality of learning, and quality of experience [18]. Domingo and Gargante [19] conducted a study to assess the teachers' perception about using mobile technology and how learning could be influences. The study reveals that content learning applications are used more frequently compared to the informational applications. It reflects the opportunity to streamline m-learning platforms to more detailed content learning applications, which can focus on specific contexts rather than integrating various contexts in a single platform. Nonetheless, Bird and Stubbs [20] identify the challenges from adoption strategy perspective for scaling m-learning applications into institution-wide learning technologies. The study focuses on integrating m-learning into the IT Strategy of institutions and universities explained through Law/Collon model [20].

On the other hand, pedagogy is deeply rooted in m-learning. There are various pedagogical approaches in education; however, the need for identifying a sufficient pedagogical approach is rarely recognized. Lozanzo et al. [21] developed a framework for assessing the pedagogical approaches in relation to various competences in m-learning contexts. Dennen and Hao [22] developed M-Cope framework for designing effective mobile learning by considering the following five critical areas: Mobile affordances, Conditions, Outcomes, Pedagogy and Ethics. However, pedagogical approaches vary across the regions, and therefore implementation approaches need to consider and reflect cultural differences. Hao et al. [23] focus on assessing how students perceive m-learning across three culturally different regions including USA, China, and Turkey; although all students preferred m-learning approach, they raise few concerns such as support, infrastructure and embedding the cultural aspects (the local pedagogical approaches) in m-learning platforms. Kearney et al. [24] investigated the use of distinctive m-learning pedagogies by teachers and identified that online collaboration and networking were rated unpredictably lower than expected, in spite of enhanced connection and flexible learning opportunities afforded by mobile technologies. However, Lindsay [25] found that opportunities for pedagogical transformation that collaborative learning offers appear to be partially realized, but the potential for situative learning using authentic contexts.

To conclude, the majority of the reviewed literature assures the positive perceptions about adopting m-learning platforms. However, socio-cultural issues, pedagogical approaches, design and technology are the main issues identified with m-learning. Such issues are related to the users of m-learning platforms; hence, the user-centric features are one of the major aspects that are not being considered in the current m-learning platforms. Additionally, the design and technology issues concerning privacy and security, usability etc. are very common concerns that need to be addressed. Considering these concerns/factors, a user-centric design framework is proposed in the next section.

III. USER-CENTRIC FRAMEWORK FOR M-LEARNING

There are various frameworks proposed by various researchers [26]-[28] for m-learning applications. Out of which UCD (User-Centered Design) [27] and mLUX [28] are the most commonly used design frameworks. The UCD includes a series of phases including knowing the users; analyzing users' tasks and goals; developing usability requirements; prototype and design concept; usability testing; and repeating the stages for more features [26]. mLUX approach has three layers [28] which include the role players, the context of use; and the process. The role players includes all stakeholders of the m-learning application who are involved in one or more stages. The term role player defines not just the users or actors but also considers the roles of the users in relation to the application. There are also invisible role players which include individuals, organizations, systems, developers, testers etc., who are not the actual users of the application, but play important roles in the design and development [26]. The context of use is the capability of the application to create an effective user-centric learning environment. Several factors are to be considered in this aspect including the Social (social acceptance of application); physical (time & location constraints), and educational (learning, outcomes, pedagogical approaches). The process is a methodology for developing m-learning application which includes four stages: User Study; Data Analysis; Idea Creation; and Product Concept as shown in Figure 1.

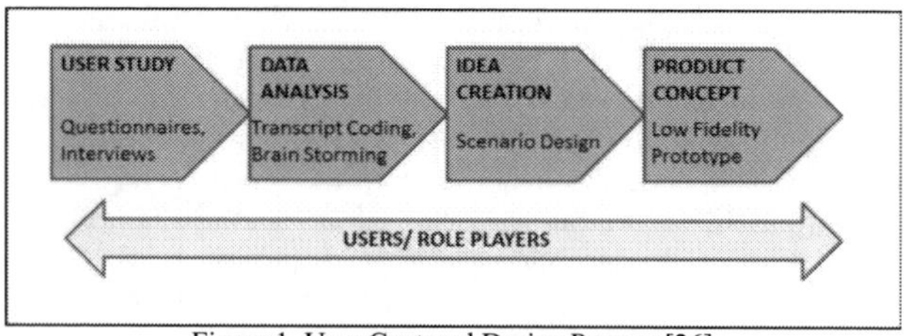

Figure 1. User-Centered Design Process [26]

The UCD framework includes some user-centric features; however, it does not cover all of the issues outlined in the above in Section II. Therefore, there is a need to develop more detailed user-centric framework and design methodology, in order to address the continuously emerging concerns. Accordingly, a user-centric layered framework is proposed as shown in Figure 2. The proposed framework aims at helping developers in adopting a streamlined approach in developing m-learning applications. It consists of the following four layers: (i) user-centered layer, (ii) socio-cultural layer, (iii) technology and design layer, and (iv) system development layer.

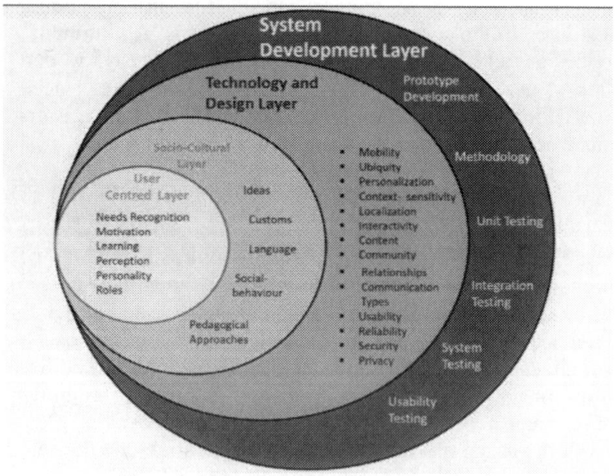

Figure 2. M-Learning User-Centric Framework

A. User-Centered Layer

This layer represents the core of the framework and reflects the user-centric aspects which need to be considered in the development of the m-learning applications. Assessing user needs and expectations is one of the first and foremost tasks in the development process. There are other behavioral aspects which include motivation (i.e., factors that enhance the user engagement); learning (i.e., factors that enhance learnability); perception (i.e., ideas and beliefs of the users about the application); personality (i.e., behavioral attitudes that define the users); and roles (i.e., various roles played by the users, such as: teachers and students).

B. Socio-Cultural Layer

Learning is a process often influenced by the cultural settings and social environment. As cultures vary across regions, so do the pedagogical approaches. Therefore, the concept of *one-size-fits-all* would be impractical in developing m-learning applications. Therefore, this layer includes the key socio-cultural aspects, which increase the adoptability and enhance the learning process using m-learning applications. These include ideas and customs which are practiced by a particular group of people or a community. Examples on such aspects include language used in the community, social behavior that defines the attitudes and behavioral aspects of a community, and pedagogical approaches followed by the community in learning process [29].

C. Technology & Design Layer

The user-centric aspects and the socio-cultural aspects must be enbeded into the design of m-learning application with the support of technology. The aspects that need to be considered in this layer include mobility (i.e., the ability of the application to be accessed on various mobile devices), ubiquity (i.e., availability of devices to receive service from anywhere on a real-time basis), personalization (i.e., ability to personalise features specific to individual users), context-sensitivity (i.e., localization and interactivity), content (i.e., the content on the application measured with completeness, accuracy and sustainability), community (i.e., users of the application), relationships (i.e., interactions between the users of the application), communication types (i.e, ways of communicating like messaging, messenger etc.), usability (i.e., ease of use, interface, enjoyability, learnability), reliability (i.e., how reliable is the application), security and privacy (e.g., data protection).

D. System Development Layer

The system development layer focuses on the factors that need to considerd for the application development. These include developing a user-centric methodology; designing a prototype and reviewing it before the actual development; adopting testing stragies like unit testing (testing individual unit/module), integration testing (testing integrated units/modules), system testing (testing the whole application), and usability testing (testing if the system meets all the user requirements).

IV. User-Centric Design Methodology

The development methodology proposed for m-learning applications engages the users in the development process along with other stakeholders including designers, developers, testers, etc. This methodology, depicted in Figure 3, is composed of two key parts: (i) the tools used to implement such steps (e.g., interview and questionnaires) and (ii) the stages/steps (e.g., identify needs) to be taken to implement the proposed methodology. Both parts are described in the next couple of paragraphs. The most commonly used tools include the following:

A. Tools/Methods Used to Support the Methodology

First: Focus Groups, which include the actual users or acting users of the m-learning application from whom the requirements, needs and expectations can be gathered for developing the application [26]. The output from the focus groups would be non-statistical and need efficient analysts to convert them in to system requirements. The process usually involves low sample population and the cost incurred is comparatively low to the other methods [30].

Second: Participatory Design, which engages the users actively in sharing the opinions and feedbacks during the designing stage [31]. This approach is mostly used for reviewing the prototype designs, which can be used later for the actual development. The output of this step would be non-statistical and requires efficient analysts to convert it in to the design specifications.

Third: Questionnaires & Interviews, used to gather the requirements from the users before developing the application and also for evaluating the system after developing the system. They can be used in both requirements gathering and evaluation stages. The output of this step would be statistical and can be analyzed using various techniques to assess the system from various perspectives. The sample size would be large and incurs fewer costs compared to other approaches [32]. In addition, interviews are one of the effective qualitative approaches for gathering the quality data which could be the requirements or feedback. The output of the interviews is non-statistical, often involves low sample size but incurs high costs [31]. Also, they can be used in both requirements gathering and evaluation stages.

Fourth: Usability Testing, which is used for testing the designs/prototypes, and also the application as a whole. The aim of the usability testing is to assess if the design/application meets the specified user requirements [33]. The output of this usability testing can be both non-statistical and statistical, often involve low sample size, and incurs high costs.

The previously described four tools or methods are proposed mainly to engage the users over the overall software development life cycle. Such engagement brings some cost, as explained earlier, but ensures effective design, development and implementation for m-learning applications.

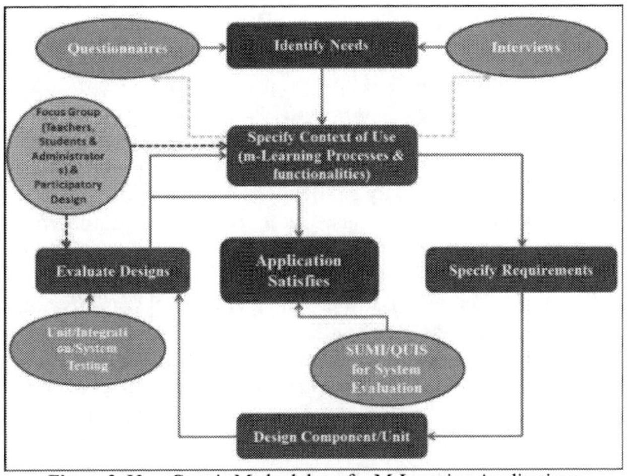

Figure 3. User-Centric Methodology for M-Learning Applications

B. Methodology Steps/Stages

The proposed methodology uses agile/iterative approach for mitigating the issues and errors during the application development. The user-centric approach specified in ISO 9241-210:2010 [34] standard is integrated with user-centric aspects in specific to M-Learning and includes the following stages of development.

Stage I – Identify Needs: Identifying the requirements of the m-learning users is the first step in the methodology, which uses interviews and questionnaires as a tool for identifying the needs, requirements and expectations of the users. Focus groups can also be involved at this stage for a more detailed assessment of needs based on their roles.

Stage II – Context of Use: At this stage the context of application is assessed by analyzing the users and their roles, location, community (i.e., socio-cultural aspects, pedagogical approaches) of using application, the purpose of developing the application, and the conditions in which the application would be used. Focus groups can be used at this stage as well to seek their ideas and opinions.

Stage III – Specify Requirements: After carefully assessing the users' needs and expectations and the context of use, the system requirements would be specified.

Stage IV – Design Component/System: The requirements outlined in the previous stage are used for designing the component/unit of the system.

Stage V – Evaluate Designs/Prototypes: At this stage, the designed components can be evaluated by using participatory approach (c-design) or by using focus groups. Unit and integration testing can be done by the testers at this stage. Repeat the process again from the context of use stage for other components till the final application is developed.

Stage VI – Application Satisfies: Once the application is fully developed, methods like SUMI/QUIS can be used for evaluating the application to ensure its completeness, correctness and consistency.

To conclude, both parts (i.e., Tools and Steps/Stages) complement each other and lead to user-centric design for m-learning applications. The proposed framework and methodology are generic to respond to the significant variety of requirements in learning domain [35]. Implementing this framework in such a complex domain will include certain challenges. One of the key challenges could be managing the user-centric approach because more frequent requirements will continuously evolve; therefore, better requirements management approaches are required. This is expected to delineate requirements conflict and specific risks associated with that. In addition, the subtle conceptualizations of some of the factors bring further complexity to the implementation of this framework. For instance, pedagogical approaches refer to different concepts for different stakeholders. Moreover, cross-layer interaction needs to be handled. This is needed to understand for example the relationship between motivation, in the core layer, and pedagogical approaches, in the next layer. A potential recommendation to manage this concern, is to have a detailed-enough instantiation process on the top of the above-introduced user-centric design methodology.

V. CONCLUSION AND FUTURE WORK

M-Learning is one of the most emerging research areas since it simplifies the learning process with the help of mobile and communication technologies. However, learning is an aspect which is influenced by the culture and pedagogical approaches specific to a particular community or region. Literature evidences identified various user-centric concerns, such as privacy, security, adaptability, usability, learnability with respect to m-learning applications. Considering these concerns, this paper proposed a user-centric design framework and m-learning development methodology in order to address the requirements of the end users effectively and efficiently. The proposed framework addressed the concerns identified via introducing: (i) user-centric and socio-cultural aspects in the process of designing the system, and (ii) an m-learning tailored development methodology by integrating the user-centric design methods in to the agile user-centric development stages. The study can be further extended by using the proposed framework and methodology for developing m-learning applications, which remains as future work.

REFERENCES

[1] Towards Maturity CIC Ltd., "Mobile Learning at Work – A New Towards Maturity In-Focus", Towards Maturity Report, 2017.

[2] S. Adkins, "The 2014-2019 Worldwide Mobile Learning Market", Ambient Insight Report, 2015.

[3] Gartner, Inc. "Gartner Identifies the Top 10 Strategic Technology Trends for 2014", 2013. Available: https://www.gartner.com/newsroom/id/2603623

[4] Google Inc., "How People Use Their Devices: What Marketers Need to Know", think with Google, 2016. https://www.thinkwithgoogle.com/consumer-insights/ [Accessed: 07-Mar- 2018].

[5] Gartner, Inc. " Gartner Says Consumers in Mature Markets Will Use and Own Three to Four Devices By 2018", 2015. Available: https://www.gartner.com/newsroom/id/3176217

[6] S. MacNaught, "Smartphone Usage Statistics 2014 - UK Survey of Smartphone Users | Tecmark", Tecmark.co.uk, 2014. [Online]. Available: http://www.tecmark.co.uk/smartphone-usage-data-uk-2014/?utm_campaign=elearningindustry.com&utm_source=%2Fsurprising-mobile-learning-statistics-elearning-professionals-know&utm_medium=link. [Accessed: 07- Mar- 2018].

[7] N. Wang, X. Chen, G. Song, Q. Lan, and H. R. Parsaei (2017). Design of a new mobile-optimized remote laboratory application architecture for M-learning. IEEE Transactions on Industrial Electronics, 64(3), 2382-2391.

[8] E. Ko, D. Chiu, P. Lo, and K. Ho, "Comparative Study on m-Learning Usage Among LIS Students from Hong Kong, Japan and Taiwan", The Journal of Academic Librarianship, vol. 41, no. 5, pp. 567-577, 2015.

[9] J. Moore, S. Oussena, and P. Zhang. "A portable document search engine to support off-line mobile learning" At IADIS International Conference Mobile Learning 2009, Spain.

[10] S. McQuiggan, L. Kosturko, and J. McQuiggan, J. Sabourin, "Mobile learning", 1st ed. New Jersey: John Wiley & Sons, Inc., 2015.

[11] J. Keengwe, and M. Bhargava, "Mobile learning and integration of mobile technologies in education", Education and Information Technologies, vol. 19, no. 4, pp. 737-746, 2013.

[12] M. Ally, and J. Prieto-Blázquez, "What is the future of mobile learning in education?", RUSC. Revista de Universidad y Sociedad del Conocimiento, vol. 11, no. 1, p. 142, 2014.

[13] M. Al-Emran, H. Elsherif, and K. Shaalan, "Investigating attitudes towards the use of mobile learning in higher education", Computers in Human Behavior, vol. 56, pp. 93-102, 2016.

[14] H. Chung, S. Chen, and M. Kuo, "A Study of EFL College Students' Acceptance of Mobile Learning", Procedia - Social and Behavioral Sciences, vol. 176, pp. 333-339, 2015.

[15] A. Khan, H. Al-Shihi, Z. Al-khanjari, and M. Sarrab, "Mobile Learning (M-Learning) adoption in the Middle East: Lessons learned from the educationally advanced countries", Telematics and Informatics, vol. 32, no. 4, pp. 909-920, 2015.

[16] H. Abachi and G. Muhammad, "The impact of m-learning technology on students and educators", Computers in Human Behavior, vol. 30, pp. 491-496, 2014.

[17] A. Garcia-Cabot, L. de-Marcos, and E. Garcia-Lopez, "An empirical study on m-learning adaptation: Learning performance and learning contexts", Computers & Education, vol. 82, pp. 450-459, 2015.

[18] A. Yousafzai, V. Chang, A. Gani, and R. Noor, "Multimedia augmented m-learning: Issues, trends and open challenges", International Journal of Information Management, vol. 36, no. 5, pp. 784-792, 2016.

[19] M. Domingo, and A. Garganté, "Exploring the use of educational technology in primary education: Teachers' perception of mobile technology learning impacts and applications' use in the classroom", Computers in Human Behavior, vol. 56, pp. 21-28, 2016.

[20] P. Bird, and M. Stubbs, "It's not just the pedagogy: challenges in scaling mobile learning applications into institution-wide learning technologies ". 11th International Conference Mobile Learning 2015. ISBN: 978-989-8533-36-4

[21] R. Lozano, M. Merrill, K. Sammalisto, K. Ceulemans, and F. Lozano, "Connecting Competences and Pedagogical Approaches for Sustainable Development in Higher Education: A Literature Review and Framework Proposal", Sustainability, vol. 9, no. 12, p. 1889, 2017.

[22] V. Dennen and S. Hao, "Intentionally mobile pedagogy: the M-COPE framework for mobile learning in higher education", Technology, Pedagogy and Education, vol. 23, no. 3, pp. 397-419, 2014.

[23] S. Hao, M. Cui, V. Dennen, Y. Türel, and L. Mei, "Analysis of mobile learning as an innovation in higher education: a comparative study of three countries", International Journal of Mobile Learning and Organisation, vol. 11, no. 4, p. 314, 2017.

[24] M. Kearney, K. Burden, and T. Rai, "Investigating teachers' adoption of signature mobile pedagogies", Computers & Education, vol. 80, pp. 48-57, 2015.

[25] L. Lindsay, "Transformation of teacher practice using mobile technology with one-to-one classes: M-learning pedagogical approaches", British Journal of Educational Technology, vol. 47, no. 5, pp. 883-892, 2015.

[26] A. Dirin and M. Nieminen, "Assessments of User Centered Design Framework for M-learning Application Development", Lecture Notes in Computer Science, pp. 62-74, 2015.

[27] S. Wood, P. Romero. "User-centred design for a mobile learning application". Proceedings of the 3rd Mexican Workshop on Human Computer Interaction. Pages 77-84. November 08 - 10, 2010.

[28] A. Dirin, M. Nieminen. "mLUX: Usability and User Experience Development Framework for M-Learning". International Journal of Interactive Mobile Technologies. Volume 9, Issue 3. 2015.

[29] R. Hammad, M. Odeh, and Z. Khan, eLEM: A Novel e-Learner Experience Model. The International Arab Journal of Information Technology 14 (4A), 2017, pp. 586-597.

[30] R. Krueger and M. Casey, Focus Groups: A practical Guide for Practical Research. SAGE, 2014.

[31] K. Eason, "User-centred design: for users or by users?", Ergonomics, vol. 38, no. 8, pp. 1667-1673, 1995.

[32] Serco, Inc., Performance Measurement Handbook: Serco Usability Services , 3rd edition, London: Serco Ltd., 1995, pp. 80-170.

[33] N. Bevan, "ISO and Industry Standards for User Centred Design", Serco Ltd., 2000.

[34] International Organization for Standardization, "ISO 9241-210:2010 - Ergonomics of human-system interaction -- Part 210: Human-centred design for interactive systems", ISO, 2010.

[35] R. Hammad, M. Odeh, and Z. Khan, "Towards a generic requirements model for hybrid and cloud-based e-learning systems," The IEEE 5th International Conference on Cloud Computing Technology and Science (CloudCom), 2013, pp. 106-111, Bristol, UK.